Hirsch and Nelson bring to this book a wide ⟨...⟩ mobilize a rich learning to offer a telling critique ⟨...⟩ what my Dad used to term "the acids of modern⟨...⟩ ⟨...⟩ they go beyond expose to offer a thick direction for reenchantment. They appeal to narrative (whereby we may speak and hear of one-off impossibilities), imagination (that opens new worlds beyond our control), and repentance (that may yield fresh reframing.) This is a timely book for the current flattened, frightened world in which we live.

—WALTER BRUEGGEMANN, COLUMBIA THEOLOGICAL SEMINARY

When I finished reading *Reframation* my first thought was to wonder whether the authors now miss the actual process of writing it. It is both whimsically beautiful and stunningly thoughtful, helping the God-imagination to soar without changing or damaging the meaning of the Christian faith one iota. I am left pondering the retelling of the intersection of my own story with Scripture.

—LINDA BERGQUIST, CHURCH PLANTING CATALYST IN SAN FRANCISCO; CO-AUTHOR OF *CITY SHAPED CHURCHES* AND *CHURCH TURNED INSIDE OUT*

The church is in the middle of a reckoning. We need *Reframation*. In this book, Hirsch and Nelson probe the depths of theology and culture to offer us a faithful reframation of the gospel. They walk us through a wonderfully fresh journey that opens new spaces for Christ's presence to make himself known in our lives and to the world in which we live. Amidst the struggling vineyards of mission in the West, *Reframation* is good fruit, ripe for this cultural moment.

—DAVID FITCH, BR LINDNER CHAIR OF EVANGELICAL THEOLOGY, NORTHERN SEMINARY, CHICAGO; AUTHOR OF *FAITHFUL PRESENCE*

In *Reframation*, Alan Hirsch and Mark Nelson set about to undo reductionist readings of Christianity. With C. S. Lewis, Martin Buber and Hans Urs von Balthasar acting as Sherpas, Hirsch and Nelson guide us through winding mountain paths, leading to an eventual summit vista from which we are able to take in the full grandeur of the biblical imagination.

—MARK SAYERS, SENIOR LEADER OF RED CHURCH, MELBOURNE, AUSTRALIA; AUTHOR OF NUMEROUS BOOKS INCLUDING *DISAPPEARING CHURCH* AND *STRANGE DAYS*

I originally planned on only giving *Reframation* a "quick read," but I seriously couldn't do it! Every page pulled me in! Packed with eye-opening and potentially life-transforming insights, this wonderfully written treasure trove of research is as intellectually engaging as it is spiritually encouraging, to say nothing of being incredibly practically helpful. Having read this book, I don't see how anyone could possibly give Hirsch's and Nelson's masterpiece a serious read and *not* find themselves reframing their conception of God, the world, and everything else in a more "enchanted way." If it doesn't cause you to reframe things in a significantly more beautiful way, *you weren't paying attention.* Five plus out of five stars!

—GREGORY A. BOYD, SENIOR PASTOR OF WOODLAND HILLS CHURCH, ST. PAUL, MINNESOTA; AUTHOR OF NUMEROUS BOOKS INCLUDING *LETTERS FROM A SKEPTIC* AND *CRUCIFIXION OF THE WARRIOR GOD*

No one has influenced my understanding of the mission of God more than Alan Hirsch! So when Alan teamed up with Mark Nelson to write *Reframation* I knew I wanted to read it. In these pages you will discover a new frame around an aging picture that allows you to grasp a new understanding of God, people and mission. Read this book and you will get a fresh perspective on how to tell the story of the "good news."

—DAVE FERGUSON, LEAD VISIONARY OF NEWTHING; CO-AUTHOR OF *HERO MAKER: FIVE ESSENTIAL PRACTICES FOR LEADERS TO MULTIPLY LEADERS*

Reframation is so refreshing. It throws open all the doors and flings open every window on the gospel, to broaden our vision and deepen our responsibility as God's people. Alan and Mark have opened our eyes to the stunning, complicated, beautiful truth of Christ.

—MICHAEL FROST, AUTHOR OF *INCARNATE* AND *SURPRISE THE WORLD*

A deep and meaningful theological reflection that was both a joy and a relief to read. Finally, something that expands our view of God, opening us up to beauty, creativity, complexity, and ultimately hope.

—BRIAN SANDERS, FOUNDER OF UNDERGROUND CHURCH; AUTHOR OF *UNDERGROUND CHURCH*

In a time when more people are turning away from the church, *Reframation* helps us rediscover the beauty of the gospel and artfully extend it to those who need it the most.

—GABE LYONS, PRESIDENT OF Q IDEAS; CO-AUTHOR OF *GOOD FAITH*

In *Reframation*, Alan Hirsch and Mark Nelson survey the cultural forces that have stripped us of our spiritual instincts and any sense of the divine. Related to this loss of the transcendent, they throw a much-needed light on the many ways we have reduced our understanding of both God and the gospel. These reductionisms have severely limited the ways in which we think God is to be encountered and communicated in the world. This book is not only desperately needed by the body of Christ, but it's also vital for those outside the church who don't yet know Jesus as the Creator of all things. *Reframation* provides a significant step towards once again having eyes to see and ears to hear.

—BRAD BRISCO, CO-AUTHOR OF *NEXT DOOR AS IT IS IN HEAVEN* AND *THE MISSIONAL QUEST*

Kierkegaard, Bonhoeffer, William Blake, Anthony Hopkins, the Camino de Santiago, Burning Man, Hans Urs von Balthasar, and Jesus of Nazareth—Hirsch and Nelson have served up quite an intellectual feast. Exotic, penetrating, and challenging to pedestrian perceptions of life, pull up a chair, this is a seven-course meal—take some time and enjoy.

—BILL HULL, CO-FOUNDER OF THE BONHOEFFER PROJECT; AUTHOR OF *CONVERSION AND DISCIPLESHIP* AND *THE DISCIPLE MAKING PASTOR*; CO-AUTHOR OF *THE DISCIPLESHIP GOSPEL*

In *Reframation*, Hirsch and Nelson's call to reenchant the story of God is inspiring and compelling, though also unsettling. This is a challenge to break away from our preconceived ideas of how we encounter God and rediscover the awe and wonder of the divine presence in every person, place, and thing. Their call to constantly pay attention to the presence of God propels us out of our confining spiritual boxes into a reframed spiritual freedom. This is an important book that I recommend to all church leaders.

—CHRISTINE ARONEY-SINE, AUTHOR OF *THE GIFT OF WONDER*

If faith were a proposition, then intellect might suffice. But God gave us stories, because faith is a life to be lived. Hirsch and Nelson are storytellers who expand our view of reality. They move us from a flat, one-dimensional story to a reenchanted world where our imagination is stirred and our desire for God and his kingdom is renewed. Read this book if you want to break out of a reductionistic narrative and awaken to the beauty and mystery of God and the wonder of life. Then immerse yourself in the story of Scripture afresh and enter into the vibrant adventure of joining God in the renewal of all things.

—JR WOODWARD, NATIONAL DIRECTOR OF V3 MOVEMENT; AUTHOR OF *CREATING A MISSIONAL CULTURE*; CO-AUTHOR OF *THE CHURCH AS MOVEMENT*

Reframation is *so* good that I want everyone to read it! Alan and Mark show that the good news has relevance to every aspect of humanity's brokenness. They help us to see God, people, and mission, through reenchanted frames. The whole picture is stunning. This is going to help so many understand so much about what has been so misunderstood. A timely book for every Christ follower.

—CHRISTINE CAINE, FOUNDER OF A21 AND PROPEL WOMEN

For the sake of the church, consider the preciously ancient gospel Alan and Mark have extracted from the rubble of bad news that the church has settled for.

—HUGH HALTER, AUTHOR OF *FLESH* AND *BRIMSTONE*; CO-AUTHOR OF *THE TANGIBLE KINGDOM*

Alan Hirsch and Mark Nelson have written an important and timely book that addresses the unique challenges contemporary culture presents the church as she seeks to extend Jesus' mission in the world. With penetrating insight, they identify how certain reductions and distortions of the gospel within the church have severely weakened her ability to communicate her own story. Their prescriptions for overcoming these obstacles are compelling: the need to recapture the power of narrative and the nature of mythic truth; the need to re-awaken the church to the wonder, shock, and glory of the Christian message; the importance of a fully incarnational understanding of the gospel; and the need for cultivating a listening ear in order to better understand the religious longings and language of our contemporaries. I hope this book gains a wide reading across the whole body of Christ. It has the potential to help set a new and fruitful direction for the mission of the church in our time.

—PETER HERBECK, LEADER OF CATHOLIC RENEWAL US

It seems that every 500 years the church experiences some sort of upheaval and renewal. Don't look now but we are at the 500-year mark. Be prepared: this book could usher it in—not by ripping and tearing, but by radically altering the way you see. Hirsch and Nelson have such a bold vision of Jesus that it reframes everything, literally everything, even the church. Change is happening. Let *Reframation* help you see, wide-eyed, the future of God's mission in the world.

—DAN WHITE JR., AUTHOR OF *LOVE OVER FEAR*, CO-AUTHOR OF *THE CHURCH AS MOVEMENT*; MISSIONAL COACH WITH V3 MOVEMENT

Cogent and compelling, this book is a treasure trove of fresh metaphors that scatter the debris choking out our staid Christian imagination. The Grand Story is indeed much more mystical, poetical, and mythical than we've come to believe. This is your invitation to rediscover something your soul has been whispering to you all along.

—PRESTON POUTEAUX, AUTHOR OF *THE BEES OF RAINBOW FALLS: FINDING FAITH, IMAGINATION, AND DELIGHT IN YOUR NEIGHBOURHOOD*

A rollicking ride down the *via negativa*. In *Reframation*, Alan Hirsch and Mark Nelson remind us that, despite the truth of our creeds and dogmas, they can never fully capture the fullness of the Living God. Answering their call to reframe how we conceive, experience, remember, and communicate the essence of the Christian faith will be vital for the reformation of a renewed missionary identity throughout the church of Jesus Christ, in the hearts of believers from all Christian traditions.

—FR. JAMES MALLON, CATHOLIC PRIEST; AUTHOR OF *DIVINE RENOVATION: FROM A MAINTENANCE TO A MISSIONAL PARISH*

Poetic, provocative, and profound … reading this totally refreshed my passion for the gospel of Jesus that alone can change hearts and minds.

—PAUL HARCOURT, NATIONAL LEADER OF NEW WINE ENGLAND

The prophet Elisha had to pray for his servant, "O Lord, please open his eyes that he may see," before the young man could see the full reality around him. In this strategic book, Alan and Mark invite us to open our eyes to see the full reality of God, the gospel, and the human condition in our shrunken times. Their book is a vital resource for all those who long to engage contemporary culture/s with the gospel, but struggle to know how to reach their heart.

—BISHOP GRAHAM CRAY, FORMER LEADER OF THE UK FRESH EXPRESSIONS TEAM; ASSISTANT BISHOP IN THE DIOCESE OF YORK

I'll never forget reading *The Shaping of Things to Come*; it was a turning point in my ministry. I literally resigned and changed the trajectory of our church. It's impossible to read a book by Alan and not walk away rethinking, well, everything. I can't wait to see this new book (now with Mark) do the same.

—JOHN MARK COMER, PASTOR FOR TEACHING AND VISION AT BRIDGETOWN CHURCH, PORTLAND, OR; AUTHOR OF *THE RUTHLESS ELIMINATION OF HURRY*

Echoes of transcendence—rumors of glory—this is the trail the authors pursue in this warm and inviting exploration of the deep longings in the human heart. Plumbing the insight of writers from Bourdieu to Lewis and on to von Balthasar, they demonstrate that the crisis of interpretation of our time can only be answered by reenchantment, naming the real wonder and the real beauty of the Christ we adore. In reaching for a richer anthropology, they forge a path we can follow on the missional renaissance—one that can answer the deepest longings of the human heart. Move over Viktor Frankl—here is a text for the new millennium!

—LEN HJALMARSON, ADJUNCT PROFESSOR, TYNDALE SEMINARY, TORONTO AND PORTLAND SEMINARY, PORTLAND; AUTHOR OF *BROKEN FUTURES: LEADERS AND CHURCHES LOST IN TRANSITION*

Too many Christians are color blind, only seeing the world in black and white. In recent decades the world has changed, and we need new lenses to view the world around us. This is the book so many of us have all been waiting for! In *Reframation*, Alan and Mark offer us a new lens, a new way of seeing a holistic framework from which we can view God, people, and the world in Technicolor. Read this book and take your place in the Great Reframation of the twenty-first century!

—WINFIELD BEVINS, DIRECTOR OF CHURCH PLANTING AT ASBURY THEOLOGICAL SEMINARY; AUTHOR OF *MARKS OF A MOVEMENT*

Alan and Mark brilliantly argue in *Reframation* that the church has a solar ecliptic view of God that greatly limits our ability to seek, know, and reveal God to a spiritually starving generation. Their missiology challenges our little heresies, smashes our idols, undercuts our simplistic notions of the gospel, and replaces these with a fresh new vision that reframes and enlarges our perceptions. I believe that they have their hands on the pulse of a critical conversation that we need to have if we are to address the decline of biblical Christianity in the West.

—DR. JOSEPH MATTERA, AUTHOR, CONSULTANT, AND THEOLOGIAN; FOUNDING PASTOR OF RESURRECTION CHURCH; LEADER OF THE US COALITION OF APOSTOLIC LEADERS AND CHRIST COVENANT COALITION

As any Christian leader in North America is well aware, ours is a time of extreme cultural upheaval and polarization. The great tragedy, however, is that so many of our churches are more likely to get caught up in the turmoil than they are to transcend it by offering a compelling alternative. *Reframation* helps us understand why this is the case, but more importantly, it provides an insightful vision for what it will take to move beyond the reductionisms that plague our thinking and toward a more faithful future grounded in God and his mission in the world.

—DR. JR ROZKO, NATIONAL DIRECTOR OF MISSIO ALLIANCE

Let this book blow your mind and awaken your heart's desire. You will hear the whisper in the wind of its words, you'll recognize the original tune—it's a gospel melody and it's a holy invitation. I hope it offends you, moves you, infuriates you, awakens you, alarms you, invites and inspires you to repentance. Because there is no time to waste. Alan and Mark have set themselves on fire. Come warm yourself to life by the holy flame.

Alan and Mark call us to repent of our reductionist gospels, readily codified and commodified for mass distribution. They invite us into a grander story and a fuller life. Here is an invitation to leave a stunted Christianity and a diluted life to step into a larger life; a life well-lived as "a Jesus-saturated affair." This is a book that needs to be read slowly and prayerfully and then read again.

For anyone disenchanted with the confines of faith and practice, Hirsch and Nelson awaken our hope and enliven our vision with new frames for the expansive story of the good news of Jesus and God's dream for a renewed world. *Reframation* is a gust of inspiration bringing a deep breath of relief.

Alan and Mark turn to the apostles of the imagination—literary visionaries such as C. S. Lewis and Hans Urs von Balthasar—to reframe the gospel and reenchant the people of God with the beauty and meaning of our core message and mission. Read and you too will be rekindled in your love for God and the gospel.

Reading *Reframation* is a constant inhale and exhale. An inhale of truth, conviction, and heart connection. An exhale of yes; dreaming and longing for more for myself and for the church, and a holy angst for a new day. Alan and Mark's vision for listening to the cultural rhythms and the breadcrumbs of God woven into the souls of our world has grown my desire to connect more intentionally with others. *Reframation* has awakened in me a dormant call for beauty and poetry in how I read, study and, create. It makes me want to dig deeper and seek more of the Lord. This is a phenomenal work!

Every once in a while a book comes along that is so audacious, so sprawling, so visionary, so learned, so fascinating, that one almost wonders what wild prophets could come up with such a work. Hirsch and Nelson have been at this ministry, playing in these fields of the Lord, for a long time, and they offer us a deep and wise manifesto of how we might reframe our view of God, God's work, our human vocation, our hope, and yes, the church's mission—so we might be faithful and full and fruitful in these times. Uber-contemporary reports such as Hirsch's taking in The Burning Man festival and Nelson's moving account of hiking the El Camino trail, to scholarly engagement with extraordinary thinkers like von Balthasar, C. S. Lewis, and Charles Taylor, will add to the urgent conversations of our day about the quest for meaning, the proper understanding of gospel-centered faith, the nature and scope of redemption, the joy of beauty, and the goodness of longing for a better world. Serious scholarship is illuminated by the transcendental vibe of Blake's poetry and awesome exegesis of biblical praise songs, by tender stories and great quips and quotes. In a hurting, searching, God-haunted world, *Reframation* is itself a signal of transcendence. *Semper reframation!*

—BYRON BORGER, HEARTS & MINDS BOOKSTORE, DALLASTOWN, PA

Hirsch and Nelson bring more than sixty years of diverse ministry experience to reflect upon the task of how the church works in the postmodern cultures of the twenty-first century. Each author demonstrates an understanding of the fundamental issues that go beyond snap answers or easy bromides. They make accessible to an audience that cuts across disciplines and professions a truth that has circulated within the academy for some time—that we see, we "know," what we are programmed to see. This view cuts the heart out of the modernist way of looking at the world and of presenting the gospel. They propose that the gospel cannot be contained in a modernist frame of "propositions," but is discovered, and has currency, in the narratives of living out God's work at putting the world back together. To see this work requires a "reframing," a "Reframation" to use their term, of how one sees the world and the gospel. Listen and live to the glory of God.

—GARY WEEDMAN, PRESIDENT EMERITUS, JOHNSON UNIVERSITY

RE-
FRAM-
ATION

SEEING GOD, PEOPLE,
AND MISSION THROUGH
REENCHANTED FRAMES

ALAN HIRSCH & MARK NELSON

MOVEMENTS
PUBLISHING

First published in 2019 by 100 Movements Publishing
www.100mpublishing.com
Copyright © 2019 by Alan Hirsch and Mark Nelson

ISBN 978-0-9986393-3-8

Cover design by Karen Sawrey

For bulk orders or bookshop orders, please visit reframationbook.com

DEDICATION

Alan

To the loving memory of John Smith (1942–2019). Unquestionably one of the foremost missional evangelist-prophets ever to emerge from Australian Christianity, John impacted me (and countless others) in hugely significant ways. I am forever grateful for his weird and wonderful life. Vale John Smith.

I also want to acknowledge my love and indebtedness to one of my living heroes, the irrepressible Hugh "HooDawg" Halter. Thanks for the in/credible witness, Hugh. "I'll have what he is having!"

Mark

For Monica, the love of my life.

ACKNOWLEDGMENTS

Alan:

Thanks to my friend (and now co-author), Mark Nelson, for his patience as well as his quiet urgency in getting this book to print. And also for Monica Nelson for putting up with Mark!

As always, to my best friend and wife of thirty years, Deb Hirsch. She continues to inspire and challenge me to be more like Jesus every day.

Mark:

I am grateful to my faith community, Crossings, and the greatest staff and leaders in the world for allowing me the space to bring this book to life. Thank you for being willing to continue to wrestle with the ideas in this book for the last twelve years as a community.

Thanks also to my dear friend Alan Hirsch. Thank you for this four-and-a-half-year journey we have shared. I have learned much and have loved the challenge of bringing this project to fruition alongside you. *It has truly been a great joy.* (Sorry, Al—I wanted to add a few more italicized words just for you.)

Alan and Mark:

Our sincere thanks and gratitude to our *brilliant* publisher/editor/friend, Anna Robinson, for her heroic effort, not least for putting up with the two of us. Truly she has earned her right to be called "our queen." Long may she live and prosper!

Thanks to Danielle Strickland and Michael Frost for their contributions, not only in the foreword and the afterword, but in their influence upon each of our lives. You are not only dear friends, but exemplars and heroes because of the way you live, teach, and breathe a wi[l]der gospel.

CONTENTS

FOREWORD

DANIELLE STRICKLAND

If you lived 2,000 years ago or so and heard the ruckus John the Baptist and his revival movement was stirring from the margins, you'd probably want to go have a look for yourself. Picture yourself there, hearing the widely popular, wild-eyed prophet, camel hair shining in the brilliant sun, hair flowing in the desert wind as his voice booms through the swarming crowds, popping back protein-packed, snack-sized locusts between speeches to keep his game on. There is no doubt, as you listened to his fiery message, you'd be faced with a decision.

Imagine yourself standing at the edges of the crowd, your brain forced into a debate about the validity of the package as the aesthetics probably offend your religious modesty. Your ego rages at the nerve of the man to invite you to a public repentance (full immersion … really?), *and*, at the exact same moment of offense, your heart starts thumping, your spirit leaping, even soaring, as your eyes and ears open to a heightened sense of something coming, something real emerging. Maybe, just maybe, your heart tells you, it's true. The kingdom is coming. The promises are genuine. Maybe it's not too late and not too hard for God to show up—for the kingdom to come. Maybe there is hope for this broken world, healing for the wounds of humanity, a future for you and the people you love.

The change that John the Baptist introduced was made flesh in the person of Jesus. And Jesus was unlike anyone who had come before. He was so different that the people most dedicated to the Scriptures and the prophets didn't recognize him. Even dear old John sent questions for confirmation from a prison cell as he felt his own end approaching: "Are you the One we've been expecting?"[1]

I'm still not sure how we expect God's kingdom to come in our time and in our current world. I have a hunch that, like those early religious leaders, we study the Scriptures with expectation but peer at the world with disdain. Jesus never did that. Jesus saw the world through a kingdom lens, a divine perspective, a holy paradigm. And the way Jesus saw every situation and every person changed every *thing*. It made every blind man an opportunity for divine encounter, every woman a potential apostle, every beggar first place for discipleship, every religious leader a seeker, and, well, the results were extraordinary. The upside-down nature of God's kingdom entered the world and has continually ebbed and flowed in increasing force and impact ever since. And yet, we still find ourselves at the mercy of our infantile intellects, bloated sensational news outlets, and the amazingly irritating human capacity for small-mindedness. We remain contained within human constructs and religious boundaries. We forget that the kingdom emerges and advances in the most unlikely of ways, through the most irritatingly unqualified people; it spreads like wildflowers planted whimsically by a love-crazed Gardener, and is brought to fullness by a truly wild King.

I'm trying to prepare you for the book you are about to read. Alan and Mark mean to reframe how you understand God and gospel, and a lot in between. And this prophetic call could not have come at a better time. I believe that if we have eyes to see and ears to hear, we will understand that there has never been a more opportune time for the kingdom of God than right now. I still believe that Jesus is calling people to follow him into the wild edges of this blazingly beautiful world, and he's calling them *now* like he called them *then*: "The time has come [...] The kingdom of God has come near. Repent and believe the good news!" (Mark 1:15). The original call of Jesus sounds out loud and clear through the pages of this book. It is the Jesus invitation, and the only possible thing to unleash authentic carriers of his wild gospel. The implications are quite simply the spreading beauty and transformation of this good news everywhere and to everyone. *Reframe* is a perfect word for a time in which repentance couldn't be more important or strategic. I do not mean the old-fashioned evangelical version of repentance, preached with angry fervor to a crowd of wayward "sinners," warning them of the fires of hell. But the original kind of repentance. The kind Jesus spoke of to the first disciples at the start of his gospel mission. It was not weary sinners that Jesus called to first follow him. It was the disciples of John the Baptist whom he first invited to *repent*. In Greek the word *repent* is *metanoia*, which means to "change the way you see." And how fitting is that?

The first calling is not to sinners but to saints. To disciples. To the folks who were present in the wilderness, seeking God's kingdom and so close to the truth they could taste it in the sandy desert grit blowing in the breeze and the holy fire burning into their souls. The thing is, Jesus doesn't call the disciples of John from a place of religious fervor at the height of their popular revival movement. He finds them much later, in fishing boats at the Sea of Galilee. No doubt these disciples had returned to fishing after the arrest of their prophetic leader. Having faced the inevitable disdainful voice (external or internal) of shame, they licked their wounds and stopped trying to change the world. Instead, they just focused on feeding their own people, picking up the family business like their mothers had always hoped, and started plodding their way to retirement. It's right at *this moment* that Jesus shows up and reframes them. Repent. Change the way you see. Jesus is calling, and he has a kingdom coming. Now is the time.

Let this book blow your mind and awaken your heart's desire. You will hear the whisper in the wind of its words; you'll recognize the original tune—it's a gospel melody and it's a holy invitation. I hope it offends you, moves you, infuriates you, awakens you, alarms you, invites and inspires you to repentance. Because there is no time to waste. Alan and Mark have set themselves on fire. Come warm yourself to life by the holy flame.

PREFACE

You may be wondering why we have called this book *Reframation*. Well, in this made-up word, we are drawing attention to the idea that each of us sees everything through a *frame*. Whether it be God, creation, people, the good news, or the call to mission, each and every "picture" we encounter is surrounded by a frame, and that frame in some way determines what and how we actually see. Our goal in sharing what we as authors have been learning is for us all to consider what it might look like to put some new frames around these pictures: to reframe our understandings of God, people, and mission.

In what we hope is obvious to the reader, the title is also something of a play on the word *Reformation* ... as in the major sixteenth-century revolution that shook the Western church. This wordplay is intentional, as we want to lovingly reinvoke (and playfully reframe) one of the central mottos of the Reformation, known simply as *semper reformanda,* which states that, "The church reformed ought always to be reforming, according to the Word of God."[1] We somewhat cheekily propose our own version called *semper reframanda* and suggest that, "The church reframed ought always to be reframing, according to the Word of God." Just as the church needs to engage with ongoing re-*form*-ation, we believe a continual re-*frame*-ation is similarly required. Every new context the church finds itself in necessitates a reframing of theology and gospel, so that it resonates with contemporary culture. As Helmut Thielicke noted,

> The gospel must be proclaimed afresh in new ways to each generation, since every generation has its own unique questions. The gospel must constantly be forwarded to a new address, because the recipients are repeatedly changing their place of address.[2]

The missional church conversation has made it abundantly clear that women and men are changing their "place of residence," not merely geographically, but philosophically and spiritually as well. It is therefore essential that the gospel is reframed, so that it might be heard, understood, and received afresh.

IF YOU WANT TO CHANGE SOMETHING, YOU MUST FIRST LOVE IT

This book will highlight the deep concern we both have for the church. However, let there be no misunderstanding—we really do love Jesus and his people, and both of us have given our lives to serve the body of Christ. It is because of this we feel called to address the frames through which we, as the church, view God and his world. In our opinion, evangelicalism, the theological tribe we hail from, has often displayed spiritual, moral, and theological bankruptcy in its portrayal of God and gospel over the last few decades or so. It's likely the same critique can equally apply to other sectors of Western Christianity as well.

From what we can discern, the core of the problem is that the church does not sound or act a whole lot like our Founder, Jesus. Evangelicalism in particular seems to have arrived at a form of what Bonhoeffer termed "Christless Christianity," in which Jesus is celebrated as Savior but rejected as Lord.[3] As a result we have ended up with a gospel that excludes the necessity for discipleship. In addition to this, we have lost the disciple's sense of responsibility to actually embody (incarnate) everything that our Founder and Lord represented and taught. Even a cursory reading of the Gospels indicates that Jesus himself would never allow people to bypass his sovereign claim on their lives. He clearly taught that to be a follower and a disciple required death to self, submission to his lordship, and a decision to grow in increasing levels of conformity to his own life and teachings—a life of love, humility, servanthood, forgiveness, justice, holiness, and mercy. When we have arrived at this point, a form of Christ-less Christianity, we can be sure *it is time for a reframation.*

This apparent Christlessness is all too readily confirmed by the very people to whom we are called to be witnesses in the first place: across the Western world, Christians are often perceived as being unloving, bad-tempered, and at times even a hateful people. How do we possibly square this with the kind of witness that Jesus called us to embody and represent? How is it that the very people who claim to have experienced the amazing grace of God can have such a narrow application of it when dealing with others? When we have arrived at this point, a graceless faith and witness, *it is time for a reframation.*

None of this is new, of course. Reductionisms (for that is what they are) have plagued religious people ever since there have been religions. Consider the Jews of Jesus' day: they made exactly the same mistake—reducing God, people, and the world into religious formulae and legal code. They were unable to see what God was doing in Jesus. As a result, they missed the very Person that everything in their difficult history as God's chosen people ought to have formed them to recognize ... and this blindness remains true to this day. As a Jew, I (Alan) lament this deeply! When we have arrived at this point, a place of cramped religion, *it is time for a reframation.*

If we follow the Jesus-logic, "you will know a tree by its fruit" (see Matthew 7:16–20), we can safely assume that any organization is perfectly designed to produce the fruit or outcomes they are currently producing. Applying the same rationale, we conclude that if what we offer to the world is a grumpy and constricted belief in God, then it is probably because we have a grumpy and constricted *view* of God in the first place. Something is deeply wrong with our fundamental conception of God here! When we have arrived at this point, a place of a profoundly reduced experience of God, *it is time for a reframation.*

ABOUT THE AUTHORS

It has taken us over four years to complete this book, partly because the themes within its pages are so very personal to both of us, capturing something of both our spiritual journeys over the last decade. This book is a collaboration, and as in all such partnerships, we both bring a unique contribution to the common voice. It is perhaps worth briefly introducing ourselves and some of our reasons for spending so long in the process of writing.

I (Alan) have been in various forms of formal ministry for around thirty years now. The first fifteen years involved local church leadership, church planting, developing missional training systems, and denominational renewal. The latter fifteen have been primarily spent on the international scene, pioneering the development of missional forms of church, largely within Western cultural contexts. I have written extensively on-topic and have had the privilege of serving God's people in many of the major denominations and organizations.

What has gone into the writing of this book has been intensely personal. In some ways it has been a means for me to try to resolve a serious existential faith crisis, precipitated by some of the reductionisms stated above. The last four or so years have involved a very painful reassessment of my own evangelical heritage. I have sought to work out why so much of evangelicalism seems to be so utterly impoverished from the roots up. In this book I have tried to identify and name much of what I perceive to be the causes for this spiritual bankruptcy. I ask the reader to please receive my observations in the spirit I offer them ... in humility before Christ ... as one confessing my own sins and complicity in it all. Thankfully, I do believe there are some key ways to address the problem—there is hope, but it will require repentance and reframation.

Those concerned about the orthodoxy of what they are about to read, need not worry. Ironically, I now feel more deeply grounded in the historic, orthodox faith than I have at any other point in my life. I totally believe! But I believe in a bigger and deeper way now—I've been duly reframed and continue to be so. I can honestly say I have grown in my understanding of God, people, mission, and gospel as a result. T. S. Eliot's words, always among my favorite, have never seemed truer ...

> We shall not cease from exploration
> And the end of all our exploring
> Will be to arrive where we started
> And know the place for the first time[4]

One more point is worth mentioning here: I have to admit that my infamous obsession with Hans Urs von Balthasar continues unabated. Over the last few years of devouring his writings, I feel I have completed my own personal PhD (in the university of my heart) by trying to grapple with all that this incredibly profound theologian has taught me. I have *never* read anyone who has loved the Scriptures more than von Balthasar. The Holy Spirit has used him to connect me to the deepest possible currents of Christian faith and theology. His influence is felt throughout this book ... I will have to ask your indulgence on this, and hopefully by doing so, I can pass on something I have received. To make the text more readable though, most of the pure Balthasarian explorations are in the endnotes. Theology geeks, take note.

Similarly to Alan, I (Mark) have been engaged in full-time ministry for over thirty years. I've progressed slowly through a vocational path that has included youth ministry, ministry on a university campus, and for the last dozen or so years, launching and leading a faith community in the city center of Knoxville, Tennessee.

I have come to recognize that giving myself in community alongside so many others trying to participate in a movement to restore all things has been a beautiful gift. The oft-quoted words of Frederick Buechner describe well my experience for the past three decades:

the kind of work God usually calls you to is the kind of work (a) that you need most to do and (b) that the world most needs to have done [...] The place God calls you to is the place where your deep gladness and the world's deep hunger meet.[5]

The writing of this book is, in some ways, a culmination of these last thirty plus years lived in this very intersection of my "deep gladness and the world's deep hunger."

In fact, the "new frames" phraseology, the very idea behind a reframation, has been a part of a specific calling I have been drawn to for a long time. It has played itself out in a variety of ways in my life, in many artistic forms (theatre, storytelling, preaching, and teaching) but has always come back to this urgent call to be a part of a great reframing of the beautiful story of Jesus. Again, this book is intended to bring much of this experience to fruition.

Each stage or season of our lives hopefully teaches all of us new and transformative truths, things we could never have fathomed earlier in life. This has often been confirmed in my own life as I continually find myself repeating the phrase, "I have learned more in the last ten years of my life than in all the previous years combined." This particularly describes my past few years, and this book is part of the fruit of that education, which I am desperate to continue.

As Alan has described his healthy obsession with von Balthasar, I too have had my share of fanboy influence from the aforementioned writer, novelist, poet, preacher, and theologian Frederick Buechner. It is Buechner's skill at reframing the sacred, whether through fiction, memoir, or sermon, that has drawn me into a wider and deeper experience of God that continually takes my breath away and causes my "heart to leap" and my "eyes to fill."[6] Alan and I both believe, at least partially, that it is this odd combination of these two great thinkers and writers that brings a broader depth and breadth to this book, that might otherwise have been missing.

AS TO MATTERS OF STYLE

Speaking of key influences, the reader will quickly discern that we use C. S. Lewis heavily. Both of us have always loved Lewis, but we have found him particularly useful in the writing of this book on reframing; his suggestive use of imagination, poetry, myth, and spiritual longing, as well as his profound reflections on the nature of heaven and hell, are so pertinent to the themes we explore. We use him extensively because we believe there is something of an implicit missiology in his approach that is critical for us, as evangelicals, to understand and apply in our mission and witness within our current context. His form of apologetics goes beyond the overused rationalistic techniques to appeal more directly to the more immediate existential registers that reside deep within every human heart. We believe we all need to follow in Lewis' footsteps; in doing so, we will not only connect with contemporary culture but also reflect more of the way of Jesus, who always speaks directly to the human heart.

Furthermore, the reader will find we quote from an unusually wide range of sources (Judaism, religious poets, pop culture, and arts) and we draw from within the broad Christian tradition (Protestant, Catholic, and Orthodox). We are deliberate in doing this. If we simply spoke as evangelicals and quoted only evangelical insiders, we would only confirm the linguistic frames and the theological blind spots or biases we already have. We need outside voices to wake us up to the treasures we already possess but fail to understand, let alone access.

We have also drawn ideas from beyond the Christian realm to illustrate that the search for transcendence really is universal and is expressed through various philosophers, poets, and mystics—be they Christian or not. We do this not because we don't believe in the priority and authority of the Scriptures in all matters of faith (we totally do), but because we want to show that the issues the gospel addresses—the longing, the yearning, and the ongoing attempts to make meaning—are built into the universal experience of *all* humans. These longings are keys to the human heart and therefore we can (and indeed must) begin to speak into these to find cultural resonance. We need to attune ourselves both to God and to the real issues of our time in order to bring a faithful witness to bear.

We both have a common love of great theology, poetry, story, and mystery. This isn't simply because we are so very tired of the small, domesticated, churchly god of pious platitudes, but because literature engages and forms the human imagination, allowing knowledge of the head to become knowledge of the heart. Knowledge therefore ceases to remain theoretical and instead becomes integrated into our whole life.

As lovers of all things God, we have kept our hearts in a state of holy restlessness in a search for a God big enough to change everything. We refuse to settle for the initial, partial experience of God we had when we first came to believe. We seek to know God as he wishes to be known ... through ever-expanding and enchanting frames, through eyes of wonder and love, believing with Augustine that, "If you understand, it is not God" (*si comprehendis, non est Deus*). God is ever greater, always bigger, than anything we think we know of him.

This holy restlessness, the kind that leads to a reframation, is laced throughout this book. Our hope is that you will feel somewhat disturbed, challenged, and stretched throughout. As Franz Kafka writes,

> If the book we're reading doesn't wake us up with a blow to the head, what are we reading for? So that it will make us happy? Good Lord, we would be happy precisely if we had no books, and the kind of books that make us happy are the kind we could write ourselves if we had to ... A book must be the axe for the frozen sea within us.[7]

In order to highlight the idea of the framing/reframing theme, we are going to sometimes play around with words in a way that allows for a double-take, two-frames-at-once kind of experience. So, for instance, we will play with words such as "wi[l]der," "in/credible," "w/holiness," "re/enchanted," etc. It's a literary trick we devised to make you read the sentence twice, each time in a different frame.

Another quirk of this book is the extensive use of endnotes. We do this largely for two reasons: first, to give those interested, a deeper exploration of the particular line of thought referenced. If an idea piques your interest and has an endnote, we trust that this will lead you to greater insight. But because it is an endnote, it ought not to hinder the flow in the main text. The other reason for using endnotes is that we want to provide proper references to the many resources we have found useful. While this is not intended as an academic text, we do want it to be a substantial (as well as a fruitful) one.

We fully realize our own limitations as we write. In trying to expose some of the Western church's most dangerous reductions, we have become all too aware, as two middle-aged, middle-class, white guys, how our own thinking is greatly reduced. So much of Protestant thinking, certainly that of evangelicals, is left-brained, functional, and technical; many of our problems in perception have arisen from a form of theological dysfunction or "exaggerated male brain syndrome."[8] We have very much been on a liberating journey of learning and of correction in this regard. W/holiness is a wonderful thing.

On topic, while we sought to be gender inclusive in our own language, we do feel it is necessary to genuinely apologize to our female readers for the numerous quotations from writers who use exclusively masculine language when referring to human beings ("man," "him," "he," etc.). We did not feel we had the right to adapt their language to suit our real needs for more gender inclusive language. Please continue to forgive us, sisters—we have so much work to do in this regard.

This book is not intended to be directive and formulaic; however, we do want to point you, as fellow followers of Jesus, lovers of God, and seekers of his glory, to what we think will lead to a greater, more Christ-like way to be his people in the world. What we very humbly offer to you are potential pathways by which perhaps, by God's grace, we might see and experience more of God in every aspect of our lives—individually and corporately. We hope as you engage with the words in this book, not only with your mind but also with your heart, that you will somehow become a little more like Jesus and a better representative of his good news.

> I ask him that with both feet planted firmly on love, you'll be able to take in with all followers of Jesus the extravagant dimensions of Christ's love. Reach out and experience the breadth! Test its length! Plumb the depths! Rise to the heights! Live full lives, full in the fullness of God. God can do anything, you know—far more than you could ever imagine or guess or request in your wildest dreams! He does it not by pushing us around but by working within us, his Spirit deeply and gently within us. Glory to God in the church! Glory to God in the Messiah, in Jesus! Glory down all the generations! Glory through all millennia! Oh, yes!
>
> EPHESIANS 3:14–21 MSG

The good news comes knocking on doors that we didn't even know we had; it flings open the curtains on windows we didn't know existed to reveal the rising sun flooding the room with glory when we had imagined that all light came from candles; it woos our cold hearts and awakens them, like someone falling in love for the first time, to a joy and fulfillment never before imagined.

—N. T. WRIGHT

INTRODUCTION

A TALE OF TWO PILGRIMS

Two summers ago, I (Mark) walked across Spain: over a period of twenty-eight days, my twenty-three-year-old son and I hiked over 450 miles through countryside and city, plateaus and mountains to complete a spiritual pilgrimage on the Camino de Santiago (the Way of St. James). An estimated 250,000 "pilgrims" walk at least a portion of the Camino every year. For me, it was a deeply spiritual experience, giving me invaluable time with my son, as well as a sabbatical from my busy day-to-day life as a pastor.

On our journey we met, walked, ate meals, and stayed in hostels with hundreds of different people. It was a genuine pleasure (in most instances) to meet and learn about each person. It took only a day or two of being on the trail to come to the conclusion that every initial conversation with other "pilgrims" always began with some variation of the following two questions: "Where did you start walking?" and "Why are you walking?" After those initial conversation starters, the discussion usually expanded to a broad range of topics, including the inevitable questions about home, family, and vocation.

I still remember the first time I tried to explain what I do in life, a life spent in vocational ministry for at least the last thirty years.

"So, what does that mean ... you're like ... a priest?"

"No, not exactly. I lead, teach, and take care of people in a faith community that gathers once a week in the heart of the city and tries to live out what they believe about Jesus throughout their whole lives."

"So, yeah, you're a priest."

And that was that. They had found their category for me.

Being outed as a "priest" always seemed to kill the conversation from that point on. For these pilgrims on the Camino, somehow my vocation as a "priest" had little to do with their own search for God, beauty, truth, or justice. Their notion of what constituted a spiritual life clearly had no place for people like me in it, and their spirituality had no way of viably engaging with, or interpreting, mine or any other form of Christianity they had ever seen represented.

This was somewhat alarming to me because I considered myself a decidedly spiritual person, but I apparently had no meaningful way to communicate any overt Christian understandings of God with the people I met on the Camino. Yet I felt like each and every one of us "pilgrims" on our way to Santiago de Compostela was *searching* for something.

Part of the pilgrimage involves a 5,000-foot climb to Cruz de Ferro, a "monumental Calvary" implanted in the Mountains of Leon. Each hiker carries with them, either from their home or from along the trail, a rock or multiple rocks that they leave at the foot of the sixteen-foot-high cross. Most have a word or a message to someone or about someone written on them. The base of Cruz de Ferro is simply an accumulation of rocks left by pilgrims throughout the years. At the peak, alongside the mound of rocks, are a variety of other items, such as clothing, shoes, and notes. For many people these objects represented some of the baggage that weighed them down in life, whether that be family, relationships, or physical or mental health issues. Many were emotionally overcome as they symbolically left behind this difficult aspect of their lives. From my perspective, and seemingly unbeknown to them, this whole process was a confession of a search for something or Someone beyond their understanding—a quest for some meaning to their existence.

Undoubtedly, all of us traversing the Camino had some sort of yearnings for divinity, community, beauty, justice, truth, and the like. Regardless of our differences in beliefs, there was an overwhelming sense we were all part of the same spiritual narrative in some way. These and other existential issues form this human experience—they are the very stuff of spirituality. Yet I found myself, the "professional Christian," walking this spiritual journey on the Camino, with no idea how to connect my experience of God in any way that might resonate with whatever these fellow pilgrims were searching for, as they walked those hundreds of miles through rural Spain.

What was it about my spirituality that did not seem to translate to Larissa from Germany, or Phil from Ireland, or Rosa from Spain? What was I missing? What wasn't I communicating correctly about this calling upon my life and the God I followed? I had done the educational and spiritual training, and most of my adult life had been spent in vocational ministry. My experiences and opportunities to communicate the good news of Jesus were far ranging and, I thought, extensive. So, what was I failing to see and to express?

We should all be forced to wrestle with a plethora of these types of questions, many of which are deeper and broader than we have ever thought to consider: what indeed is spirituality? Who or what is God? Where do I find meaning? And how do we come to know what is true and meaningful in a world of deception? And what exactly are we all looking for? What road ought we to take? Who is trustworthy enough to guide us?

These are some of the all-too-human issues we seek to bring to awareness at the very start of this book. We do so in the hope of making new and surprising connections between God's mysterious ways of reaching out to us and the myriad of human ways of experiencing God.

ANOTHER KIND OF PILGRIMAGE

For the past ten years or so, I (Alan) and my wife, Deb, have made a regular pilgrimage of a somewhat different nature. While hardly being as overtly religious as the Way of St. James, the Burning Man gathering remains, in my opinion, one of the most explicit spiritual quests in current Western culture. Every year, around 70,000 people from every walk of life descend on one of the most remote and desolate places in Black Rock Desert, Nevada: an ancient dried-up lake bed called Black Rock City, or simply "The Playa" by the "Burners" themselves.

While the die-hard Burners insist that things are changing and the gathering is becoming way too mainstream, by far the majority of participants are there not simply to party. Instead, they view the whole experience as something of a personal pilgrimage. For some this involves a whole year of preparation and planning.

In many ways far more energetically spiritual than the average church service, the real religious quest behind Burning Man is not at all hard to discern: conversations about God, spirit, meaning, love, and beauty are everywhere present and encouraged. And not only is Burning Man a celebration of some of the most beautiful art I have ever seen, it is also what is called a "gift economy." It is an incredibly generous place where nothing is for sale and everything can be given. In fact, everyone is *expected* to bring something to share with others, be it a piece of art, an act of service, an idea, music, dance, or simply a meal or a libation shared with random people walking past your tent. Collectively, Burners end up donating tens of millions of dollars by sharing some of the most magnificent artwork ever seen (just look online at images of "Burning Man Photography" and be amazed). Remarkably, many of these art pieces will be burned during the week to signify that art cannot be possessed by the wealthy; it is to be experienced equally by all and then relinquished—itself quite a statement in the obsessively acquisitive world we all inhabit.

Participants are encouraged to experience radical self-reliance where each Burner brings everything they need for the event, as well as radical self-expression—each individual is at liberty to express themselves in whatever way they see fit. Because all are accepted for who they are, or as who they present themselves to be, Burning Man is somewhat of a celebration of human creativity, with people dressing in some of the most original costumes seen anywhere. It is weird, wild, and intriguingly wonderful.

The week climaxes with two major experiences, which define the whole event: the first is the burning of "The Man" on the Saturday night. The Man is a huge, fifty-foot, cruciform statue, symbolically situated at the very center of the camp, and it functions as the reference point for the week, hence the festival's name. The second major event, the burning of "The Temple"—itself a magnificent structure that any wealthy art collector would probably pay many millions of dollars to own—exemplifies the deeply spiritual nature of the Burn. During the week, the Temple is the designated place where people "do business with God" (or the "Universe," the "Universal Spirit," the "True Self," or whatever). They mourn the loss of friends that year, make restitution, or bring something—a shrine or some other symbol—that represents an event that is significant for them. Burners can write poems or prayers on the walls, or construct a little personal shrine to remember a loved one or a broken relationship—it's a very special place and people treat it with reverence.

Whereas the burning of the Man releases what can only be called Dionysian energies—it is a wild party that goes all night—the burning of the Temple on the Sunday night is a completely different affair. Over 70,000 people gather together in reverent silence. Then, at sundown, the Temple is lit on fire, and the stunningly beautiful, fire-dyed flames consume the building. At this point, people begin to openly weep, wail, and mourn. As misdirected as much of this seems to be to a Christian, it is nonetheless an incredibly sacred, genuinely "religious" moment where the whole city opens itself to "otherness," to God, to others, to their own suffering, to the affirmation of life, and to the yearning for forgiveness.

IN SEARCH OF SO MUCH MORE

Most Christians would probably dismiss Burning Man as a debauched pagan festival, fueled by drugs, nudity, and sex, and the Camino as a misguided appropriation of the Christian understanding of pilgrimage—a vain attempt to create meaning in an increasingly meaningless world. And while these various dimensions are most certainly present, in our experience they are by no means the primary dynamic going on at the Playa or on the roads to Santiago. Implicit in these modern-day pilgrimages is a search for God, even if the participants cannot fully name what is really going on.

These contemporary pilgrimages are far more spiritual than might first appear to the critical onlooker. In fact, these experiences, and the numerous others like them scattered across our cultural landscapes, might well contain clues vital to unlocking both the power of the gospel and to accessing the real desires of the human heart in our time. In the process of coming to grips with the nature of the spiritual quest going on in the world, we might well also renew our own tired, middle-class, churchly, adventure-less spiritualities. Avoiding engagement with communities like those of the Playa or the Camino will, in the end, undermine our own experience of God and diminish our understanding and application of the gospel. Genuine missional engagement with culture always ends in renewal of the church and its spirituality.

Most people remain highly interested in God/Being/Spirit; most will readily affirm, even inevitably propose, that Jesus is one of the greatest people who ever lived—often he would be at the top of the list; and most people are searching for identity, meaning, belonging, and purpose in whatever pilgrimage they find themselves on. They are spiritually searching in all corners of culture, much more than might appear at first glance. What has become clear is that many simply cannot draw a straight line between these spiritual pilgrimages and the church or those who represent this Jesus. This is partly because they cannot readily interpret their own actions as questing, but also because they cannot see any relevance in the church today and the story of God being told. This goes some way to explaining why Mark's fellow pilgrims on the Camino failed to recognize either him or his vocation as "spiritual."

Perhaps more alarming for Christianity than atheism is the rise of the so-called *Nones* and *Dones*. The *Nones* can be categorized as those professing no particular religious faith, not because they have no belief in God or gods but because they simply perceive no real need for it. *Nones* see no ultimate reason for any particular religious beliefs about a divine being and in fact reject the claims of all religions to be able to make such assertions. In comparison, the so-called *Dones* are a rapidly increasing demographic who no longer believe they need the institutional church to practice whatever belief in God they may have left. Many in this category claim they had to leave the church in order to find God. In addition to this, there is also an increasing cultural gap between the church and Millennials—who are looking for purpose, community, and authenticity in faith communities—and yet for many their only experience of the established church is of religious activity, judgment, and hypocrisy.[1]

These current cultural analyses obviously shed some light on why the average person on the Camino discounts the spirituality of someone in a religious vocation. If the message, whether perceived or actual, is one of hypocritical, heartless judgment, then no one desires an encounter with someone giving that kind of "good" news.

Taken together, these are not just problems of perception, or ones of church attendance in decline, but a serious spiritual crisis. This is a missionally profound moment of truth because our capacity to function as credible witnesses of God and gospel is at stake. We are not witnessing to the incredibly good news of Jesus in ways that either make sense or resonate.

Culture is telling us something here: whatever we appear to be expressing through our standard churchly offerings (traditional or contemporary) is simply not connecting with increasing portions of our populations, who are in search of something so much more.

The human quest for God can take many forms. We need to learn to construct ways to recognize this, and, as witnesses, help when and where necessary. We believe humans are wired for this search for God from the start, and express that intuition in countless ways. We also believe that God, who has made us and knows us more deeply than we know ourselves, has communicated to us and is actively reaching out to us in ways far too numerous to list. In fact, human beings are haunted by God and simply cannot escape the fact that life is lived under the auspices of eternity. The passageways are simply everywhere, if searchers are willing to open their hearts—the doors of their spiritual imagination and consciousness.

In this universal search, it is not that God has stopped making himself known. Rather, it is that people (both those with belief and without) are unfortunately seeking the right things in the wrong places. The ability to discover and experience God in this search has been greatly diminished because, as Christians, we have invariably reduced the reality down to a religious formula or some church/clergy-bound sacrament, forgetting what a biblical encounter with God looks and feels like. In this book, we will spend a lot of time trying to name and identify the religious quest taking place in the husk of everyday life, and we will seek to reconnect these quests to the many-sided grace of God that comes to us in the wonders of creation, in the complex mysteries of culture, and throughout the human story.

A CALL TO REFRAMING

We live in a world that is constantly on a pilgrimage, searching and longing for so much more. Yet, as we will attempt to describe throughout the book, followers of Jesus struggle to articulate the story of God in a way that brings clarity and understanding to these longings, this world, and our place within it. This inability to recognize and respond aptly is what Walter Brueggemann refers to as a "crisis of interpretation," a crisis that results in followers of Jesus being robbed of the capacity to speak, to care, and to notice those in the Nevada desert, on a trail in rural Spain, or anywhere in between.[2]

Our driving force, the "why" behind the following pages, is the deeply held conviction that there is a great need for a reframation that allows us to see God, people, and mission through re/enchanted frames. We want to seriously consider how it is that we tell and live the story of God in the midst of this pervading "crisis of interpretation."

This is not simply an evangelism problem, nor a "give me a new zappy formula so I might share the gospel" type of discussion. This is not about telling a story designed to get people to "sign up," but instead to begin to reframe how we see and understand all sorts of pilgrims' tales. We want to consider what it might look like to enter into the story of God, allowing that good news to personally transform us in such a way that any communication of that story recognizes and addresses the deep longings and hungers of those around us. It is therefore a vibrant story of God that we invite others into—one that literally changes and transforms everything about them and their world.

THE FLOW OF THE REFRAMING CONVERSATION

As you will soon see, we believe many of our problems arise from the narrowing reductions in our framing of God, people, gospel, and the world. This has already been a significant theme in Alan's writings to this point, but in these pages we will more thoroughly explore this idea. In the first half of the book, we will identify and name what we perceive to be critical reductions in our framing of God and the world, and in the second, we will suggest ways to enlarge the frames.

So, the flow of this reframing conversation will be as follows:

In section one, we attempt to make the case that a *reduction* has taken place throughout cultural Christianity. We will explore how these reductions affect our beliefs about God, the story we tell others, and the life we live.

Section two attempts to explore the *longings* for truth and beauty that are innate to all. We also expose just how narrow and limited our perceptions of truth have become.

In section three, the turn is made into a *re/enchanting* of what it might look like to move toward seeing differently, learning to tell a better story and to live a more beautiful life.

And in section four, we conclude with a *re/learning* of some rhythms and practices that will help us find ways to perceive and understand the keys to culture.

Through this book, we want to be able to help followers of Jesus enter into a more authentic dialogue, a conversation with pilgrims on the Camino and the Playa and everywhere in between—conversations that "deepen the argument of being alive."[3] We also want to acknowledge our impoverished stewardship of both the good news of Jesus and the rule and reign of God, of which we all share responsibility. Remember, our goal is not to change the story, but rather, to take a picture we have all grown accustomed to, and surround it with a new frame, one that allows us to see the picture afresh. This reframing does not actually change the picture, but it allows for a second thought, and a third. It enables us to see a picture we have too easily defined and contained, siphoning out the breadth of mystery and meaning that every pilgrim on any trail longs to experience.

In the 1989 movie *Dead Poets Society*, John Keating told his students, "I stand upon my desk to remind myself that we must constantly look at things in a different way. The world looks very different from up here. You don't believe me? Come see for yourselves."[4] In the same way, this reframation that allows us to see God, people, and mission through ever-expansive frames, does not change the picture; it is simply standing on the desk, enabling our perception and perspective to be changed. It is not modifying the meaning; it is bringing out the color, texture, and vibrancy already present. And to do so will require a fresh approach. As the French artist Henri Matisse said, "To look at something as though we had never seen it before requires great courage."[5]

If we are able to consider a reframing of this extraordinary story of good news, we believe the beauty, the mystery, the wonder, and the glory will return, and it will connect and resonate with real human longings and desires.

May we be so courageous.

SECTION 1

A REDUCTION

What are the origins of our struggle to communicate the sacred story? Who or what is responsible for this disconnect between the longings of the world and the good news of a God who desires his people and all things to be restored to himself?

It is the root of these challenges that we seek to address in these first three chapters. If we are to effectively share the story of God into a world that includes searching pilgrims from rural northwest Spain to the desert of Nevada to our churches, coffee shops, workplaces, and everywhere in between, it will require more than a few simple tweaks to our message here and there. Instead, there must be an honest and careful exploration into a series of reductions, recognizing the domino effect a reduction in one area has on another, and then another, and so it continues. Or, more specifically to the content of section one: our framework of God has been reduced, which has led to the reduction of the radical story of Jesus, which in turn results in a life that reflects those same reductionisms.

An urgent response to this searching involves a radical rethinking and revisioning of our way of seeing, thinking, and experiencing God, the world, and the mission of God. We readily admit that this radical reframing can appear to be somewhat overwhelming. But we urge you to keep your mind and heart open, and to ask the Holy Spirit to reveal his truth to you as you begin to see and identify some of the long-held reductions we, as the people of God, have made.

MOVING THE MOON

(A GOD GREATLY REDUCED)

The greatest heresies do not come about by straightforward denial; most of the church will see that for what it is. They happen when an element which may even be important, but isn't central, looms so large that people can't help talking about it, fixating on it, debating different views of it as though this were the only thing that mattered.

— N. T. WRIGHT

Alas! the world is full of enormous lights and mysteries, and man shuts them from himself with one small hand!

— BAAL SHEM TOV

If you comprehend God, he is not God. A comprehended God is no God at all.

— THOMAS AQUINAS

In his book, *Eclipse of God*, Martin Buber points out that a solar eclipse is something that concerns the relation of our eyes to the Sun, rather than a movement or changing of the Sun itself. Although an eclipse *appears* to impact the Sun, in fact it has no influence on it at all.[1] Seen from the perspective of Earth, a solar eclipse is caused by the Moon moving between the Earth and the Sun and therefore blocking all or some of the Sun from Earth's view. Similarly, an "eclipse of God" occurs not because God moves away from our sight, but rather because objects, ideas, and idols insert themselves into our viewpoint, obscuring our capacity to view God in all his fullness.

THE ECLIPSE OF GOD

We now understand that after a short period of time the Sun reappears at the end of an eclipse, as the Moon moves out of its path. But our understanding has not always been this advanced. Primitive beliefs viewed an eclipse as an apocalyptic event. As the darkness came upon the people in the middle of the day, and as they saw the Sun disappearing and felt the cold breezes starting to surround them, their limited understanding caused them to believe that the Sun had died and the world was ending. Although this is an inaccurate scientific interpretation of a solar eclipse, there is metaphorical significance in suggesting that a world that has lost connection to its radiant Sun (God) is a world that is ending, and that it is a dark and precarious place.[2]

The eclipse (or concealment of God) is therefore a powerful twenty-first-century metaphor because it explains so much about the struggle we face to know God. The eminent philosopher Charles Taylor talks about the secular West as being trapped in what he calls "the immanent frame"—meaning that we find ourselves enclosed (framed) within a view of the world that locks out the possibility of transcendence. Our awareness of God is therefore obscured and eclipsed, and we find ourselves cut off from the enchanted, theistic, sacramental worldview that has been lost in the last 500 years or so.[3]

The process by which we arrived at this unfortunate state has been considerably analyzed by some of our greatest thinkers.[4] In summary, it is the net result of the confluence of cultural and intellectual forces that have been growing for the last 500 or so years and have snowballed in the middle to late twentieth century.[5] Rather than pointing creation toward their Source, a host of influences, including ideologies, events, idols, and people, are in fact obscuring a culture's awareness and perception of God.

And this fading of God from human consciousness has been catastrophic. Benjamin Mann, a one-time atheist, now a Catholic priest, laments:

> God's eclipse means the loss of an infinite horizon, and its replacement with a purely finite sphere: in which our freedom has no higher goal or reference point, principled values are indistinct from mere preferences, and technical ability becomes the criterion of truth.

> Man was never meant to live in such a world; he cannot make sense of it, or make sense of himself within it. Yet this—despite the persistent personal faith of a great many individuals—is the kind of world in which we increasingly live our common life.

> The crisis of the modern world is not primarily its moral disorientation—which is serious, but largely symptomatic. Nor is it the loss of specific, traditional religious faith—which is also alarming, but is really one part of a greater whole. The crisis of the modern world is the "eclipse of God."[6]

The issue is not just a loss of traditional religious faith and a declining church but a more profound loss of our whole sense of transcendence, our spiritual instincts, and our consciousness of the divine. It is a growing blindness and deafness to the Eternal, and we find ourselves tragically limited to the horizon of this finite world, such that we "no longer grasp the 'transcendent' character of [our] 'existence as man.'"[7] People (both in the church and out of it) increasingly lack the plausibility structures to make sense of faith in God, or their place in the world. Seminal British missiologist John V. Taylor names those who reduce every vertical to a horizontal, all language to the literal meaning of words, and all relation with God to a relation with others, as "contemporary flat earthers."[8]

This loss of a sense of the divine can be traced to numerous cultural forces prevalent in our day, such as:

- the ever-present secularism as a dominant worldview that eliminates religious expression (Charles Taylor's "immanent frame")
- the philosophical atheism that has dominated the arts and science over the last 120 years
- the specializing tendencies of scientific methods that reduce a total vision in order to study the parts
- the rampant materialism that has very effectively supplanted the role of religion
- the anti-religious bias of psychology and the social sciences
- the pervasiveness of capitalism and the associated market forces that inevitably reduce people to economic units of consumption
- the domination of depersonalizing technique and data, and
- the polarizing political propaganda that we are subjected to every day.

It's no wonder people can't seem to find God—so many things have moved in to obscure our vision.

As a result of the coalition of these and other forces, we now see the world as an object to be categorized and consumed—a significant move away from the premodern perception, which considered the world to be the realm of the sacred. In many ways, it is this shift in perspective that has destroyed the opportunity for intimacy with an eternal, ever-present God. God is still here (he never moved); it is we who have lost our sense of spiritual attunement. God is revealing himself to us but our senses are blunted, and we no longer have the eyes to see him. God is speaking to us but we have lost the ears to hear him and lack the language to respond.[9] When an animal can only hear certain ranges of sound, or a person is color blind, it is not that the sound or the color is absent, but that there is an inability to *perceive*. So it is with the silence and speech of God: we can no longer "see" (recognize) or "hear" (respond to) God. We have little in terms of common language or concept within which to frame a true knowledge of God. The real problem at this moment in history is that God is "disappearing" from the human horizon. Consequently, the light that comes from him is dimming, and humanity is losing its bearings, with increasingly destructive effects.[10]

THE GREAT REDUCTION

Alongside the eclipsing of God, there has been a corresponding loss of the whole due to a focusing on the parts. In other words, we have lost a sense of the big story that makes sense of all our little stories. It is this loss of wholeness that contributes to the eclipse, concealing and alienating us from the truth of the one God—and it is this loss of the whole that lies at the core of heresy.

In its original meaning, the word *heresy* does not infer that someone is wrong or has believed a falsehood. Rather, it simply refers to a particular truth or belief that has been extracted from its true and complete context and is subsequently treated as if it were the whole truth. This explains why every heretic in the history of the church has had a verse or two of Scripture they rigidly hold to. Or, as N. T. Wright notes:

> The greatest heresies do not come about by straightforward denial [...]
> They happen when an element which may even be important, but isn't
> central, looms so large that people can't help talking about it, fixating on
> it, debating different views of it as though this were the only thing that
> mattered.[11]

The point is that the so-called "heretic" really has (re)discovered some truth that has been lost, ignored, or suppressed. That is something to get excited about. However, the error in the heresy is in the exaggerated enthusiasm or preoccupation that ensues. The heretic becomes increasingly obsessive and sectarian by making the newly recovered particular truth into the *whole* truth. Its real meaning is obscured because it is separated from the greater Truth from which it has been extracted.[12] Truth thereby becomes fragmented.

The poet Rumi lamented this shattering of truth:

> The Truth was a mirror in the hands of God.
> It fell, and broke into pieces.
> Everybody took a piece of it and they
> looked at it and thought they had the truth.[13]

Heresy is not exclusive to theology and religion. If we look into just about every other domain of knowledge, we can see that this sort of reductionism affects everything. For instance, it happens when ideas—be they theological, political or sociological—are reduced and distilled into a singular controlling "ideology" through which the insiders interpret their world and organize their purposes in order to act on it.[14]

In the fields of science and philosophy, heresy occurs when knowledge becomes over-specialized and fractured, leading to various specialties warring with one another about who is really correct. Bemoaning this very fact, the philosopher E. F. Schumacher quotes the renowned psychiatrist Viktor Frankl as saying that:

> The present danger does not really lie in the loss of universality on the part of the scientist, but rather in his pretense and claim of totality [...] What we have to deplore therefore is not so much the fact that scientists are specializing, but rather the fact that specialists are generalizing. The true nihilism of today is reductionism [...] Contemporary nihilism no longer brandishes the word nothingness; today nihilism is camouflaged as nothing-but-ness.[15]

Reductionism can very definitely lead to a preoccupation with one thing—the monomaniac or fanatic is the result. The fanatic is a person with little empathy, humility, or humanity. Consider the suicide bombers of our day as the exemplary fanatics. Such people are "radicalized" by over-focusing on a reductionist Jihadist ideology by which all else is subsequently measured. They become radical sectarians, losing all meaningful relationship and perspective. And in case we are tempted to assume that ideological fanaticism is limited to those "Muslim crazies," consider the current state of "uncivil war" in the United States. The "either/or" ideology of the monomaniacal conservative or the arrogance of the elitist liberal becomes prohibitive to even "seeing" the truth in/of the other, let alone finding the ability to engage them as fellow humans. Refining that thinking down further to Christian circles:

> If you consider most conservative evangelicals, they do not believe that God is a lively character and a real agent, because they've got God all packaged up into sustained systematic explanations. And if you consider most theological progressives, they don't believe that God is a real character and a lively agent either, because they really believe that God has no hands but our hands.[16]

We are so easily imprisoned by our own interpretations and so convinced of the absolute rightness of them that we close the door to engaging the ever-greater God. This was precisely the problem with Israel's leaders in the time of Jesus. Their interpretations became the theological prisons for their own souls and minds as well as for the collective mind of Israel. In Jesus' words, they had access to the keys to the kingdom but ignored them, and hindered others from entering the kingdom as well (Matthew 23:13; Luke 11:52). When this reductionism occurs today, the story we tell manifests itself as propaganda rather than theology.

Please do not misunderstand us here—the fact is, because truth is so big and complex, analytical reductions are necessary if we are going to successfully negotiate the world (or communicate the gospel for that matter). However, because they are only fragments extracted from the whole, they should never be mistaken for the whole picture, in all its unfathomable mystery.[17] We ought never to lose sight of the enormity of truth itself—especially when we are talking about God and the mystery of his involvement in our world.

THE NEED FOR A RADICAL REFRAMING

So why are we spending so much time on this here? We want to throw a torchlight on the many reductions of how we understand and experience both God and gospel. On the one hand we believe many of our problems in engaging missionally (Camino, Playa, and beyond) are rooted in reduced understandings of God that have severely limited the ways in which we think he is to be encountered and communicated in the world. On the other hand we are equally limited by a severely diminished anthropology (understanding of the human condition) and have therefore failed to fully understand the complex, existential, religiously motivated elements common to all human beings—desire, longing, and search. (This diminished anthropology is explored in section two of this book.) As a result, Christians no longer know how to connect the various dimensions of God's good news to the human search implicit in all culture and evident throughout history. We want to reconnect the dots, reframe the picture, so that God's people might once again be able to see the marvelous ways in which he is always at work in the putting back together of this broken world.[18]

I GOT ME A PIECE OF ELEPHANT

You may well know the old parable of the blind men and the elephant in which numerous blind men are set on the task of describing an elephant; each grab the piece of the elephant that is at hand and proceed to describe what they think "an elephant really is." Each of the blind men then assume their interpretation or experience is the only one, but in reality it is a very diminished (reduced) view of an elephant.

Interestingly, this parable is used in numerous religious traditions to address the tendency of religious people everywhere to think they have God under control and all nicely boxed up. As Darrell Guder says:

> If we accept Karl Barth's distinction between the Christian faith and "religion," then the human desire to exercise control would certainly be one of the major characteristics of all [fallen] religious systems. These systems can [appear to] be very pious and impressive. But, in one way or another, they are ultimately expressions of "the hidden desire of the human heart [...] to use God merely to serve [one's] human purposes."[19]

But God will not, indeed *cannot*, be put into a box. Guder rightly reminds us that God's unwillingness to be put in a box or be controlled takes us back to the very revelation of the divine name given to Moses in Exodus 3:13–15. Despite Moses' request to know God's name, God refused to allow himself to be confined by a human constraint. The meaning of his name (YHWH) is best translated as "I will be there as I will be there." The triune God cannot be conjured up; he will choose to appear when and in whatever manner he so chooses. Nothing about him can be predicted or neatly categorized. In other words, God always retains the element of surprise. YHWH claims an always unlimited and uncontrollable sovereignty. The name of God poses a constant challenge to our human attempts to master God for our own purposes.[20] God is always ungraspable in himself; he is always *more*.

We are not saying all religious claims are the same, or that God is relativized in any way—we really believe that the God revealed in Scripture, and especially through Jesus, is indeed absolute. We are simply highlighting the fact that our grasp on him can never be absolute. Humans are limited and cannot comprehend the Absolute absolutely. Therefore, our historical reductions (the pieces of the elephant we happen to be describing) are really not the whole picture, but only a part. The early church Fathers, who were theological virtuosos when it came to exploring the boundaries of what can and cannot be known about God, were right to remind us that when dealing with the Lord of the universe there is always more. Even in our best attempts, we never arrive at a totally comprehensive understanding of God. If anyone claims to have done so, then it is not God that they have understood.

It is this human tendency to control God that lies at the heart of his condemnation of idolatry. All idolatry and religious image-making are implicit attempts to limit (reduce) and thereby control God. Idolatry is the worship of the parts instead of the whole, one aspect of the universe in place of the Creator of all who transcends all. And the Bible is unrelenting in its attack on the religious roots of reductionism, as Guder highlights: "The Prophets unmasked man's religiosity as being not just a desire for God, but a desire to have a god, to possess him, to have him for their own, at their disposal."[21] This is as true now as ever.

As beings who are so concerned about control, we find the universal significance and translatability of the gospel offensive, even a shock. A translatable gospel is fundamentally not a controllable one—it's too big; it breaks our boxes. It unsettles us to discover that faithfulness to Christ can vary from culture to culture, and is expressed with different patterns than the ones we have so painstakingly evolved. Western Christianity has assumed it represents the cultural perfection of the gospel. But no particular cultural rendering of the gospel, Western or otherwise, may claim greater validity than any other, and most certainly none have yet perfected it.[22] Therefore we must always address our tendencies to suppress, own, and limit God and gospel. The church must come awake to our participation in this heresy of reductionism, especially in our attempts to communicate the story of God. "Our faithful witness can only happen when we learn to see and repent of our conformities. These conformities must be addressed when we examine the issue of gospel reductionism and open ourselves to our own continuing conversion."[23]

Ultimately, the sad (and frankly embarrassing) outcomes of accumulated reductions and codifications of the truth are seen and experienced in our lives and churches as:

- Ossified doctrines; where ideas are believed but not lived, and faith degenerates into religious ideology.
- Wooden proclamations; where little resonates with the people beyond (and inside) the church, and theological boredom becomes the order of the day.
- Empty doxologies; where ritualized religion replaces true worship, with no relationship to the eternal and universal perspective.
- Legalistic ethics; where discipleship is reduced to religious moralism, and shame and guilt replace freedom.[24]

Or perhaps if we were to be more specific, we might simply affirm what our good friend Brad Brisco states when he laments that:

- We have reduced the church to a place and a gathering.
- We have reduced mission to evangelism.
- We have reduced worship to singing songs.
- We have reduced the gospel to bullet points.
- We have reduced Christology to the cross.
- We have reduced discipleship to the transfer of information.
- We have reduced the ministry callings/functions (Ephesians 4) to shepherd and teacher.
- We have reduced spirituality to withdrawal from the world.
- We have reduced church planting to starting worship services.[25]

Have we brought about such a reduced version of the truth that we can no longer enter into a culture that is so desperately longing for something that makes sense of our lives? And if so, can we own our responsibility and culpability for allowing this eclipse to occur?

DEADLY RELIGION

We have already observed our all-too-religious penchant for locking God down to selective doctrinal formulas. The result is a safe and controlled zone of believing in belief about God rather than in believing in God himself—God is held as an objective idea rather than a holy relationship.

Matthew Skinner's exploration of the stoning of Stephen in Acts 7 suggests that, rather than identifying ourselves with Stephen the martyr and victim, we should perhaps first read the text through the eyes of the religious leaders in this passage—the ones who stone Stephen. Reading it in this way gives us great insight into the toxic ways of thinking that all religious people are susceptible to. For instance, we can probably assume that those who killed Stephen saw themselves as responsible for protecting the religious tradition, come hell or high water. They couldn't engage Stephen in authentic conversation about God because of these immovable religious commitments, pre-commitments which they would protect to the hilt before considering other ways of understanding God. So much so that they were even willing to kill people in order to protect their beliefs. These commitments implied they presumed to know *exactly* how God works, and therefore they refused to make room for anything a professed visionary like Stephen might proclaim. They lashed out in violence because they had fallen victim to the oldest sin in the book, idolatry—in this case an idolatry of the prevailing theology of the religious tradition and of the temple itself.

> Idolatry worships a creation instead of the Creator. Idolatry loves symbols more than the thing to which a symbol points. Idolatry satisfies itself with knockoffs and shadows. Idolatry imagines God can be contained and therefore controlled and owned. Because idolaters think they know where the treasure resides, they allow no alterations to their maps and they punish explorers—with violence, if necessary.[26]

Stephen's speech to the high priest warns about idolatry by reasserting what the prophets continually declared: God's dwelling encompasses all of heaven and earth and it cannot be limited to a geographically located temple on a hill (e.g., Isaiah 66:1–21). Stephen does not say the Jerusalem temple is inherently idolatrous; rather, he claims that the members of his audience have come to treat it in an idolatrous manner. They assigned disproportionate importance to the temple and in doing so were unable to glimpse other places and ways God promised to be present.

> The idolatry perverting Stephen's foes hardly afflicts them alone. It connects to more than a high regard for the Temple and rightly interpreting the Law of Moses. It involves temptations that beset probably all religious people (including Stephen?): to turn a quest for God into an enterprise of self-assured arrogance instead of a search requiring humble reliance on fellow seekers and openness to new and old ways of finding

God. Steven's story is not about the bad guys. It's about coming to terms with the reality that all of us are prone to reject God's messengers and cling ferociously to what we already know, or think we know, very well.[27]

Skinner suggests the antidote to idolatry is not to avoid being religious, as violence and self-assurance are hardly limited to religious people; nor does it mean we should suppress our passionate convictions about our beliefs; nor are we to distrust all we think we know, or can know, about God. Rather, the answer involves keeping in view the object and purpose of our convictions, namely the possibility of encountering God, the Maker of the universe. The invitation from God is always an invitation to relationship, not an invitation to the "right way" of adhering to rules and regulations. We fall into danger when we slip into idolatry, esteeming religious rules above relating to the living God. Reductionism happens when we make following God anything less than relationship with him. We need to understand that love (for God as well as for others) and relationships *really* matter (Mark 12:30–31). When the defending of truth is done in a loveless way, it violates the very purposes of truth—to make us more like Jesus who is "the way and the truth and the life" (John 14:6). Or, as Skinner puts it, "If our convictions leave broken bodies in the wake, or if our pursuits of our religious values and prerogatives snuff out people's vitality in other ways, then we are almost certainly doing something wrong."[28]

Are we sure we would not have been among the stoners had we been privy to the events surrounding Stephen? Are we too defending reduced truths, a "system" of belief, a god-in-a-box? Have we grasped the leg of an elephant and made a calling out of proclaiming we have procured the entire animal? Have we taken a truth that is *this* big (hold your hands out as far as possible) and reduced it to something *this* big (the smallest space between your thumb and forefinger)? Would we have responded, do we respond, in similar ways to the religious leaders in Acts 7 when we are introduced to a God who is "outside of our frame"? C. S. Lewis warns us of this very issue: "My idea of God is not a divine idea. It has to be shattered time after time. He shatters it Himself. He is the great iconoclast." Lewis goes on to say that this "shattering" is actually one of the sure signs of God's presence, with the incarnation being the ultimate example, leaving "all previous ideas of the Messiah in ruins."[29]

Reductions, restrictions, and limitations are much more easily managed than interpreting a truth and grace that confounds our sense of logic and fairness, a truth that is always bigger, never smaller. Have we placed God in a box and, in doing so, have we created an ossified, wooden, empty, and legalistic religion that has reduced the reality and truth of God?

For all those with a penchant for boxing God up nice and tight, we'd do well to remember that the God of the Scriptures is not a being who will endure such blasphemous reductionisms. That is why in Scripture he is revealed as Spirit and Fire—whoever approaches God approaches the uncontainable fire of a holy love that cannot and will not be contained. This holy love will upend a life obsessed with safety and security (Hebrews 12:18–29). God is not safe, nor containable, and he claims us, body and soul, but this is what we are made for. In acknowledging God as a consuming fire, we recognize he can never fit in any box we try to place him in. He is always the ever-greater God, and the Seducer of our hearts.

MARTIN LUTHER'S PANIC ATTACKS

We suggest that one of the reasons for our current eclipse of God among Protestants is that, by-and-large, we are so keyed into the theological-anthropological frequencies of a different era that we cannot seem to grasp, let alone name, the existential issues evident in our own time. Strangely enough, this blindness partly came from a reduction arising from Martin Luther's profound struggle before God—his *anfechtung*—in the distinct theological context of the sixteenth century. (*Anfechtung* is the word Luther used when describing his own personal times of spiritual terror, despair, and religious crisis.)[30]

Now to be sure, Luther was a very spiritual man living in medieval Europe, part of a culture that was enchanted by its immersion in all things God. Furthermore, the prevailing worldview was shaped by the long tradition of Christendom Europe, meaning the church and its symbols were present everywhere. A professor of the New Testament, Luther ended up experiencing an existential crisis as he grappled with Romans 1:16–17, which references God's "righteousness" being revealed in the gospel of Jesus. But Luther could not work out how God's righteousness could possibly be good news to an unrighteous sinner. Surely it meant that we were hopelessly lost because we could never rise to God's level of righteousness. At the heart of his *anfechtung* was the terrifying feeling that God was ultimately going to judge and condemn the sinner—of which he felt the foremost.

Luther then (re)discovered that Paul's revelation in Romans was that righteousness was to be received as a gift of God's grace, through personal faith—and boom!—the rest is history. It's not too far-fetched to say that the whole Reformation was born out of the recovery of this single insight. Everything changed.

The problem was that this formulation of the gospel was so powerful in the context of the guilt-ridden medieval consciousness of the time, it soon became the only way that "the gospel" was formulated.[31] It was as if the question of objective guilt before God was the only issue human beings ever deal with. In other words, "the gospel" was so reduced to only resolving human guilt that it inadvertently left so many other dimensions of the human condition untouched by the good news. And therein lies the problem we attempt to address: the evangelical gospel has become one-dimensional— it has for such a long time been minimized and narrowed to "the Romans Road," "the Four Spiritual Laws," "the Two Ways," and the like.

Again, we don't want you to hear what we are *not* saying. We *do* believe that humans are indeed desperately separated from a holy God and very much in need of God's forgiveness; we *do* believe that Jesus died vicariously in order to reconcile and restore his creation to himself. These are absolutely vital dimensions of the good news of Jesus Christ. But what we *are* saying (throughout this entire book) is that this is not the only dimension of the gospel. As astonishing as forgiveness of personal sins is, God has done even more than that in the incarnation, life, death, and resurrection of his Son, Jesus Christ. The good news has relevance to *every* aspect of humanity's brokenness, not just personal guilt before God.

The consequence seems obvious: if justification by faith is the only way we are allowed to articulate the good news, then in order to tell the story of Jesus to a group of people who don't experience themselves as guilty-before-a-holy-God, we feel the obligation to make people feel bad about themselves before they can feel better. And so evangelicals (good news people?) come off as the tongue-clucking, finger-wagging moralizers that everyone seeks to avoid (the antithesis of good news people). Besides, when did we assume the role of the Holy Spirit? Is it not the Spirit's task to convict people of sin and righteousness (John 16:8–11)? Our job is to announce and demonstrate good news in a bad news world.[32] When we play the Pharisee, we become part of the bad news. God wants to forgive people of their sins and has already provided a way for that, but guilt need not always be the singular starting place in an individual's life.[33]

Deb Hirsch recounts hearing a speaker once pose the question, "What should be the first thing that can be said about any human being?" The overwhelming majority of the (Christian) audience answered by saying that people are first and foremost fallen sinners, capable of evil, and in need of salvation. The speaker then challenged their response and went on to explain that, while it is true that all have sinned and fallen short, there is still a more fundamental truth: each and every person is "like God"—we are all created in his image. This truth is the primary truth that precedes and qualifies the secondary truth—that we are indeed fallen sinners in need of redemption.[34] The story must always start at the beginning.

> Christianity too often begins by emphasizing a problem (original sin) instead of beginning with the wonderful unity between creation and Creator (original blessing). We first remind you that you are "intrinsically disordered" or sinful—which then allows us to just happen to have the perfect solution. It is like the vacuum cleaner salesman first pouring dirt on your floor, so he can show you how well his little Hoover works. As if the meaning of the universe or creation could start with a foundational problem![35]

So often the evangelical culture falls into the trap of starting its proclamation of the gospel in Genesis 3 (original sin) rather than in Genesis 1 (original blessing). When this happens, the good news simply becomes about how we get rid of all that guilt and all that sin. But if we desire to start at the beginning (a simple proposal that aligns with any storytelling technique … "once upon a time"), then we must begin with Genesis 1. Humanity is created in the image of God and that creation was good and right until separation from God happened in Genesis 3. Then the good news becomes about how God brings his family back together and restores the world, both as they were intended. If we reduce the gospel by beginning with the problem, then the whole search for God becomes a negative problem-solving journey. And to those who are desperately searching for something more, reducing the good news to problem-solving and moralism presents itself as an exercise in futility.

In chapters to come, we will explore how we can broaden the conversation beyond simply talking about guilt and sin. For now, we simply note that human beings have a much larger register of religious and existential need than *just* guilt before God, as real as that is. A holistic approach to God's total and saving response to each and every one of these issues is far more expansive than our limited view has allowed.

ONE SIZE FITS ALL

Procrustes, whose name means "he who stretches," is arguably one of the most intriguing characters in Greek mythology. He was a devious villain who kept a house by the side of the road in which he would offer hospitality to passing strangers. The guests were invited in for a pleasant meal and a night's rest in his "very special bed," which Procrustes described as having the enchanting property of matching the exact length of anyone who lay down on it, magically of course. What Procrustes left out of the description was the method by which this one-size-fits-all miracle was achieved: as soon as the guest would fall asleep in the special bed, Procrustes would begin his villainous procedure, stretching the guest on the rack if they were too short for the bed or chopping off their legs if they were too long—a rather unfortunate way of making everyone conform to his one-size-fits-all bed.

Procrustes' infamous allegory has found its way into our language when we describe something as "a procrustean bed" or "procrustean effort," or simply call something "procrustean." It denotes an asserting of a set of assumptions and subsequently forcing everything to fit those assumptions even when they do not fit—like forcing a round peg to fit a square hole.

It should come as no surprise that people guilty of "the procrustean way" also tend to formulate problems in such a way that the solutions to those problems demand precisely the very tools and processes that they (rather providentially) just so happen to have at hand, and which they are already skilled at.[36]

Social psychologist Abraham Maslow wrote of interpreting the world through a similar single lens when he developed what he later called "the law of the instrument" or "the law of the golden hammer." This describes the consequence of over-reliance on a particular idea, tool, or interpretation. In *The Psychology of Science* in 1966 he suggested that, if the only tool you have is a hammer, then you will treat everything as if it were a nail.[37]

It is a one-size-fits-all approach to life.

A relatively harmless example of this is in the 2002 movie *My Big Fat Greek Wedding*, where the patriarch of the family, Gus Portokalos, believed that a squirt of Windex was the solution to all that ails humanity. Any ailment "from psoriasis to poison ivy" could be cured with a quick spray of Windex.[38] No matter what the presenting problem was, Gus would point to his bottle of Windex and then spray: a classic forced-to-fit strategy of dealing with reality. And we in the church do this very same thing whenever we become enamored with a single defining solution or formula and then reformat all our theology to suit—whole theological systems and denominations are built on precisely this impulse.

Von Balthasar suggests that many theologians throughout history have had a bad habit of isolating some fragment of knowledge upon which they begin imposing their own speculations ... procrustean theology is the result.[39] We see this throughout the centuries as numerous historical players and agencies have scrambled to make the message of the Scriptures fit their prior experiences, understandings, organizational brands, or preferences, and then demand compliance from their respective adherents. And God help the poor wretches who did not fit. Christendom (the name itself implies an imperial assumption of *dom*ination and control) has subsequently forced, often with great violence, much of reality and culture to fit the formulas. Christendom managed to do even more violence to its dissenters than Procrustes himself—their methods of torture also included the stretching of, or the removal of, limbs, but went way beyond this to include flaying of the skin, emasculations, drownings, and, the ultimate torture … burning people alive in the public square in the name of God.[40]

Or consider some other forms of reductionism … such as reductions in our concept of church. There are now more than 25,000 denominations worldwide—each of these constructed around selective visions drawn out from the grander view of the church in the Scriptures.[41] Many of these define and distinguish themselves based on structure, leadership, on baptismal mode, understandings of atonement theory, belief in predestination or free will, whether adherents speak in tongues or not, whether one uses musical instruments in worship or not, etc. Each of these have their favored Bible verses but therefore they are reductions.

It is surely an act of God's sheer grace that over its lifetime the church has managed to get a lot of things right, but it must also be acknowledged that we have managed to force fit the greater biblical truths into innumerable reduced doctrinal formulas, which are then in turn used to bolster the reduction of a greater truth. One can say that almost every denomination is in some way a victim of Procrustes.

A WAY PAST THE ECLIPSE

In section three of this book, we will propose ways to reverse the effects of the eclipse and to move past our procrustean ways. For now, in these first three chapters, we need to explore and recognize that it is a problem both contemporary believers and unbelievers alike must face—a reduction of truth, a reduction of the story, and the natural result, a reduced way of living. These reductions are at the heart of our own incapacity to see and experience God's transcendence, as well as his immanence, in all things. Not only do we struggle to readily discern God at work on the Playa and the Camino, we equally struggle to see God at work beyond the narrow and privatized confines of the domain of church.

We believe that each and every one of us has a responsibility to move the moon or, at the very least, begin to adjust our perspectives and allow a reframation to begin. Because again, in an eclipse of God it is not God who moves; the darkening comes when we insert or interpose anything that obscures and conceals the truth of God in his totality.

A CURD MADE FROM MASHED SOYBEANS

(A STORY GREATLY REDUCED)

God made man, because he liked to hear a story.
— **AFRICAN PROVERB**

Here we have our present age ... bent on the extermination of myth. Man today, stripped of myth, stands famished among all his pasts and must dig frantically for roots, be it among the most remote antiquities.
— **FRIEDRICH NIETZSCHE**

Telling stories is as basic to human beings as eating. More so, in fact, for while food makes us live, stories are what make our lives worth living.
— **RICHARD KEARNEY**

Old Testament scholar Walter Brueggemann writes, "The gospel is [...] a truth widely held, but a truth greatly reduced. It is a truth that has been flattened, trivialized, and rendered inane."[1] When we reduce God and truth, what naturally follows is a reduction of the *story* of God that we tell. The telling of a reduced story takes the always impressive and authoritative story of Jesus, and siphons it of its transformative power, drains it of its restorative influence, or simply bleeds it dry until it is lifeless. This happens all the time in Sunday School when Jesus' stories are used to bolster middle-class morality rather than unleashing the revolutionary call to transformation they're intended to do; hence the prevalence of the so-called "Sunday School Jesus!"

It is these reductions and the shrouding of truth that have left us completely unprepared for the missional moment and context we find ourselves in. All this makes a meaningful proclamation about God putting the world back together again so very difficult—this is true whether the context is a church gathering, the Camino, the Playa, or simply a conversation with our next-door neighbor.

TOFU V WARHEADS

Author Don Everts believes that in our telling of the gospel story we have made Jesus into a "Tofu Savior": square, tasteless, bland ... "a curd made from mashed soybeans." (Apparently we eat tofu only because it is good for us, not because we necessarily enjoy it or like it. No disrespect to tofu-eaters intended.) Likewise, we have bought into a reduced story in such a way that it can be equated to the worst that tofu is ... a "flavored sponge"; something that doesn't have much taste itself but simply absorbs the flavors of the foods that surround it.

In contrast Everts asks, "Have you ever had Warheads Sour Candy? You put a Warhead in your mouth and immediately your body has two reactions, either 1) 'I feel alive; everything is now in color!' or 2) You spit it out of your mouth as fast as you can, because you cannot handle the 'jarring taste.'"[2] We propose that this somewhat ridiculous comparison (tofu v Warheads) illustrates the different ways the story of Jesus is retold. The Jesus story ought to be experienced like Warhead Sour Candy—it should jolt us. It should startle us. This jarring dimension of theological truth applies to all the manifold revelations of God in Scripture and history, but it is especially applicable to the life and ministry of Jesus. A cursory reading of the Gospels shows that anyone who got a "taste of Jesus" either wanted to spit him out as quickly as possible, or they ended up intrigued saying, "I don't know where this is going, but I feel strangely alive!" An encounter with the incarnated story of God-in-Christ always changed lives, one way or another.

In the same vein, Tim Keller writes:

> Jesus's teaching consistently attracted the irreligious while offending the Bible-believing religious people of His day. However, our churches do not have this same effect, which can only mean one thing. Our preaching and practices are not declaring the same message that Jesus did.[3]

The temptation when communicating the story of God is to settle for "a curd made from mashed soybeans" because, well, we have come to believe that even a tasteless religiosity is better for us than having no religion at all.

Evangelicals especially seem to want to reduce the story to the point that it can easily be written on a napkin. A preference for tofu-Jesus tries to cut the gospel story down to manageable size and in ways that merely confirm our lifestyle and political preferences. We seem to do this for two key reasons: first, because of a fear of presenting a Jesus who is far too counterintuitive and offensive to our already settled lives; and second, because we have an incorrect belief that if we tell of a Jesus who is more palatable and culturally applicable, it will be much easier for people to accept him and his teachings. Either reason results in us telling a reduced story siphoned of its transformative power and drained of its restorative influence.

WIRED FOR STORY

So why is story important? What is passed on in and through telling a better story? And what is lost when our stewardship of God's story is dissolved into religious formula?

All human beings are formed through narrative. It is what shapes our identities as people—corporately as in tribal history, and personally through events that impact our sense of who we are and what our roles are in the world. We are wired for story.

Human beings live inside stories. Stories are how we communicate with each other; how we connect with each other. They are how we learn, how we think.[4] The stories we consume shape so much of who we are, what we do, how we act, and what we believe. Stories are not simply a way to communicate; they live in and around us in a way that allows humans to advance.[5]

All cultures and societies use story to pass on cultural DNA, to form identity, and give context for meaningful engagement in the world. "Telling stories is as basic to human beings as eating. More so, in fact, for while food makes us live, stories are what make our lives worth living."[6] As philosopher Alasdair MacIntyre points out in his classic *After Virtue*, I can answer the question, "What am I to do?" only if I can answer the prior question, "Of what story or stories do I find myself a part?"[7] Story is a vital part of the frame.

We would do well to consider why stories like *The Lord of the Rings*, or *Harry Potter*, or *The Chronicles of Narnia* have captivated the imagination of millions of people. We would argue that these stories capture our imagination and provide us with new ways of seeing the world—with new possibilities and questions to explore. Their characters are three-dimensional and credible. We sympathize with them when they fail or are wounded. We feel joy when they succeed or fall in love. We are drawn into the plot, the bigger narrative, because the characters and story are plausible, carrying universal significance. They allow us to enter into worlds we couldn't see on our own, and in a very real sense to inhabit those worlds. Stories allow us to seriously confront questions, such as: what if I lived in a world where magic was real? What if I encountered a piece of furniture that transported me to a different world? What would I do if the "one ring" came into my possession?

> Maybe above all they are tales about transformation in which all creatures are revealed in the end for what they truly are—the ugly duckling becomes a great white swan, the frog is revealed to be a prince, and the beautiful but wicked queen is unmasked at last in all her ugliness. They are tales of transformation where the ones who live happily ever after, as by no means everybody does in fairy tales, are transformed into what they have it in them at their best to be.[8]

Ultimately, stories like these enable us to ask, if I entered this story, who would I be? In the same way, when we tell the story of Jesus with similarly rich metaphors, it provokes questions and thoughts, such as: how would my life change if I lived in a world where it was truly better to give than receive? What would it be like to live in a world where the first shall be last and the last shall be first? If I really did believe that God had power over death, would that alter the way I lived? What would it be like to live in a world where death didn't have the final word?[9]

Why is it that these questions, central to the Jesus story, are scarcely considered? Is it because, as Christians, we so often present a one-dimensional story, with our formulaic points and doctrine inserted in?

God's revelation is not some storyless event that can be observed and then filed away in neat categories; it is the record of his dramatic rescue of the world, a rescue that is still unfolding in our world every day. We are participants in this story, and whether we like it or not, we are in the drama as it is being performed. "We have no real objective viewpoint from which to merely observe."[10] This is not to say that theological formulas are not important, but on their own, and divorced from the living context of narrative and testimony, they can become stultifying and dangerous ideologies. Story and narrative communicate truth, and form identity in a way that rational code simply cannot.

Our attempts to distill the Bible—which is bursting with life, intrigue, and drama—to a series of principles is equivalent to trying to reduce a living person to a diagram. The exodus from Egypt, or the revelation at Sinai, or Miriam's slander against Moses, are all events, not an idea; a happening, not a principle. Conversely, attempting to reduce the Bible to a catalog of events, a sacred history and nothing more, will equally fail.[11] This is precisely why, in Jewish tradition, *halakhah* (conceptual ideas and ethical code) is always held in balance with *haggadah* (story, parable, and history). Each one interprets and makes sense of the other. And both are needed to make sense of the world. It also accounts for why Jews traditionally have generated some exceptional thinkers as well as some of the world's greatest storytellers.[12]

This role of story was undoubtedly significant for Israel. The biblical story of faith provided a narrative in which an individual would discover who God was, who they were, why they existed, and where they were going. The covenant was given to a particular people and it is to be passed on in living memory through the telling and retelling of the story. And they are urged again and again to recover and reappropriate the story—Isaiah 40–55 is a case in point. That story is remembered annually in the regular liturgy of Israel and is dramatically reenacted in the reading of the Passover Haggadah.

When the biblical characters forgot their narrative, they lost their way. They no longer knew who they were, where they came from, or where they were going. According to the prophets, the "losing of their story," their constant forgetting of the covenant relationship established in the patriarchs and at Sinai, was the root of their rebellion and sin (e.g., Judges 8:33–34). It might well be the root of ours as well.

THREE WAYS TO MAKE TOFU

In further understanding our tendency toward reductionisms, we suggest that specific practices have contributed to this "crisis of interpretation." In the telling of God's revelatory story and how that story intersects with all of culture, we have been guilty of:

- *demythologizing*—through shrinking revelation to reduced-to-fit, anti-supernatural, atheistic/deistic presuppositions about life
- *demystifying*—by eliminating mystery, wonder, love, and awe from the equation of how humans can rightly approach and know God, and

· *depoeticizing*—through dangerously narrowing our perceptive range and our linguistic capacity to talk about God, thereby reducing theology to rational code and religious formula.

These are key factors related to what has been called the "disenchantment of Western culture" as it moved from the premodern openness to the divine, to the closed, rationalistic, secularized, technique-based culture we currently inhabit.[13] Each of these three elements has contributed to a crisis of interpretation because each directly impacts our capacities to recognize, understand, and respond to the story of God as it unfolds in Scripture and history.

We don't need to look into the unfolding of history to find these three reductionistic practices at work; we need look only into our own soul. As you read the following pages, try to discern the impact of these reductions on you and the people around you. We all are infected with the virus. The crisis is universal in scope.

DEMYTHOLOGIZED

One of the strongest forces in the overall disenchantment of the world and the reduction of story is what has been called demythologization. In relation to the narrative of God, this has involved a systematic attempt to weed out all elements considered "primitive" and "legendary." The gospel has instead been articulated purely in terms of the rationalistic or existentialist worldview of the twentieth century. To fully grasp this claim, it is important to understand what we do, and do not, mean by the word *myth*, and why it is so vital to theology and culture, as well as spirituality in general.[14]

The popular use of the term *myth* carries with it a negative connotation, especially when brought into conversation about common religious beliefs and superstitions. This widely held definition of myth relates to outdated convictions held by people regarded as "primitive" and "irrational." So, when people using this nuance dismiss something as a myth, they are dismissing it as untrue.[15] (Obvious examples could be applied to holiday myths, such as the Easter Bunny, Santa Claus, and Cupid.) We are certainly not referring to this interpretation; rather, we are using the term in the same way C. S. Lewis, J. R. R. Tolkien, Roland Barthes, and Joseph Campbell (among others) have applied it.

Understood in this way, myth describes those stories that have a "super-meaning"—stories that contain the roots of defining themes that have cultural, religious, or spiritual significance for those who tell them.[16] They are the stories that guide, orientate, and illuminate whole peoples and generations. They are narrative frames through which we understand our roles in the world. Evangelical theologian James Menzies notes that:

> Throughout human history, myth has served as a source to explain questions of creation and human origins, making sense of tragedy, finding meaning for one's existence, and to help prepare for life after death. And whether one examines indigenous cultures steeped in religion or highly technological cultures espousing many (or no) religions, there is frequently an evidence of myth handed down through generations resulting in ideas and beliefs that intentionally and unintentionally become part of such cultures and societies.[17]

To say that a story is mythic (in this sense) therefore is not to say that it is mere fantasy. Quite the opposite. By appealing to the power of myth, we give ordinary, everyday things new vitality and meaning by which life is reoriented and reframed. This is because myth reaches into the innermost levels of human consciousness, something we are actually wired for—there is a "myth receptor" in each one of us. Myth resonates with us because it contains universal and fundamental truth, but mythic stories also have power because they reach beyond the filters of the rational mind and go right into the human heart, that barely conscious place where all our deepest longings are rooted. That's why humans can't get enough stories and drama. It's what takes you back to the bookstore, Netflix, or to the cinema again and again. And this is why, when we speak with mythic resonance, deep calls unto deep.

> Literature that engages and forms our imaginations allows knowledge of the head to become knowledge of the heart; situated not in cold abstraction but in a way that is integrated and organic. This type of knowledge doesn't just change our minds, it changes our lives. Fictional worlds may consist of things which do not exist materially (e.g., hobbits, trolls, elves, dwarves, fairies, wizards, and talking animals), but are built of real transcendentals like truth, justice, and beauty, and in this way can be truer worlds than our own. When we can see that fiction is sometimes fact, we come to understand our experiences in a new and

more meaningful way. Emotions such as courage and desire, awe and enchantment, sorrow and guilt, long since dismissed by materialists as simple biological mechanisms, can be true guideposts for a life of faith. And if we are willing to enter this newfound story, we see that the author is none other than God himself, and he has written it just for us.[18]

And so we can see how God can readily address people in and through mythic story. The church has long believed that authentic myth contains truths and ideas seeded in and through all creation and history, and can be traced back to Jesus as the Logos (the Word), through which the world was created in the first place (John 1:1–14). We can therefore say that all that came to light in the life of Christ was already hidden "in myths and conjectures concerning the beginning, end, and meaning of life."[19]

> Divine grace, predestined in Christ to be given to the whole world, is secretly at work in the whole sphere of history, and thus all myths, philosophies, and poetic creations are innately capable of housing within themselves an intimation of divine glory.[20]

Assuming this, we can say that a work that contains mythological elements will inevitably draw a reader out of themselves and into something greater. For instance, Lewis explains that a reader, after entering into an experience with a real myth, may well say, "I shall never escape this. This will never escape me. These images have stuck roots far below the surface of my mind."[21] We feel ourselves somehow eternally impacted by the mythic. It speaks to us and our situation one way or another in a never-ending way.

But Lewis says that the real value of the myth is that it takes all the things we know and restores to them the rich significance that has been hidden by the veil of familiarity.

> The child enjoys his cold meats (otherwise dull to him) by pretending it is a buffalo, just killed with his own bow and arrow. And the child is wise. The real meat comes back to him far tastier for having been dipped in a story: you might say that only then is it the real meat. If you are tired of the old real landscape, look at it in a mirror. By putting bread, gold, horse, apple, or the very roads into a myth we do not retreat from reality, we rediscover it.[22]

When we lose a sense of the mythic dimensions of story, we end up with a low-resonance proclamation that fails to scratch the itch—the splinter in the mind—that people feel lies at the very core of who they are. We lack a message that reaches into the soul—collectively or individually.

The Disenchanted Mind

So much for what myth is. But what is de*myth*-ologization and how did it come about? Simply understood, demythologization removes and/or rationalizes the perceived "mythic" elements of a story, rendering it more consistent with a supposedly scientific understanding of the world. Stories thus become "disenchanted." This has happened primarily in the last five centuries or so of Western history as part of the overall disenchantment or desacralization of our understanding of the world.

When demythologization has been applied to the biblical story, it has sought to separate and remove what is considered an obsolete understanding of the origin and development of the universe. This demythologization has deeply impacted the collective Western mind-set—including yours, much more than you are aware of. This systematic elimination of myth intended:

- to reinterpret events that are overtly supernatural in terms more consistent with what is considered natural law and admissible science[23]

- to extricate what are considered crude folklore and superstition from historic records in order to render them as rational accounts of history, and[24]

- to disengage philosophical principles and ethics from outmoded theological claims in order to provide a religious or moral aspect to life.[25]

We are sure many readers will quickly recognize these forms of rationalism present in their churches and theology. Whether we like it or not, the vast majority of people reading this book will have been taught to think of faith largely in rationalistic terms and, in many ways, to practice faith devoid of a radical openness to the supernatural work of the Holy Spirit. Both mainline Protestant and conservative evangelical cultures are dominated by the language of the scientific and the rational, and because of this there has been a loss of this deeper mythic dimension. The story of God creating the world, ultimately restoring the world and everything in between has been disenchanted ... the "magic" has been siphoned out.

Scripture is reduced to a dusty book containing dry history, doctrine, and ethics. The story of God contained in the Bible no longer inspires and resonates; we no longer engage with it as a call to a wide-eyed adventure of which we are a part. Our theology is no longer performed on its knees, but rather at the desk and in the academy—seldom at church or on the streets. The academic approach allows us to think that we can pick God apart like we would a frog specimen in science class. This kind of scientific theology does not often require much of us. It allows us to think about God without having to become like Jesus. We can read our books and prepare our sermons without much changing within us.[26] Thus, divorced from prayer, worship, and the passionate pursuit of God, theology quickly degenerates into scholasticism. Our theology manuals run dry, our commentaries become fussy and artless, and our proclamation no longer resonates with its intended audience. Our communication lacks any appeal to the real issues of the human longing for salvation and fullness. And if this is not bad enough, the removal of the narrative strength and mythic resonance impairs the disciple's ability to see, hear, and respond to God with body, heart, and soul. A flattened story results in a flattened response. Yet the narrative of God in Scripture is an evolving drama in which all are called to actively participate.[27]

Joseph Campbell, the American author renowned for his work in mythology, warned us that wherever myth is interpreted as mere biography, history, or science, its impact is annulled. The living metaphors and images it contains turn into remote facts. He maintained that when a civilization begins to reinterpret its mythology in this way, the life goes out of it, temples become museums, and the link between the historical and the mythical becomes dissolved. When this deeper dimension is lost in the telling of the gospel, a story that is "too good to be true" is exchanged for a one-dimensional, rational, and believable narrative rather than one that is multi-dimensional and mind-blowing.

The result of this systematic demythologization is that the myths that help us make sense in a senseless world, and give significance to our existence, are consistently drained of their potency, and simply absorb the flavors of the foods that surround them. We end up with that darn tofu again. As a result, people turn away from the story of God to just about any other source, in an attempt to find a meaningful alternative. Hollywood and the video gaming and advertising industries have understood all too well the identity-shaping power of myth—and profitably exploit it to great effect. They are on to something the church has forgotten. There is something significant about the way culture tells stories—more than the mere entertainment they provide.

This search for an abiding myth to live by, for mythic living itself, is precisely what is going on in the innumerable new religious movements in our day—the Playa and the Camino are just two cases in point. It also accounts for the popularity and influence of Joseph Campbell and others like him. People will get their defining stories somewhere. The church's demythologized, rationalistic message, void of story, just does not fill the soul, inspire the heart, or call us to adventure and journey. Our unwillingness to even consider the place of myth in the story of the gospel contributes to a great vacuum in evangelical culture.

DEMYSTIFIED

All great stories have a sense of mystery, of unresolvable "magic," an enchantment that draws us in. A story that transforms us carries with it a mystery that expands the possibilities of what we know, but does not defy reason.

Once again, the problems of perception and interpretation of the divine can be best understood in light of the greater practice of demystification that has been at work in our culture over the last five centuries or so. Modern technological society, in an effort to name, classify, control, and exploit, has effectively demystified the world. The premodern world was a thoroughly enchanted place where people confronted mystery throughout. Despite all the terrible conundrums of suffering and death faced throughout history, when premodern people looked out into the world they were aware of an unfathomable mystery that pervaded every aspect of life. They experienced this world as immediate, personal, and often very threatening. The sense of the divine blazed throughout. But they also intensely experienced the beauty and harmony of the universe.[28] Their myths projected all kinds of mysterious meanings to the planets and stars. In terms of religious experience, they were much more open to the divine and to the possibility of theophany (the visible manifestation of God to humanity). They were also open to experiential encounters that led to asking and engaging in spiritual questions. Their "enchanted" world was thus responsive, full of a spiritual radiance, for which we moderns have neither name nor concept. To a great extent we now live in a largely desacralized (or sacred-free) world.[29]

While rejecting outright animism (the practice of assigning a soul to inanimate objects) and polytheism (the worship of multiple gods) as ways of understanding and encountering God, the Scriptures affirm the fact that all of reality is, or can become, a theatre for the holy. Theophanies are littered throughout Scripture, from the burning bush in Exodus 3 to the powerful demonstration in the Incarnation of the Word. The Bible is written from within what is called the premodern worldview. Nature is not to be identified with God. But neither is nature neutral; rather, it is "charged with the grandeur of God" (Hopkins).[30] God is both transcendent and immanent and therefore permeates absolutely everything, as J. V. Taylor, in his remarkable book *The Christlike God*, points out:

> Wherever God exists he exists wholly. In his infinitude he cradles the universe, yet he knows every atom of its structure from within. The truth of God transcendent and of God immanent, his mystery and his availability, must be held together as a single reality, dialectical to human thought but indivisible in itself. The God who is within things is not secondary or less than the God who is beyond. His unfathomable otherness addresses each of us with an intimacy surpassing all other relationships.[31]

"Woe is Me! For I am Undone"

Any genuine encounter with God—what Rudolf Otto calls "the Numinous"—brings about a sense of utter holiness, awe, and wonder, different from anything we experience in ordinary life.[32] According to Otto, an encounter with "the Numinous" is comprised of the three components contained in the Latin phrase: *mysterium tremendum et fascinans*—the encounter with a holy mystery that is both awe-inspiring and fascinating. Let us define what we imply:

Mysterium involves a sense of the wholly Other, of unadulterated holiness, of limitless incomprehensibility, and is responded to with blank wonder, stupor even.

Tremendum comprises a sense of holy dread, reverential awe, of unapproachability because of the sheer majesty, might, and vitality that is encountered in the Numinous.

Fascinans is made up of a sense of potent charm, attractiveness. In spite of the fear and terror, we are held in awe.

You can see all these dimensions in every theophany and encounter that humans have with God. For example, "'Woe to me!' I cried. 'I am ruined! For I am a man of unclean lips'" (Isaiah 6:5); "When Simon Peter saw this, he fell at Jesus' knees and said, 'Go away from me, Lord; I am a sinful man!'" (Luke 5:8); and upon seeing his vision of Jesus in the figure of a Warrior-Judge, John falls on the ground as though dead (Revelation 1:9–18). This is the pattern of all theophany in Scripture.

The three elements of *holiness/otherness*, *awe/dread*, and *fascination/attraction* are so intimately related that they form an irreducible, synthetic whole. These aspects of the Numinous and the otherworldly are so often conspicuously absent in the demystified story of God, or the reduced version of Jesus, that we so often communicate.[33]

When someone has an authentic experience of the Holy, they find themselves caught up in two opposite movements at the same time. They are both daunted by, and yet irresistibly drawn into, the mystery they have encountered. We both draw back from and are pulled forward into a kind of liminal space where we are not at home at all and yet totally at home for perhaps the first time.[34]

> The paradoxical tension between the fear inspired by the otherworldly Sacred and the irresistible attraction it exerts at the same time on the believer was the very essence of religious consciousness. Since human reason is unable to break its code, the numinous also always appears as the mystery.[35]

The profound mystery of God's inescapable presence ought to evoke wonder and should be a part of the story we tell. Abraham Heschel calls this a "sense of the ineffable" and without it, we will never be able to comprehend God or the things of God.[36] The Bible consistently teaches that the fear, or awe, of God is the gateway to the love and knowledge of God (e.g., Proverbs 9:10). And it is this aspect of mystery, respect, and awe that is missing from our modern sense of interpretation.

DEPOETICIZED

This attempt to gain a rational grasp of God, and to manage and systemize the story of this God's incarnation, has left our experience and proclamation of the divine with little originality, creativity, and artistry. Such a tragic but very true reduction has not only demythologized and demystified the story, it has "depoeticized" it as well.

In what should be a powerful and beautiful story of creation, separation, rescue, and restoration, we have reduced the magnificence and grandeur; instead of being spiked with a dash of Warhead, it's been laced with tofu. David Lipscomb, an important religious leader and educator in the second half of the nineteenth century, warned his hearers that they were to read the Bible narrowly, always taking it in its most literal sense. Such an approach he claimed, "keeps man on safe ground [...] and *clips the wings of imagination and speculation* and makes the Bible the only and safest teacher of duty to man" (italics ours).[37] Lipscomb's mentor was an influential man named Tolbert Fanning, and it appears it was from him that Lipscomb inherited his negative assessment of imagination. In his eulogy to Fanning, H. R. Moore said, "He waved no plumes, wreathed no garlands, but struck from the shoulder and at the vitals. He was destitute of poetry and barren of imagination."[38]

Now, just to be clear, eulogies are intended to represent the highest of praise for someone; a summary of their life. What boggles the mind then is trying to comprehend what kind of reasoning and logic considers the words "destitute of poetry and barren of imagination" as high praise and worthy of a eulogy.

Read that tragic line one more time: *He was destitute of poetry and barren of imagination*. Such a sorrowful lament.

The question for us then becomes, is this poverty of imagination and poetry still prevalent in our circles? We think it is. From our experience it seems that most classic evangelical education fails to pass on any appreciation of poetry, or a hermeneutic that understands how it is that revelation impacts the godly imagination. Students are often told what to believe and are schooled in analytical/rationalistic approaches to theology and exegesis. This is a huge deficiency in our capacity to enter into a relationship both with God and his story. As Robert Frost reportedly noted, "Poetry is what gets lost in translation."[39] But what a loss!

Consider this: much of the Bible is written in poetic form—prophecy with its fertile symbolism and rhetorical rhythm; the apocalyptic with its multitude of images and metaphor; the Psalms with their lyrical cadence of joy and lament. Symbols, metaphors, and other verbal tangents are the very stuff of poetry, and these are loaded throughout Scripture. We cannot expect to grasp what is being communicated if we fail to interpret these in the way they are intended to be read. Poetry cannot, and must not, be read in the same way one reads rational and systematic code.

"The imagination," John Piper writes, "calls up new words, new images, new analogies, new metaphors, new illustrations, new connections to say old, glorious truth—whether from the world or from the word of God. Imagination is the faculty of the mind that God has given us to make the communication of his beauty beautiful." To communicate breathtaking truth in a boring way is "probably a sin," he says, for God is "infinitely worthy of ever-new verbal, musical, and visual expressions."[40]

Because its appeal is precisely to the imagination, the story of Jesus is obviously not meant to be read without an understanding of metaphor and other language forms. Furthermore, all the prophets were poets. If you doubt that, just try reading them in a purely literal manner and see where it gets you. They pile metaphor upon metaphor. Metaphor really is a remarkable tool because it means what it says but also what it *doesn't* say. You don't try to figure a metaphor out; rather you try entering into what's there.[41]

For instance, when Jesus is called "the Lamb of God" in John's writings, he is not saying Jesus is a literal lamb, a baby sheep. Or when Peter calls Jesus a "living Stone," it does not mean Jesus' chemical makeup had changed into a new form of rock. Rather these are types of creative speech designed to communicate something much more meaningful regarding Jesus' person and work, and to encourage us to respond. All forms of language (narrative, poetry, prose, etc.) are found to be destitute and barren when read one-dimensionally—in fact it can be outright dangerous to do so. How can we ever come to grips with either the content or the purpose of God in his story if we don't understand how to engage poetry and prose?

Consider the effects of siphoning and draining the power of story in the Gospels. Whether it is misinterpreting Jesus when he uses the metaphor of the yeast of the Pharisees (Matthew 16), or Jesus returning to a place where they could not go (John 14), or the eating of the body and drinking of the blood of Christ (John 6), or the meaning of being born again (John 3), and a host of others, people "destitute of poetry and barren of imagination" can never seem to grasp what Jesus was really saying. People mishear what Jesus said precisely because of their inability to think poetically and metaphorically. They are trying to make sense of Jesus' use of parabolic logic within the concrete logic that has no means to interpret the big story or access the content of what is being revealed. Too often people cannot grasp Jesus because he speaks poetically (evoking imagination), and by interpreting him literally they are bound to doctrinally predetermined templates devoid of imagination.[42]

A failure to engage God and the Bible poetically and imaginatively means we will likely misread both because we are forcing our experiences to conform to linear, informational categories as opposed to entering into a world of metaphors, parables, word-play, and evocative language. It's like trying to interpret multi-dimensional reality with a one-dimensional method. It flattens the revelation.

How many times do we make the same mistake and force a univocal literalism (only having one meaning) on a multivocal text? When we do so, the Bible becomes an echo of our own voice and mentality. It is all cut and dried. Predictable as opposed to surprising. Religious as opposed to spiritual. Benign as opposed to liminal. The Word is entrapped in the hermeneutics of literalism—the resonance and the sheer voluptuousness of Truth is gone.

It is this depoeticized ("destitute and barren") perspective of theology, God, and the story of Jesus that contributes greatly to a story that has been reduced to "a curd made from mashed soybeans." Unfortunately, we have all been effectively blinded to this great reduction.

THE RED TERROR

We cannot allow the story to be reduced. We cannot allow it to be demythologized, demystified, or depoeticized. We must resist the reductionist tendencies and instead recognize the power of story in our lives and especially in the proclamation of the gospel.

The *October Revolution* is one of the labels given to a socialist revolt in Russia in the year 1917. Led by Vladimir Lenin, the Bolshevik Party overthrew the existing autocratic government in a seizure of state power that contributed to the eventual rise of the Soviet Union. The Bolsheviks took control over multiple government agencies and seized control of rural areas. In order to suppress any dissension to the revolution, the security organization "Cheka" was created. This Bolshevik secret police, Cheka, was given the task of ensuring the revolution continued accordingly by quashing anything resembling a rebellion by workers or peasants throughout the countryside. Many thousands of Russian people (some estimates reach 500,000) were arrested, detained, tortured, or executed by the Cheka over a three to four-year period in what has been labeled "The Red Terror."

This is one of the stories passed down throughout the years of this horrific time of unspeakable violence:

> One day into a small rural village in the shadows of the Ural Mountains rode a lone horseman who asked to meet with some of the leaders of the town. Once gathered he inquired of those in leadership, "Do you have many storytellers here in your village?"
>
> Of course they did. The narratives of history and culture had to be passed down from generation to generation, and the telling of stories was one of the best ways this was accomplished. They told the stranger how the men would gather in one part of the town and some of the most accomplished of storytellers would command an audience with their tales of village heroes and mighty accomplishments that gave the community a sense of pride and dignity. The leaders described how the children would gather in the very small town square multiple times throughout the week and listen

as others told stories and weaved magical tales of hope and meaning and purpose into the fabric of these young lives.

"Well," the stranger said in response, "I would like to recognize and give honor to your storytellers and all the storytellers from villages throughout this region. My comrades and I would like to celebrate all storytellers with a festival just for them." The town leaders loved the idea and a date and time was established. Word traveled fast and far as the excitement grew for what would be, surely, a grand celebration.

The day eventually arrived for the festival, and the town was decorated beautifully, and into the town flooded the best of the storytellers for miles and miles. They gathered in the town hall in the center of town at the appointed time and waited for the party to begin. Finally, the man who initiated this whole event arrived at the town hall, along with a few associates who remained near the rear of the hall.

Stepping to the front of the crowd the man proclaimed, "Welcome, I am thrilled that all of you were able to make it to this celebration today. For today we want to pay special attention to all the storytellers throughout this land. We ask simply that you wait just a few more moments for the festivities to begin." At that moment, the man stepped out of a door near the front of the hall. And his associates did the same in the back of the building.

There was a quiet buzz in the room, an anticipation of what might happen next. After a few moments, the room became eerily quiet. Then suddenly, the sound of horses entering the courtyard surrounding the building could be heard.

When the people looked out of the windows they saw torches being used to set the town hall on fire. Smoke began to seep into the room. As they tried to escape they realized the doors had been sealed from the outside, evidently by their "hosts." The building burned to the ground. And every storyteller for miles was mercilessly killed.[43]

Unbelievably, events similar to this happened in village after village across the countryside of Russia during this time of Red Terror. It seemed as though the Bolsheviks understood a real truth: if you take away a people's story, they no longer know who they are. They lose any sense of values, or where they come from or where they are going. Remove a people's story and you can put anything in its place.

We need an unreduced and unleashed story to make sense of God, our lives, and the world. The influence of story over our identity, behavior, and calling cannot be underestimated. And our inability to invite people into *the* definitive story of life by extracting the myth, mystery, and imagination has resulted in a surrendering to the reduction of both truth and story, and a failure to comprehend what is really at stake.

STRANDED IN GREY TOWN

(A LIFE GREATLY REDUCED)

Hell is a state of mind—ye never said a truer word. And every state of mind, left to itself, every shutting up of the creature within the dungeon of its own mind—is, in the end, Hell. But Heaven is not a state of mind. Heaven is reality itself. All that is fully real is Heavenly. For all that can be shaken will be shaken and only the unshakeable remains.

— C. S. LEWIS

"It is not sufficient for us to be once called by the Lord, unless we live as new creatures. This is the long and short of it" (Calvin). The word given and received in the gospel announced to us "begets" a new people whose life together might itself become, in turn, good news to the world.

— DOUGLAS HARINK

The most beautiful experience we can have is the mysterious. Whoever does not know it and can no longer wonder, no longer marvel, is as good as dead, and his eyes are dimmed.

— ALBERT EINSTEIN

In the 2006 movie *Stranger Than Fiction,* Will Ferrell (in his most atypical of roles) plays a "seemingly average and generally solitary IRS agent." Ferrell's character, Harold Crick, starts to hear a disembodied female voice narrating his every action, thought, and feeling in alarmingly precise detail, which only he can hear. His carefully controlled, OCD life as a tax agent is turned upside down. The narrator seemingly begins to determine his entire life, from his work to his love interests, and even to his death. When the voice suddenly declares that "the character Harold Crick is facing imminent death," Harold realizes he had better find out who it is who has taken hold of writing his story and, by whatever means, persuade her to change this fatalistic ending.

Much to his chagrin, Harold is told there's really nothing he can do, and that he is to just let the story take him: "Just do what you want to do, you really have no choice ... Harold, you could just eat nothing but pancakes if you wanted."

Harold emphatically responds, "I don't wanna eat nothing but pancakes. I wanna live. Who in their right mind in a choice between pancakes and living ... chooses pancakes?"

He is advised, "Harold, if you'd pause to think, I believe you'd realize that that answer's inextricably contingent upon the type of life being led and, of course ... the quality of the pancakes."

"You have to understand," Harold says, "that this isn't a philosophy or a literary theory or a story to me. It's *my life*."

Harold recognizes that in order to change this impending tragic ending, he must proactively enter into the story and change it by involving himself, rather than allowing lazy indifference and empty rituals to determine him. In other words, Harold determines to live a better story. The result is seen near the end of the movie, when the narrator comments:

> Harold Crick became stronger in who he was, what he wanted, and why he was alive. Harold no longer ate alone. He no longer counted his toothbrush strokes. He no longer wore neckties. And, therefore, no longer worried about the time it took to put them on. He no longer counted his steps to the bus stop. Instead, Harold did that which had terrified him before. That which had eluded him Monday through Friday for so many years. That which the unrelenting lyrics of numerous punk-rock songs told him to do: Harold Crick lived his life.[1]

Stranger Than Fiction is the story of a man who has been asleep for most of his life and suddenly wakes to realize he has very little time left in a life he's barely lived. He grasps hold of the reality that he has the chance to do something that is universally desired—to actually live a better story.

A THIRD REDUCTION

In so many ways this is a parable of our contemporary Christian experience. If we are honest we, as the church, have by and large failed to live the fullness of life we have been given by Jesus.[2] This eclipsing of the grandeur of truth (chapter one), and the failure to live into a Warhead-infused story as it unfolds (chapter two), have a sad and inexorable outcome: a severely cramped existence, eking out a life as it passes by.

In this chapter—as part of this first section of the book exploring various reductionisms—we want to consider how so many of God's people end up with a rather sad, attenuated, moralistic, adventure-less, and churchy spirituality by which they scrape out something of a spiritual existence. Why would *any* pilgrim on *any* trail or at *any* art festival have *any* interest in the type of reduced life that is portrayed to them by the average churchly Christian? Why do we talk about the satisfaction of eating pancakes when the story we have been called to was described by Jesus as a "real and eternal life, more and better life than they ever dreamed of" (John 10:10 MSG)?

HELL'S DOORS ARE LOCKED FROM THE INSIDE

Perhaps one of the most disconcerting portrayals of the reduced life is found in *The Great Divorce*. This book by C. S. Lewis is not only a brilliant parable about how the dynamics of heaven and hell play out in everyday human life, but is also an outstanding example of the sheer power myth, imagination, and story have to renew life. The story is set against a backdrop of Grey Town, a rather loveless, grumpy, and alienated "place," where the miserable inhabitants of the town—Lewis calls them the "shrunken souls of the damned" and "greasy stains on a window pane"—live increasingly insubstantial, ghostlike lives.

Early in the parable, we learn that Grey Town is ever-expanding because the inhabitants inevitably quarrel and are constantly moving further and further apart to get away from one another. This is a relatively easy accomplishment because, in this hell of a place, all they need to do to build a new house is to *think* it. Apparently, in Grey Town "you get everything you want (although of poor quality, of course) by just imagining it." There are no constraints: the undisciplined desires of the insiders create an unreal and disordered world, well-suited to their preferences.

> But evil desires are at odds with joy, so that even though in some sense the damned get what they want, they are left empty and frustrated. What they want is to be happy on their own terms, but that is impossible, so strictly speaking they do not get what they want after all, even though Grey Town endlessly adapts and expands to their wishes.[3]

This description of Grey Town is strikingly different to Lewis' version of heaven, where everything is available upon request but is only given on God's terms. These substantial, authentic gifts and graces of God are in stark contrast to the flimsy, poor-quality reality of Grey Town.

What if, Lewis wonders, these damned souls were permitted to ride a bus from hell toward heaven? And what if, when they got halfway there, they were met by the souls of the blessed who, arriving from heaven, try to convince them, even at this halfway point, this place of decision, to give up their sin and pride and embrace the mercy of Christ? What would they do? Astonishingly, we find that in all but one instance, the unrepentant sinners freely choose to return to hell (Grey Town) where they will carry on their ghostlike, thin existence until finally they are infinitely alienated from God, each other, and therefore ultimately from their own selves. Their rejection of grace has not only blinded them to the truth, it has robbed them of their own humanity. To borrow a phrase from *The Last Battle*, they are so afraid of being taken in by the saints sent to help them that they cannot be taken out of their self-imposed imprisonment and willful exile from God.[4]

One of the more startling aspects of *The Great Divorce* is that many live in hell without even knowing it. The problem is that this hellish existence passes off as normal for all those who are in it. And what is more shocking is that, according to Lewis, this would include many who claim to be believers but who refuse the way of following Jesus.

An implicit message of Lewis' book is the implications our choices have on the direction of our life. Where we find ourselves has a lot to do with whether we choose to retreat into the alienated and reduced life (i.e., Grey Town) or venture into a larger experience of life offered to us in God. Hell involves a mind-set that comes about through the willful narrowing of life until what we have left is insubstantial ... unreal ... fractured ... and hellish. "Hell *is* a state of mind [...] And every state of mind, left to itself, *every shutting up of the creature within the dungeon of its own mind*—is, in the end, Hell" (italics ours).[5] Therefore Lewis warns us that:

> Every time you make a choice you are turning the central part of you, the part of you that chooses, into something a little different from what it was before. And taking your life as a whole, with all your innumerable choices, all your life long you are slowly turning this central thing into a heavenly creature or into a hellish creature.[6]

The key idea of *The Great Divorce* is that the damned are, in a real sense, successful rebels to the end; and that people actually do get to choose hell over heaven. What Lewis is saying to us here is that hell's doors are locked from the inside.[7] It is all in the little choices we make on a daily basis, in our daily accepting or rejecting of God's grace.

Our choices and perspectives matter ... hugely. There is a quality of heaven or hell in the decisions we make that determines the meaning and trajectory of our lives. Both these processes begin long before death. "The good person's past begins to change so that his forgiven sins and remembered sorrows take on the quality of Heaven: the bad man's past already conforms to his badness and is filled only with dreariness."[8] And herein lies the danger of the shrunken or reduced human life—the life in Grey Town. It is this "state of mind" that we are hoping to address in the call for all people everywhere to learn what Harold Crick learned.

LIVING CIVILIZED IN THE UNITED STATES OF GENERICA

Timothy Tennent, President of Asbury Seminary and one-time missionary laments that:

> Our long sojourn under the spell of Christendom has also meant that we find ourselves adhering to a rather domesticated version of the gospel. One of the legacies of Christendom is that it is willing to provide a safe haven for Christianity, but only at the cost of the steady domestication of Christianity, gradually smoothing down most of its rough prophetic edges, so that Christian identity and cultural identity became virtually seamless.[9]

The seminal missiologist David Bosch likewise observes that, "Christianity has become nothing but the religious dimension of the culture" and "listening to the church, society hears only the sound of its own music."[10] The problem is that contemporary Christianity is the product of the long-term, religious domestication process that has been going on for hundreds and hundreds of years. In the words of Mickey Goldmill, of the *Rocky* movie franchise, who gruffly tells Rocky after a defeat, "The worst thing happened that could happen to any fighter: you got civilized."[11] A similar fate has fallen on those of us following Jesus: we have become civilized and domesticated in both our living and telling, and in doing so the gospel itself has been likewise domesticated. Like the proverbial frog in the kettle, Western Christians are now largely unaware that they are living out a significantly reduced experience of the good news of Jesus than the one portrayed in the New Testament.

UNCA LONNY SAYS

Lonny Davis, a zany friend of Alan's who goes by the tag "Unca Lonny," claims that most Christians experience their faith as *deists*. He says:

> Deism pretty much sums up the present state of things with regard to the faith posture of the Western world. It goes like this: God created the world, sent Jesus, gave us the Bible, and then walked away, left it up to us to work it out from there. We have to settle for a religion pretty much void of wonder, the supernatural, and an unmediated engagement with God, but we get to go to church instead. As long as we get this basic "theory" correct, and as long as we maintain a keen desire to exert moral order, we're good to go.[12]

Sociologists Christian Smith and Melinda Lundquist Denton agree with Unca Lonny. In their 2005 book *Soul Searching*, they suggest a form of deism that has entrenched itself in our time—they call it Moralistic Therapeutic Deism (MTD).[13] The research shows that MTD involves a simplistic, formulaic, and moralistic creed to which many people's faith can be reduced.

- It is *moralistic* in that faith is reduced to *rules for a happy life*—do not intentionally hurt anyone and be decent to people around you.
- It is *therapeutic* insofar that religion is reduced to a *self-help tool* that is used only when needed. The goal is to live in a way that "makes you happiest."
- It is *deistic* because God is reduced to a *removed and distant being*. It is not atheistic, as there is a creator "out there somewhere," but this god is perceived to be somewhat indifferent to human concerns and uninvolved in the drama of life, except maybe to grant a child a wish now and then.

The problem with deism is that it lacks radical openness and receptivity; it is closed to the possibility of God's involvement in real life and history, and does not cultivate the personal vulnerability required to truly know God and be known by him. It claims to have knowledge *about* God—more like *facts* about God—while lacking any knowledge *of* God. It certainly has no real experience of living in a covenantal relationship with God, one that has a dynamic give and take. In other words, it is an inherently closed and codified religion. Reduced.

It is rather like living a day-to-day faith akin to a carefully controlled, OCD life as a tax agent named Harold, counting toothbrush strokes because it is the pathway not only to better dental hygiene but a nice, good life. It is a reduced belief that participating in the *right* things (moralistic) will result in *controlled happiness* (therapeutic) for which you will be glad to give thanks to *the God above and beyond* (deistic). It is simply living a life of church-going goodness that never questions if there is more than dutiful participation in programs and ministries designed to bring about a feeling that you are achieving your best life now, (i.e., eating pancakes). Why would anyone we meet on the Camino or on the Playa come to desire a spiritual life that is centered on simply putting moralistic rules in place so we can be happy and sing songs to a distant God?

A civilized, domesticated, MTD approach implies that life's great longings and questions are responded to with a shrug and a "meh ... whatever." This "whatever shrug" is the result of sinful pride, but it is also caused by a lack of understanding and desire to enter into a much more dynamic (theistic) experience of God—a God who is fully involved in all the dimensions of individual and corporate life. Recognize it now?

This latent MTD that literally pervades middle-class evangelical Christianity has domesticated and civilized faith by locking it down in tight, largely moralistic formulations—the god in the back pocket, the god who doesn't mess with our plans, a god appropriately reduced to fit to a reduced life.

Perhaps a major force undergirding this latent domestication is the combination of the self-protective obsessions of safety and security (derived from middle-class interests) and comfort and convenience (derived from the worldliness of systemic consumerism).[14] Make no mistake, these forces that are so prevalent in our culture will always tend to reduce the effect of discipleship and weaken what the Bible would define as appropriate faithfulness and abundant living.

This desire to seal ourselves off from the life God intended will actually take some careful planning if we are to avoid any distress or danger, but it will also lead to a meaningless life marked by lovelessness. As C. S. Lewis says in his characteristically potent way:

> There is no safe investment. To love at all is to be vulnerable. Love anything, and your heart will certainly be wrung and possibly be broken. If you want to make sure of keeping it intact, you must give your heart to no one, not even to an animal. Wrap it carefully round with hobbies and little luxuries; avoid all entanglements; lock it up safe in the casket or coffin of your selfishness. But in that casket—safe, dark, motionless, airless—it will change. It will not be broken; it will become unbreakable, impenetrable, irredeemable. The alternative to tragedy, or at least to the

risk of tragedy, is damnation. The only place outside Heaven where you can be perfectly safe from all the dangers and perturbations [distresses] of love is Hell.[15]

To shut ourselves off from the world inevitably leads to this "lovelessness," which is itself hellish. Some in broader culture seem to have woken up to this hellish lovelessness, seemingly more than the church, as indicated by the popularity of Brené Brown's studies on love and vulnerability:

> I define vulnerability as uncertainty, risk and emotional exposure. With that definition in mind, let's think about love. Waking up every day and loving someone who may or may not love us back, whose safety we can't ensure, who may stay in our lives or may leave without a moment's notice, who may be loyal to the day they die or betray us tomorrow— that's vulnerability.[16]

A hellish existence means we experience a reduced life, which in turn implies that we settle for all sorts of substitutes. And when the substitutes become the norm, we find ourselves living very comfortably, embracing the art of settling.

> Human beings are settlers, but not in the pioneer sense. It is our human occupational hazard to settle for little. We settle for purity and piety when we are being invited to an exquisite holiness. We settle for the fear-driven when love longs to be our engine. We settle for a puny, vindictive God when we are being nudged always closer to this wildly inclusive, larger-than-any-life God. We allow our sense of God to atrophy.[17]

Our aptitude for "settling," and our skillfulness at dodging the transformative dimensions of an encounter with God, have led to a reduction of living that settles for that which is secondary, not that which is primary. We settle not for what is *best*, but what is *okay;* not for "first things," but "second things."[18]

Even when Western Christians talk about "life ... to the full" (John 10:10), we often talk about it in very shallow terms—defining it in terms of safety, security, and prosperity.[19] And to the non-believer, this inauthentic optimism we communicate about Jesus bringing us "life to the full" often doesn't sync with the reality of our lives. It can therefore discredit our testimony, and is one way we actually flatten the story and render it impotent. Life to the full involves both death *and* life, both crucifixion *and* resurrection.

The safe, secure, and prosperous life is *not* the life followers of Jesus have been given and are called to participate in. The overwhelming testimony of the Bible is that people who come into contact with God will be swept up into a whirlwind of action, excitement, and adventure, as well as the pain, struggle, and suffering that is inevitably part of what it means to follow Jesus. This is known in the New Testament as *abiding in Christ*, being *filled with the Holy Spirit*, and *discipleship*, which, when accurately defined, is about as far from the banality of MTD as one can imagine.

Have we really become, in the words of the author Walker Percy, "the only civilization in history which has enshrined mediocrity as its cultural ideal"?[20] And yet, both those who love God and those who deny the existence of God can agree that a life settled on "second things and mediocrity" is one of despair and hopelessness. A reduced and settled life requires no faith because we control everything. It is the exact opposite of "the assurance of things you have hoped for, the absolute conviction that there are realities you've never seen" (Hebrews 11:1 The Voice).

LESS THAN ULTIMATE

Greg Boyd claims that at the source of all that is wrong with humans is a false and ugly (and we would add "reduced") mental image of God. This distortion/reduction, he says, lies at the root of the brokenness that originated in the garden—Adam and Eve believed the Serpent's narrative about God.[21] Even though God had only been a generous God who had given them all they would ever need, they accepted the lie that they could have even more if they believed a different story. Of course, the end result was an impoverished and broken life separated from God. Instead of life as it was intended to be, they ended up with a shrunken existence. We all repeat this error on a daily basis. To one degree or another, we have all internalized lies about God that have caused us to mistrust him and therefore to look elsewhere to find life. See how the "domino effect" of these reductions plays out here? Our reduction in the truth of who God is has devastating effects on the way we live out our (reduced) life. Looking at the world through hungry eyes, we, like our primordial parents, have come to see various versions of the forbidden tree as potential sources of life. And here we return to the pervading concern of the Bible ... idolatry.

Remember in chapter one we noted that one of the basic urges of idolatry is the human desire to initiate one's own relationship to God, and thereby control him and the way he intersects with our own story. Idolatry is the ancient practice of diminishing and reducing God.[22] This is what an idol is. It's anything we try to use to fill what only God can fill, which means it is anything we use to replace God. The theologian Paul Tillich defines the true evil of idolatry as "giving oneself to that which is less than ultimate," allowing the definition of self to come from the finite.[23] When anything or anyone becomes the means by which we try to fill our innermost need for unconditional love, unsurpassable worth, and absolute security, it becomes an idol.[24]

Boyd claims that:

> There are an endless variety of idols people use to satisfy their hunger. Secular Western people today typically try to get life from what they achieve, what they possess, or whom they impress. The misdirected homing device of some leads them to work eighty hours a week, sometimes sacrificing family and friends in the process of climbing the ladder of success to achieve "the American dream." Others strive to gain the applause of the crowd, performing or achieving their way to fame. And then there are the multitudes that tend to experience the inner void as a gnawing boredom with life. They chase after peak experiences, believing that the next risk-taking adventure, the next experience of falling in love, the next lurid sexual experience, or the next drug-induced high will make them feel fully alive. At best, however, these merely provide a momentary diversion from their emptiness.[25]

In the Hebrew scriptures, idols and images were forbidden in order to prevent the chosen people trying to fill the space that God wanted left open. This prohibition was to keep them yearning for a future consummation of God's promises, to keep them expectant, hopeful, and ready, and in relationship with the one, true God. The issue is the same today: we try to diminish the power and presence of God and minimize his impact in our lives by allowing idols to fill the same space only God can fill.[26]

Idolatry both reduces our understanding and experience of God as well as diminishing the quality and meaning of our lives. The Scriptures explicitly warn us about the reducing power of idolatry, saying that we who worship idols become like them ... empty and without meaning (Psalm 115:8, 135:18; Isaiah 44:9). In a famous commencement speech at Kenyon College, the author David Foster Wallace addressed this very issue:

> There is no such thing as not worshipping. Everybody worships. The only choice we get is what to worship. And an outstanding reason for choosing some sort of god or spiritual-type thing to worship [...] is that pretty much anything else you worship will eat you alive. If you worship money and things—if they are where you tap real meaning in life—then you will

never have enough. Never feel you have enough. It's the truth. Worship your own body and beauty and sexual allure and you will always feel ugly, and when time and age start showing, you will die a million deaths before they finally plant you. On one level, we all know this stuff already—it's been codified as myths, proverbs, clichés, bromides, epigrams, parables: the skeleton of every great story. The trick is keeping the truth up front in daily consciousness. Worship power—you will feel weak and afraid, and you will need ever more power over others to keep the fear at bay. Worship your intellect, being seen as smart—you will end up feeling stupid, a fraud, always on the verge of being found out.[27]

Humans think that a meaningful life can be found by creating and worshipping our own gods, but in doing so our lives become like the dwellers of Grey Town—reduced to nothingness.

THE FALSE PRESENCE OF THE KINGDOM

It is the role of those who speak of God, writes Martin Buber, to shatter the false security of idolatry and invite others into an engagement with the sovereign God who demands that his human creatures involve him in all the arenas of life. This "invasive" and demanding presence of the biblical God simply cannot be avoided. It confounds those who imagine they can find some security and comfort in the false certainty an idolatrous religious expression seems to provide.[28] The substitution of religious ritual and formula in place of the foreboding presence of God is what Jacques Ellul calls "the false presence of the Kingdom."[29]

We may all go through seasons of apparent comfort or security, protection from, or unawareness of dangers. But eventually, in the life of all believers, there inevitably comes "an hour of awakening," when a chasm suddenly looms at our feet. It might be doubt or contradiction; it might be an existential challenge, but it calls us to respond in faith, and we find ourselves afraid.[30] Our choice is either to continue with the safe life we have so carefully cultivated, with its rules, laws and formulae, or risk a life of dynamic engagement and responsibility. We must choose which of the two will master our lives—a spirit of reduction and security or a spirit of risk and insecurity. It is truly an awesome choice. Buber says that only in such "holy insecurity" can we approach the mystery of God.[31]

Buber here is reflecting on what the Scriptures mean by living in the fear of God. It is that element of faith that retains a sense of reverence, amazement, and awe; that recognizes we are dealing with a Being that is wholly Other—a Being we can never hope to control. The fear of the Lord places humans in that distance of reverence that permits true and unlimited intimacy with God (the *mysterium tremendum et fascinans* we explored in the previous chapter).[32] The Scriptures therefore rightly teach us that this holy fear is the gateway to the love and knowledge of God (Proverbs 1:7). It is this fear of God that keeps us radically receptive and responsive to God and the possibility that we're included in his story.[33]

Whatever tugs against or away from this relationship with God functions as an idol to which we pledge our allegiances. Not only is the Ultimate betrayed, but these idols will only fail in their ability to meet our deepest needs and desires. We must call people into a story that discloses both the power of idols and of God, communicating to them the perils of settling for "less than." We must no longer bury the Ultimate to get on with our lives as "best we can," for even when we try to bury God, the ache, longing, and brokenness remain. A civilized and domesticated life will inevitably only yield a numb resignation, but it can never diminish the overwhelming longing for something more, something we know is out there but we just can't find.

A LOSS OF WONDER

So much is lost when we resign ourselves to a settled life, including the ability to wonder. An invitation to enter into a "wonder-less" story will entice very few. No one, Harold Crick included, desires to live a story without wonder, awe, and mystery. "The most beautiful experience we can have is the mysterious. Whoever does not know it and can no longer wonder, no longer marvel, is as good as dead, and his eyes are dimmed."[34]

It is to a culture with dim eyes that we attempt to engage in a conversation that moves people beyond numb resignation and opens them up to the hope of finding God outside of dogmas and certitudes. Abraham Heschel, one of the most significant Jewish theologians of the twentieth century, wrote extensively on wonder and awe throughout his career. A look at the loss of wonder would be incomplete without attempting to understand Heschel's thoughts on this void in our culture.

> The awareness of grandeur and wonder has all but disappeared in the present age. Our educational system stresses the importance of controlling and exploiting reality, of deriving power from knowledge, but there is little education for wonder, for the sublime. We carefully teach children how to measure and weigh and spell, but we fail to teach them

how to revere, how to admire, how to appreciate. The sense of wonder and awe, the sense for the sublime, is such a rare gift; without it the world becomes flat and the human person hollow.[35]

He proposed that the indifference to wonder is perhaps "the root of all human failings." We have adopted the belief that everything can or will be explained and that to understand our very existence is simply a matter of aligning principles and theories of reality; for "all enigmas can be solved, and wonder is simply the effect of primordial ignorance. Wonder is thus cast aside."[36]

Heschel (as well as Harold Crick) came to the insightful conclusion that a life lived void of awe and wonder, a life that can simply be reduced to having the right answers and doing the right things can be a somewhat tragic life with a proclivity to settle for the mediocre. No one should ever give themselves over to that kind of life. It cannot be the undertaking of any faith in any god to address and provide answers to all our many questions. That wouldn't be the abundant life Jesus promised. That would be a life steeped in the art of settling; a life with all the answers would have no need for a sense of wonder. And *that* would be a reduction of truth that leads to a reduction of life, which in the face of imminent death reduces our search for life to the nearest International House of Pancakes.

THE WORST OF ALL SINS?

In Aimee Bender's "The Doctor and the Rabbi," we are given what amounts to one more caution against living a reduced life in Grey Town. Her short story begins:

> The doctor went to see the rabbi. "Tell me, rabbi, please," he said, "about God."
>
> The rabbi pulled out some books. She talked about Jacob wrestling the angel. She talked about Heschel and the kernel of wonder as a seedling that could grow into awe. She tugged at her braid and told a Hasidic story about how it is said that at the end of your life, you will need to apologize to God for the ways you have *not* lived.
>
> "Not for the usual sins," she said. "*But for the sin of living small*" (italics ours).[37]

SECTION 2

A LONGING

There is so much that has been lost in our unceasing reduction of God, story, and life. Hopefully, in section one, we have clearly stated how a variety of factors have eclipsed our perception of God, and how we have inherited a swathe of profoundly reduced truths that no longer make sense of the complexities we face as we attempt to translate this God into our contexts. As a result of these many reductions, we (the church as well as broader culture) are missing a big picture perspective to help us make sense of all the smaller ones.

Our hope in section two is to consider how we have reduced our understanding of what it means to be human in God's world. It is not only the theological frames that have been narrowed. The frames through which all people are understood (anthropology) are equally reduced. Likewise, the frames through which all people can *perceive* and *experience* God are greatly diminished. Simply stated, all of us suffer a reduced view of what it means to be human.

Before we try to provide some viable pathways forward (in sections three and four), we want to take a closer look at aspects of the human condition itself that have been affected by these broader reductions and mostly ignored from all angles, Christian or not. We need to do this for both those we meet on the Camino and at Burning Man as well as for ourselves as individual believers, both existentially and missionally. We need to look again at how *all* human beings are on a search that involves the deepest aspects of their natures, one that none can avoid, ourselves included. Humans are inherently created for the divine—that much is inescapable—and it is how we go about fulfilling this side of ourselves that makes the difference between meaning and meaninglessness.

THE HUMMING OF UNSEEN HARPS

(THE SPIRITUAL ANATOMY OF DESIRE)

To become aware of the possibility of the search is to be onto something. Not to be onto something is to be in despair.

— WALKER PERCY

The unexamined human life is a lost chance to behold the divine.

— FREDERICK BUECHNER

Earth's crammed with heaven,
And every common bush afire with God;
But only he who sees, takes off his shoes,
The rest sit round it and pluck blackberries,
And daub their natural faces unaware.

— ELIZABETH BARRETT BROWNING

I (Mark) met Alex almost three weeks into our pilgrimage at the end of one of our longest days of walking on the Camino de Santiago. Alex was from London where she worked for London Underground in some type of upper management position.[1] She was thirty-ish with a lively personality, great wit, and was generally enjoyable to walk alongside on the trail. But she did walk very slowly ... extremely slowly. Yet somehow she always found a way to get to each day's final destination. I am willing to wager that on one or two occasions a taxi gave her pace a boost.

After a long day of walking on the Camino, most evenings were generally spent sharing an informal meal with five to ten people we had journeyed with that day, or perhaps a few days earlier. The food was never the finest of cuisine, but the dinner conversations were almost always interesting (if you spoke the same language, and sometimes even if you didn't).

One particular night, eight of us ended up around one big table—one person from Germany, two from the Netherlands, one from Southern California, one from Japan, my son, myself, and Alex. Toward the end of the meal Alex took charge of the discussion. She asked us all to go around the table and answer three questions: what was the best part of your day, that day, on the Camino?; what was the most beautiful thing you saw?; and, what about your life will be different once you finish the pilgrimage and arrive at the end, in Santiago de Compostela?

Alex had the person to her left answer first and then proceeded around the table, which left her to go last. Everyone gave thoughtful answers to the questions, nothing really unexpected. When it got to Alex, she was prepared. She had evidently been thinking about these questions all day. This long and arduous pilgrimage was affecting her worldview in a multitude of ways. She began by saying, "Well, first of all, just so you know, I don't believe in God." This was an odd opening statement, but it didn't necessarily disturb or unsettle anyone; it was on a par with almost every outlook we had encountered on the Camino so far.

Alex then proceeded to describe all she had seen and experienced that day in words and phrases bursting with poetic enthusiasm, detailing the amazing beauty of creation and how she was in awe of the grand display of splendor. She described a personal transformation occurring within her, one that would probably change most things about her life, particularly her career. She was tired of living for nothing and wanted to make a difference in the world but wasn't exactly sure how she might go about implementing this. That night around the table, in an answer exceedingly longer than anyone else's, Alex was describing something in her that was restless, some kind of a deep longing that she did not know how to fulfill. There was a stirring in her soul, a soul that apparently "didn't believe in God."

Three days later, about fifteen more towns and villages down the trail, I ran into Alex again. I was sitting on a corner resting my weary body, waiting for the Advil to take effect, when Alex walked by. After briefly catching up on each other's previous couple of days (she never once mentioned a taxi), I told Alex what I had been thinking since that night she had shared her thoughts at dinner.

"Alex, there's something you said the other night at dinner that I find problematic, to the point that I think I *vehemently* disagree with you." It was a surprisingly strong statement for such a casual conversation. I had her attention though.

"You said the other night that you didn't believe in God?"

"That's right," she responded, probably a little alarmed as to where I was going with this.

"Well, I hope you hear this right, Alex, but I don't believe you. I think you actually *do* believe in God. I think you know there's Something out there bigger than you, Something that created what you are seeing every day on the trail, and Something that is calling you to a different life than the one you're living, a life that might actually play a part in putting the world back together."

And then I pulled out a phrase I've heard dozens of times: "Look, Alex, I have a pretty strong feeling that this god you don't believe in is a god I don't believe in either."

I think I made my point, but I wished I could have been as articulate as David Brooks when he wrote in *The New York Times*:

[Faith] begins, for many people, with an elusive experience of wonder and mystery. These moments provide an intimation of ethical perfection and merciful love. They arouse a longing within many people to integrate that glimpsed eternal goodness into their practical lives. This longing is faith. It's not one emotion because it encompasses so many emotions. It's not one idea because it contains contradictory ideas. It's a state of motivation, a desire to reunite with that glimpsed moral beauty and incorporate it into everyday living.[2]

That's what I should have said.

THE QUESTION AND THE QUEST

Albert Einstein is reputed to have once said that if he had only one hour to solve a problem in which his life actually depended on the solution, he would spend the first fifty-five minutes determining the proper question to ask. He claimed that if he knew the right question to ask, he could solve the problem in less than five minutes.[3]

Einstein's somewhat counterintuitive approach might well be worth considering as we seek to reframe our current ways of seeing God and people. The prevailing logic tends toward giving answers rather than asking questions, and in our experience, evangelicals are generally extremely uncomfortable with quest/ions. But if we want to understand the Alexs of our world, we must have a holy curiosity about each and every person we encounter, being more than willing to spend the first fifty-five minutes asking the right questions.

This inability for curiosity has not only led to a diminished understanding of God but is also highly problematic for an informed missional understanding. Many of us cannot comprehend what is going on in broader culture, nor do we seem interested in doing so. All this eclipse and reduction has not only led to a reduced theology (understanding of God) but also to a reduced anthropology (understanding of people). How can we begin to understand the longings and desires of the Alexs in our world if we are unwilling to engage in the hard work of exploring culture?

Hence we need a reframation. We need to "look again" at what has become all too familiar. We cannot recognize what we are seeing because we lack the perceptual capacities to make sense of it. We need a wi[l]der and deeper framing of human existence that goes beyond simply highlighting our separation from God. We need an understanding that includes a sense of the tragedy and struggle that is part of making sense of everyday life, as well as an empathetic understanding of the existential restlessness that lies at the root of each one of us. In other words, we need a renewed index of the human soul. Without this we will simply not be able to missionally exegete the culture, and our proclamation will fail to resonate in any meaningful way—once again, tofu.

A MISSIONAL ANTHROPOLOGY

In his book *The Culture Code*, Clotaire Rapaille gives a contemporary example of the importance of properly exegeting a culture. He describes how marketers—people who make it their business to know trends, conduct market research, organize focus groups, and ask hundreds of questions—can fail so miserably in their high-paid tasks. He suggests that so many "experts" fail, not because they do not ask questions, but because they simply do not ask the right questions. In so doing, they fail to understand "the culture code"—what is really going on behind people's choices and behavior.[4]

Similar to sociologist Pierre Bourdieu's notion of *habitus*, Rapaille builds his model on the assumption that, during childhood, all human beings learn given words (and the ideas connected with them) and naturally associate these various words/concepts with certain emotions.[5] He called these primal associations *imprints*, and it is these that resolutely determine a person's attitude towards a particular thing. But the imprints do not just affect individual behaviors; pooled imprints make up a collective cultural unconscious, which in turn predetermines and influences the behavior of entire cultures. These provide "the unconscious meaning we apply to any given thing—a car, a type of food, a relationship, even a country—via the culture in which we are raised."[6]

The culture code therefore contains and forms the reservoir of unconscious human emotions, habits, and dispositions from which people make the various choices in life. Therefore, Rapaille says, understanding and deciphering the culture code is the key to motivating, designing, and maintaining healthy organizations and enterprises.[7] This method of cultural exegesis is not at all dissimilar to Paul's missionary strategy, as we will see in chapters nine and ten. When seeking to develop a missional anthropology, we need to pay attention to what is not necessarily obvious, but implicit in the culture.

Rapaille describes an experience of being hired to work by Chrysler in the 1990s. His role was focused on reversing the surprising decline in sales of the Jeep Wrangler, a previously successful range of cars. Rapaille sought to understand the cultural code in the market of potential consumers. "When I put groups of consumers together, I asked them different questions. I didn't ask them what they wanted in a Jeep; I asked them to tell me about their earliest memories of Jeeps." What he heard was story after story with a strong recurring image—"of being out on the open land, of going where no ordinary car could go, of riding free of the restraint of the road." He had identified the cultural code.

> I returned to those wary Chrysler executives and told them that the code for Jeep in America is HORSE. Their notion of turning the Wrangler into just another luxury SUV was ill advised. SUVs are not horses. Horses don't have luxury appointments. Horses don't have butter-soft leather, but rather the tough leather of a saddle. The Wrangler needed to have removable doors and an open top because drivers needed to feel the wind around them, as though they were riding on a horse.[8]

The switch in marketing strategy based upon Rapaille's research proved to be a huge success for Chrysler and its Jeep Wrangler.

The people we met on the Camino and at Burning Man had each given an "unconscious meaning" to their faith in God, or lack thereof, based upon the story with which they had grown up and the emotional responses they had to it. If we had asked them, "Tell us your earliest memories of God," we would most likely have heard some strong recurring imprints— "Growing up wearing Sunday best, but never being quite good enough to be in 'the club'"; or perhaps something more damaging, such as, "Hearing the repeated message that 'the world is going to hell,' capped with a large dose of fear-producing fire and brimstone"; for others their imprint might have been an experience of Christians who said one thing on Sunday and lived an entirely different life throughout the week; or simply an impression of a distant and cold God of whom they lived in fear.

Some may have had no experience of God or church; others may have had a horrific or tragic encounter with the church or with individual Christians; for some it may be an experience somewhere between the two. But we all have an emotional and intellectual attachment, "baggage," when it comes to faith. It is these experiences, and the combination of emotion and meaning attached to them, that create in people an "imprint." And it is the blend of these imprints that defines us. We so desperately need to understand this if we are to reframe and enlarge our understanding of the people we encounter every single day.

So our question is ... can we exegete our culture's database of myths and stories, and, in doing so, unravel one of the most fundamental human drivers: desire and longing?

A DIALECTIC OF DESIRE

Perhaps the first step in developing a missional anthropology is to wrestle with the questions: what do we really desire?; what are our deepest longings?; what is it we are all searching for?

Philosopher and theologian James K. A. Smith says culture is not primarily an intellectual, heady phenomenon because we are not those kind of creatures—we are not primarily thinking beings. Smith also suggests we need a new anthropology:

> We need a retooled, more holistic approach of human persons not necessarily as thinkers, not primarily as knowers, nor primarily as believers. Human persons are fundamentally lovers and if you start here and understand this, that will generate a very different account of what culture is.[9]

Smith says if we really want to know who someone is, what really defines a person, we need to know the answer to the questions, "What do you want? What do you love? Because if I know this, I know who you are."[10] This implies we are defined by our desires.

And Smith is not by any means new in claiming this. In Western theology, it was, above all, St. Augustine who taught us that the human being is essentially motivated by desire (*eros*). Augustine said it is what one loves—

what one desires—that determines to what city one belongs, the earthly or the heavenly.[11] Passion in the negative sense (lust and covetousness) is nothing else but disordered desire, a longing that fails to acknowledge God as the subject of our heart's yearnings.

Augustine begins his autobiography *Confessions* with these timeless words: "For Thou has made us for Thyself and our hearts are restless until they rest in thee."[12] *Confessions* is the story of his own restless heart in search of fulfillment. He chronicles his first forty years, including his conversion, writing very little of what and how he believed but, instead, of his longings, his desires, and his passions.[13] His confessions are those of a life of seeking satisfaction in the wrong places, and of finding no rest until his story intersected with God's.

Augustine's argument goes something like this: human desire differs from animal desire in that it is, at root, insatiable. Humans are characterized by a hunger for the infinite, for an eternity of life, love, and joy which, whether they recognize it or not, can be nothing other than God. Assuming that God exists, it will follow that God is indeed humanity's true end, for the appetite of any living organism shows its function.

> The stomach hungers for food because its function is to digest food. As physical taste and hunger may often be mistaken as to their true object, desiring nothing but caviar instead of a balanced diet, man is often mistaken as to the goal of his life, desiring wealth, power or physical pleasure instead of God.[14]

As we discussed in chapter three, we all worship something, and when what we worship is anything less than God (i.e., an idol), it only leads to dissatisfaction and discontentment; our real appetites continue to be for God, for which these lesser goals are always unsatisfactory analogues and substitutes. "Those who set their hearts on finite goals are always discontented; they must always have more and more and more of what they desire, and failing this are frustrated and miserable."[15]

As Smith suggests, it is precisely humanity's unhappiness, our restlessness in the conditions of tedium and boredom, that affirms: "There seems to be something here that we just can't shake—that no amount of 'rational' atheism seems to be able to excise. Might its persistence be reason to think that there's something to this?"[16] Can we move closer to realizing it is this restless condition of the heart, religious or secular in approach, that leads us all in an ongoing and universal search for truth? It is difficult to deny that there is some degree of insatiable desire, longing, and restlessness present in each and every human being. We can safely say that all humans are familiar with the experience of intensely desiring some *thing* that will make life more complete, even though they may not be able to name it as such.

It would also be fair to say that most evangelicals don't have a spiritual vocabulary that incorporates *insatiable longing*, in the Augustinian understanding of the term. In fact, most would be deeply suspicious and judgmental of people pursuing their desires and longings. And yet it is precisely this dialectic of desire we need to come to grips with if we are to be faithful witnesses to God and unlock human hearts, opening them to the wonders of God and gospel. Without this understanding, we cannot correctly interpret much of what is occurring on the Playa and the Camino and around every workplace and neighborhood.

SEHNSUCHT ('ZE:N‚ZƱXT)

Alister E. McGrath, a theologian deeply influenced by C. S. Lewis, tells us that, "Like Augustine, C. S. Lewis was aware of deep human drives that point to a dimension of our existence beyond time and space, a deep and intense feeling of longing that no earthly object or experience can satisfy."[17] In his book *Surprised by Joy*, Lewis calls this experience "joy." Joy is "an unsatisfied desire which is itself more desirable than any other satisfaction [...] anyone who has experienced it will want it again."[18]

This common human experience is broadly known as *sehnsucht*. In the most basic and literal sense, sehnsucht means "longing" or "yearning"— the unexpressed sense that something is not right, so much is broken and left unfinished, and this is not the way life was intended to be. It expresses a relentless urge, a deeply emotional state of missing something, an indefinite longing that we may or may not recognize.[19] In social sciences, the idea of sehnsucht has been defined as that which "captures thoughts and feelings about past, present, and future aspects of life that are incomplete or imperfect, coupled with a desire for ideal, alternative states and experiences of life. Such thoughts and feelings are typically intense, recurring, and accompanied by a mixture of positive and negative feelings, producing an ambivalent emotional experience."[20]

Lewis describes his experiences of this in his autobiography. He relays how, as a young child, he was standing by a magnificent flowering bush, when, for some unexplained reason, a memory was triggered:

There suddenly rose in me without warning, as if from a depth not of years but of centuries, the memory of that earlier morning at the Old House when my brother had brought his toy garden into the nursery. It is difficult to find words strong enough for the sensation which came over me; Milton's "enormous bliss" of Eden [...] comes somewhere near it. It was a sensation, of course, of desire; but desire for what? Not, certainly for a biscuit tin filled with moss, nor even (though that came into it) for my own past [...] and before I knew what I desired, the desire itself was gone, the whole glimpse withdrawn, the world turned commonplace again, or only stirred by a longing for the longing that had just ceased. It had only taken a moment of time; and in a certain sense everything else that had ever happened to me was insignificant in comparison.[21]

Lewis here describes a brief moment of insight, an overwhelming instance of being caught up in something that went far beyond the realm of everyday reality. We have all experienced this, even though we can't quite pin it down. Perhaps it can best be described as a soul-wound, a longing, a desire, or an absence of something that was once present; the feeling of love for something that is lost, like the feeling of love for one who has passed away. This longing is an experience of transcendence. For example, we long for peace, justice, love, beauty, goodness—for God. Yet these things so readily slip our grasp, leaving us with a desire for that which is no longer and not yet.

There have been times when I think we do not desire heaven; but more often I find myself wondering whether in our heart of hearts we ever have desires for anything else. [...] It is the secret signature of each soul, the incommunicable and unappeasable want, the thing we desired before we met our wives or made our friends or chose our work and which we shall still desire on our deathbeds when the mind no longer knows a wife or friend or work. [...] All your life an unattainable ecstasy has hovered just beyond the grasp of your consciousness. The day is coming when you will wake to find beyond all hope that you have attained it or else that it was within your reach and you have lost it forever.[22]

But this joy is distinct from mere pleasure or momentary happiness. It must have "the stab, the pang, the inconsolable longing."[23] Human desire, that deep and bittersweet longing for something that will satisfy us, points beyond finite objects and finite persons (who seem able to fulfill this desire, yet eventually prove incapable of doing so). It points through these objects and persons toward its real goal and fulfillment in God himself. "That we are haunted by unquenchable longings points to a goal for that longing—in eternity if not in time."[24] Lewis says our longing for so much more is "no mere neurotic fancy, but the truest index of our real situation."[25] At the other end of all human longings, as our poets and mystics rightly point out, is an experience of God, who is the completion of sehnsucht. Lewis says, "We do not want merely to see beauty, though, God knows, even that is bounty enough. We want something else which can hardly be put into words—to be united with the beauty we see, to pass into it, to receive it into ourselves, to bathe in it, to become part of it."[26] Elsewhere he says that "God is what is at the other end of our wounded desire, of our experience of transcendence. If transcendence is an experience of longing, God is the object of that longing. God ... is the reason for our experience of it."[27]

Solomon expressed this very idea in his poetic writings: "He has made everything beautiful in its time. He has also set eternity in the human heart; yet no one can fathom what God has done from beginning to end" (Ecclesiastes 3:11). God has placed within each and every one of us a longing for something that lasts beyond our life here on earth. The very fact that we grieve the death of a loved one is indicative of this: we were not made to be finite, and we are wounded when we're faced with this reality. We are made for eternity—and this has been set in our hearts by God himself; our longings and desires reveal this to be true.

All poets understand sehnsucht and write of it in universal terms. For instance, D. H. Lawrence in his poem "Terra Incognita" writes:

> There are vast realms of consciousness still undreamed of
> vast ranges of experience, like the humming of unseen harps,
> we know nothing of, within us.

Sehnsucht, this universal longing, this never-ending searching that is instinctive in every single person, is "like the humming of unseen harps within us." This humming can be disregarded, neglected or suppressed, but it can never be eliminated. And so we conclude that "Alex from London," as she journeyed on her pilgrimage, is "every person"—especially those who profess no belief in a divine being. Alex's searching and longing, expressed in her awe of creation and her desire for purpose, is not unique to her. Our Creator has set eternity in each and every one of our hearts.

As we have already seen, all human beings are culturally imprinted and we act in ways we are not consciously aware of. It is these "imprints" that *really* determine a person's attitude towards a particular thing. The unbelief of many is based largely upon these latent cultural imprints—the truth is that most of what these unbelievers do not believe, Christians do not believe either. And so our professed unbelief can never turn off the humming. Whether acknowledged or not, the whole of Alex's being is a search for God, and no amount of baggage and hurt from past experiences can wash away the restlessness of the heart.

ECHOES OF A VOICE

It is this divinely placed humming that is an intrinsic part of the human soul, which in turn generates so much of the culture code. If we are to develop a missional proclamation that opens the door of human hearts in our time, one that will truly resonate, then we need to follow C. S. Lewis' advice in developing a *dialectic of desire*—one that recovers Augustine's theme of a restless heart. We will look into how we can practically tap into and access the power of directing desires in chapters nine and ten. For now, we simply have to acknowledge that we have much to learn if we are to develop a missional anthropology (and proclamation) that resonates with the real experiences of all human beings.

In his brilliant book *Simply Christian*, N. T. Wright explores four areas of desire that apply directly to sehnsucht. Wright says today's world can be interpreted by understanding there are four "echoes of a voice," each of which call us to a place beyond ourselves, that lead us toward something we may not be able to understand or articulate, but that we all desire.[28]

When we consider the communities and individuals with whom we are engaged, these four echoes are impossible to ignore:

- A *longing for justice*. Everyone recognizes the world is full of brokenness, and the universal desire is to see it repaired. It is the longing for the world to be set right.
- A *thirst for spirituality*. The awareness all humans have (whether acknowledged or not) that they are made for communion with someone or something much bigger, much greater, than anything we can know on our own.
- A *hunger for relationship*. The easiest of the echoes to hear—we all have a need for belonging, the desire to know and be known. We were made to be in relationship.
- A *delight in beauty*. All humans experience, and yearn for this, during their lives. "Beauty is to the spirit what food is to the flesh. A glimpse of it in a young face, say, or an echo of it in a song fills an emptiness in you that nothing else under the sun can. Unlike

food, however, it is something you never get your fill of. It leaves you always aching with longing not so much for more of the same as for whatever it is that makes it beautiful."[29]

We would add one more universal echo to Wright's four echoes: that of the human need for significance, meaning, and purpose. Humans are meaning-hungry creatures who will shrivel and die for want of hope and direction.

These echoes are not exhaustive to all issues of life, and N. T. Wright is clear that they do not provide proof that compels belief, nor do they definitively point to the Christian God. However, they may provide a key to help open our minds beyond the flat, scientific materialism and drab consumerism of modern Western culture. Not all truth is revealed through observation and experiment, Wright notes. We see the moral chaos around us, but we somehow know the world was made for justice—our thirst for spirituality, relationships, authenticity, beauty, and significance are real. Such knowledge requires resources beyond those available to the scientist and engineer. Whatever or whoever is ultimately responsible for these echoes is not simply another element or part of this universe. These are echoes of the voice of God.

When we take the time to deeply study human desires and longings, we easily conclude that the search is on; a quest for an experience that climbs beyond ordinary limitations and exceeds our explanation; a journey to a belief that goes beyond mere physical needs and realities. It is a universal search for transcendence in a time when "transcendence has been reduced to a rumour."[30]

Alex was seeking the transcendent on the Camino. Something beyond or above the range of normal; something that was more than just about a physical experience. Her questions that night around the dinner table were caused by an otherworldly experience. Whether she was cognizant or not, the deep desire was ever growing within her. It was as if a door had been opened that she did not know existed, and she was in the middle of something that pushed her to a new realm of possibility, beyond any previous experience; a place she longed to enter and possess. Encountering transcendence throws open the windows of the known world to a wholly different world.

A correct understanding of the human soul zeroes in on the reflexive desire toward a transcendent experience. To be fully human is to seek answers to those deepest questions about the meaning of life and of death. As Christians, the more we fail to understand these ultimate desires and longings, the more we are unable to comprehend and communicate this unifying vision of reality that finds its ultimate source in God. We remain trapped in this crisis of interpretation.

And so we need to learn how to enter into conversations about the troubled search for love and lasting connection; we need to gain some understanding of the echoes, desires, and cultural imprints—this "humming." We are not attempting to tell the story of God to a people lacking for nothing; we are simply attempting to tell a story that makes sense of, and gives true direction to, the longings that already exist. For those of us who live missionally, it's our role, as well as our privilege, to point the seeker beyond the purely temporal and earthly to that which lies beyond … and to make the holy connections.

WHAT ABOUT ALEX?

The last time I (Mark) saw "Alex from London" was on the day we arrived at our long-desired destination: the cathedral at Santiago de Compostela. On completion of their journey, almost all the Camino hikers attend the noon Pilgrim's Mass at the cathedral. It's a majestic, serene, and holy experience … some might say "transcendent."

I entered the cathedral early and wandered around, appreciating the sense of history and the beauty of the architecture, and observing the hundreds of people as they filtered in for Mass. Almost unbelievably, as I walked down the center aisle toward the front of the church, I came upon Alex sitting by herself in a pew. We hadn't crossed paths for the last few days, not since I had run into her on the street corner. She had her backpack next to her on the pew, and she was quietly weeping. I never was certain of the reason for her tears, but it apparently had something to do with the fact that the Mass administered that day was to be given in Italian, her grandmother's native tongue. This moved her deeply, more than she could express; she felt it was in some way significant.

We talked for a moment, and then she said something that acknowledged a recognition and awareness of this God she had passionately denied just a few days before. Albeit very small, I believe it was a step toward belief. She said, with a look of longing on her face, "You know, I live in a flat [apartment] in London that is right next to a church. I mean, *right next* to the church. I share a wall with them." She then stood up and held her hand out, fingers extended, as if she was touching the wall. She looked at me, as if she was about to reveal something of great magnitude, and then said, "So, when I touch the wall like this, it's kind of like I'm there, in church, with all those people who believe in God."

I looked at her, trying not to cry myself, and asked, "What do you think that means?"

"I'm not sure," she responded.

"Me, neither," I said. "But I think all of this—your pilgrimage, your deep questions about your life and what you want to change, your tears—it has to mean *something*."

Alex didn't say a word. But the look on her face of hope, wonder, questioning, and restlessness all spoke of searching, of longing, and desire. She simply turned and sat back down, her eyes fixed toward the front of the church.

THRO' NARROW CHINKS OF THE CAVERN

(THE DUNGEONING OF HUMAN PERCEPTION)

We behold something illustrious that cannot undergo an end—lofty, heavenly, infinite, older than heaven, older than primordial chaos.

— **VESPERS HYMN ON THE FEAST OF THE TRANSFIGURATION**

Unless the eye catch fire The God will not be seen
Unless the ear catch fire The God will not be heard
Unless the tongue catch fire The God will not be named
Unless the heart catch fire The God will not be loved
Unless the mind catch fire The God will not be known

— **WILLIAM BLAKE**

There is not a square inch in the whole domain of our human existence over which Christ, who is Sovereign over all, does not cry, Mine!

— **ABRAHAM KUYPER**

The nineteenth-century poet and painter William Blake considered it his life's purpose to awaken people to the divine aspects of their own natures. A genuine eccentric who performed his particular art out of a deep reverence for Scripture, Blake used poetry and bizarre paintings to break through dull familiarity, evoke imagination, and provoke response. In his epic poem *The Marriage of Heaven and Hell*, in which he explores the spiritual interconnectivity of all things, he writes:

If the doors of perception were cleansed everything would appear to man as it is, Infinite. For man has closed himself up, till he sees all things thro' narrow chinks of his cavern.[1]

This little line of poetry provides us with a major key to understanding the themes of this book. Becoming aware of the spiritual blindness in ourselves and in the people and society around us would be a major move toward a reframation. As we've already explored, human beings are wired for eternity (the humming of unseen harps), but in order to discern the source of humming and to be able respond to it, human perception needs to be "cleansed."

Allow the sheer power of Blake's images to impact your perspective on reality and imagination—"doors of perception," "cleansed," "closed," "narrow chinks," and "cavern." Blake here pictures people—people very much like you and me—as living rather fearfully in a prison-like cavity in the side of a mountain. There, as they press themselves ever further into the back of the cave, the opening appears to them as an ever-diminishing slit of light. Through this narrow opening they get only highly filtered glimpses of what they perceive as the overwhelming and threatening world outside the cave. And yes, while it might well be dank, dark, and confined inside the cave ... to them, at least, it seems safe and controllable. But in this restricted, "dungeoned" existence, the inmates' own perceptions are darkened and reality cannot be viewed as it truly is.

We ask the reader to somehow try to imagine what it is like to form one's perspectives of the world from a life spent within a very limited space. Consider one of C. S. Lewis' parables, in which he invites us to picture a woman thrown into a dungeon. In that prison, she bears and rears a son. The poor lad grows up seeing nothing but dungeon walls, straw on the floor, and a grating, which is too high up to show anything except a little patch of sky. It turns out that this unfortunate woman was also an artist, and when they imprisoned her, she was allowed to bring with her a drawing pad and a box of pencils. Because she never loses the hope of freedom, she constantly tries to help her son understand something of the outer world, which he has never seen. As he has no reference to objects outside the dungeon, she tries to teach him by drawing him pictures. With the lines of her pencil, she attempts to communicate to him what fields, rivers, mountains, cities, and waves on a beach are like. He is a devoted learner, and he does his best to believe her when she tells him that the outer world is way more interesting and glorious than anything in the dungeon. At times, he succeeds in believing this. At times, he simply cannot believe because he cannot conceive what she is really referring to. In one such event, when his imagination fails him and he confesses utter disbelief, the mother realizes that all these years he has lived under a misconception.

> "But," she gasps, "you didn't think that the real world was full of lines drawn in lead pencil?" "What?" says the boy. "You mean that there are no pencil marks there?" And instantly, his whole notion of the outer world becomes an utter blank. For the lines, by which alone he was imagining it, have now been denied of it. He has no idea of that which will exclude and dispense with the lines, that of which the lines were merely a transposition—the waving treetops, the light dancing on the weir, the colored three-dimensional realities which are not enclosed in lines but define their own shapes at every moment with a delicacy and multiplicity which no drawing could ever achieve. The child will get the idea that the real world is somehow less visible than his mother's pictures. In reality it lacks lines because it is incomparably more visible.[2]

All the boy's points of reference (the dungeon) fail to help him perceive a reality outside this limited world. Remember, this is what Blake is addressing—*perceptions*, not reality. The actual results of a cave-like existence are very tangible, as we illustrated with Harold Crick in chapter three, but here our attempt is to delve deeper, past the problems of reduced living, in order to understand that it is our reduced *thinking*—our theory of knowledge, how we perceive, interpret, and make sense of the world—which is at its core severely narrowed. It's not simply that the truth is reduced, but that our very way of *receiving* and *perceiving* the truth is confined.

A SYSTEM OF HIDEOUTS

Apart from providing shelter for prehistoric cavemen and a few random monks, caves have generally not been considered as places to live, but rather as places to hide. In the Scriptures, caves are used for concealment, for staying out of sight, and as hideaways. Metaphorically and theologically understood, therefore, the cave can be seen as the place where the Adam in all of us, the first of all of us, hides from God.[3] Afraid of the piercing light of God's presence, we prefer, as God's first creation did, secretive darkness instead.

> Adam hides himself to avoid rendering accounts, to escape responsibility for his way of living. Every man hides for this purpose, for every man is

Adam and finds himself in Adam's situation. To escape responsibility for
his life, he turns existence into a system of hideouts.[4]

In the Rabbinic tradition, Adam's decision to eat the fruit was far less
a concern to God than his attempt to hide afterwards. Adam's hiding is
representative of a world that attempts to deny the existence of a God who
"intrudes" into it and calls it to account. It is this avoidance of God that
lies at the root of rebellion and irresponsibility. "When this habit of hiding
becomes one's primary stance in relation to God, then with every new
hideout the person's situation becomes more and more questionable every
day."[5] In an attempt to hide themselves from God, the rebel/sinner creates
an illusion of safety, developing a mind-set that enables them to function
in day-to-day life. This fabricated world inevitably leads to a life evacuated
of meaning, to seeing oneself and one's life through distorted lenses, and
ultimately to the destruction of one's very identity. Sin is essentially the
choice to move away from truth. The lies we subsequently choose to live by
gradually construct ideologies (religious or otherwise). We generate these
ideologies in an attempt to fill the gaps left by the loss of Truth. In time,
these beliefs become integrated in our lives in such a way that they become
the primary truth for us.[6] We are all prone to deny truths about ourselves
and the world around us that threaten our settled convictions. This is
as true of atheists as it is of Christians, and anybody else. The actor Sir
Anthony Hopkins, a one-time atheist who also studied and acted roles that
included the demonic suppression of the knowledge of God, concluded
that being an atheist was like living in a locked cell with no windows ...
sounds awfully like a cave.[7]

In his compassion, God continues to ask, "Where are you?" That
question—addressed to Adam and to us—is designed to awaken each one of
us to responsibility and to lure us out of our respective system of hideouts.
When we hear *that* question, and when we shed our alibis and try to respond,
then the wall built by our callousness begins to crumble away. God is never
distant from the honest and repentant heart, for the biblical God is not
essentially a hidden God, but one who is always revealing himself.[8]

THE DISENCHANTED PARADIGM

As we consider what it means to be human, we'd do well to note that in
the New Testament, the word *mind* (*nous, dianoia*) constitutes "not an
instrument of thought" but "a *mode* of thought" or "mind-set." It therefore
refers to the outlook, filter, orientation, or frames, as well as the rationale

implicit in these. There are similarities here to the cultural imprint ideas
we explored in chapter four, but excavating the idea of "mind-set" takes
us even deeper toward understanding the spiritual depth of imprints. This
mind-set is "a complex of thoughts and assumptions which make up the
consciousness of a person" or their "way of thinking."[9] For instance, Paul
talks about the "cravings of our flesh" in Ephesians 2:3 as a way of talking
about a darkened perception, and in Romans 12:2 he talks about having
one's perception cleansed, "renewing the *nous*."

To translate *nous/dianoia* as simply "mind" therefore does not
fully convey the full biblical understanding. Rather, it approximates
what we might generally call a *worldview* or *paradigm*; a particular set
of frames used to view the world. And while paradigms allow us to see
the world and negotiate it, they also come along with what is called
"paradigm-blindness." By opting for one view of reality, the perceiver
automatically deselects possible alternatives.[10] It is this that either allows us
to see—or blinds us to—what is really there.

And so perhaps the most truly terrifying thing about living in a darkened
cave is the paradigm—the "cave-rationality" by which it operates—the
mind-set that is now suitably adjusted to the reduced reality of the hideout.
The narrowed and darkened confines of the cave become the very definition
of what is to be considered normal.[11] Those on the inside don't even notice,
as they have simply inherited a way of seeing things and use the same
rationality to escape their own existential culpability before God. We are
once again reminded of Lewis' image of hell in *The Great Divorce* (the
name of which, incidentally, is a direct riff off the title of Blake's poem
The Marriage of Heaven and Hell). However, now we discover that the
problem is rooted in human consciousness itself. As we noted in chapter
three, C. S. Lewis claims that, "Hell is a state of mind" and warns that,
"every state of mind, left to itself, every shutting up of the creature within
the dungeon of its own mind—is, in the end, Hell."[12]

This "darkening of the *nous*," might best be described as *disenchantment*, a darkness that has come about from a refusal to see and
acknowledge this living and active God. Such disenchantment of the
mind (the *nous*) is even more dangerous than outright revolt. In becoming
disenchanted, an individual effectively silences the only inner voice that
can keep their heart lively and alert as they grow older. They have stifled
the voice of the child they once were. It was Jesus who said that it is only
through the simple eyes of the child, the eyes that see the world through
the ever-expanding frames of wonder, surprise, and imagination, that one

can understand God.[13] "Disenchantment therefore is as full and dense as hell itself. In this icy place, all fire from above has been extinguished. The only person who can be disenchanted is the one who has not grasped that the world is a dark marvel. Disenchantment is a sign of stupidity."[14] It is "stupidity" here because, in claiming to be wise, the disenchanted have proven themselves to be fools in the most fundamental sense of the word (Romans 1:22). Disenchantment is therefore a characteristic of the darkened prison in which all deniers of God inevitably find themselves.[15]

It is therefore the *nous*—the paradigm or door of perception— that needs to be cleansed, reoriented and reimagined so that a sense of re/enchantment might prevail. And according to Paul it is this disenchantment that the gospel of Jesus addresses by restoring a right relationship with God (Romans 3–4), reconstituting a new humanity (Romans 5), uniting us with Christ, reorienting our lives around Jesus (Romans 6), bestowing his Spirit to lead and enlighten us (Romans 8), and granting us a new *nous*-paradigm (Romans 12) through which we can attune ourselves to God and his purposes. God has overcome our brokenness and rebellion, has cleansed our perceptions, and has enlightened us with a comprehensive vision of reality that includes his eternal purposes for his entire cosmos (Colossians and Ephesians). Hardly a vision of the world from the confines of a cave.[16]

SEEING IS BELIEVING AND BELIEVING IS SEEING

"To see what is in front of one's nose requires a constant struggle" (George Orwell).[17]

The story is told that when Columbus first arrived in what was to become known as the Caribbean in 1492, the indigenous people on the shore could not see Columbus' large ships sitting on the horizon. The reason for this was that the idea of "ships" was beyond their conceptual experience, beyond their knowledge, and therefore beyond their perceived realm of possibility. They could not see what was right in front of them.[18]

It should be obvious simply from any experience of looking for something that was under your nose all along … Things can hide in plain sight.[19] Even when something might be right in front of us, if we do not have the proper mental slots or receptors to process what we are seeing, we fail to see at all. Limited perceptual categories mean that people will often not "see" what is directly in front of them. Eugene Webb warns that it requires great effort for a philosopher, a psychologist, or a scientist to grasp what is lacking in their own respective spheres of expertise; they are so trained in a certain way of thinking, it is almost impossible to "see" the gaps.[20]

We've all experienced this when we have been so preoccupied with one thing that we fail to see something else right in front of our eyes. (Smartphone-obsessed pedestrians dawdling along the bike path, this means you.) We tend to see only what can be incorporated into our entrenched frame of reference, our already established frame, and to reject anything that doesn't "fit." We de/select those aspects of reality that confront our assumptions about the world and make us uncomfortable. We can only see what we believe to be possible.[21] This is a warning to us all.

In his book *Simply Good News*, N. T. Wright points out that Jesus had similar problems in proclaiming good news to his hearers; there were plenty of people who couldn't see or receive his message because it was not what they expected or what they had been trained to see. "Jesus's contemporaries—even his Jewish ones, and how much more his non-Jewish ones!—had their heads and hearts full of wrong ideas, and he constantly ran the risk that they would hear what he was saying within the context of those wrong ideas and so twist it completely out of shape." In fact this is a problem that runs throughout history. Jesus' message to his contemporaries, and the church's subsequent message about Jesus, never seems to fit what people expect. Often enough, it doesn't even fit what the church itself expects. The good news seems to baffle its hearers because it is never what people think it ought to be. For some people, it's so different (they were not expecting Warhead Candy), they can't even begin to recognize it. That is why, as Paul said, the gospel is the power of God to some and foolishness to others.[22] Some perceive the message as threatening and therefore become fearful of it or try to stamp it out. Wright goes on to say:

> How we understand things is a function of our whole personality. But if that whole personality is significantly flawed in some way—and sadly, that seems to be the case with all of us—this will affect the mental framework with which we start. It isn't, in other words, that we are flawed human beings in other respects but our minds are clear and fully operational, just waiting like a blank sheet of paper for someone to write true ideas on them. Our minds, which are intimately connected with our imaginations, our emotions, and our physical bodies in a rich and multitextured combination, need to be sorted out just like the rest of us. If we insist on keeping our mental, emotional, and imaginative world the way it's always been, the good news just won't fit. We will then either reject it or distort it, cutting off the bits we can't fit in or reshaping parts to conform to the ideas we already have.[23]

And so it is our *whole* mind-set, our *whole* way of seeing that needs to be cleansed in order to receive the good news. Jesus was so challenging to many of his hearers because he constantly pushed them to see things differently.

> He wasn't giving new or more detailed answers to questions they were already asking. He was doing and saying things designed to tease his hearers into facing new and dangerous questions, into looking at familiar ideas (such as the kingdom of God) from new and unexpected angles. Most people, then and now, find that disturbing and try to avoid it.[24]

As long-term inmates of our respective dungeon-hideouts, we really do not see reality as it is, which leads to a delusional understanding of the human condition. For example, we call the formulae of science "concrete facts," forgetting that science, though extremely valuable, is the most abstract way of apprehending nature or reality. We see everything in terms of space and time and number and miss each thing's uniqueness. We miss the startling reality of what is simply *there* ... under our noses. Between us and reality lies a heavy veil of thinking of which we are largely unaware. Most people have never given this any thought, and yet every person, just by virtue of being human, has this veil between him or her and reality. Illumination therefore involves removing, overcoming this veil, and finding the reality that is simply there.[25]

REMOVING THE VEIL

There are multiple instances in the narrative of Scripture where this idea of the "removing of the veil" can be seen. It is noteworthy that the New Testament word for truth (*aleitheia*) literally means *unveiling, unconcealment, disclosedness,* and so the concept is implied in the revelation of truth itself.[26] The writers of Scripture often use the imagery/metaphor of unveiling when it comes to the knowledge of God and to various theophanies. For instance, Paul refers to it in 2 Corinthians 3:13–18: "Indeed, to this very day whenever Moses is read, a veil lies over their minds; but when one turns to the Lord, the veil is removed" (2 Corinthians 3:15–16 NRSV); it is mentioned throughout the writings of the Old Testament prophets, including in the vision of the Valley of Dry Bones (Ezekiel 37), where God unveils Ezekiel's eyes to see what he was calling Israel toward; and, of course, we see it in the tearing of the temple veil at the death of Jesus, with all its associated symbolism.

A particularly powerful experience of unveiling occurs in Genesis, when Jacob settled in for the night after a long day of walking.

> He came to a certain place and stayed there for the night, because the sun had set. Taking one of the stones of the place, he put it under his head and lay down in that place. And he dreamed that there was a ladder set up on the earth, the top of it reaching to heaven; and the angels of God were ascending and descending on it.
>
> GENESIS 28:11–12 NRSV

This vision of angels going up and down the ladder was only a small part of Jacob's unveiling. The more significant revelation was the presence of something Divine, a presence of Something that up to this time had most likely only been a small part of Jacob's culture and tradition. Suddenly, as the veil was pulled back, this became a present reality, a reality that had *always been there*:

> And the LORD stood beside him and said, "I am the LORD, the God of Abraham your father and the God of Isaac; the land on which you lie I will give to you and to your offspring [...] Know that I am with you and will keep you wherever you go, and will bring you back to this land; for I will not leave you until I have done what I have promised you."
>
> GENESIS 28:13, 15 NRSV

God graciously grants assurance to Jacob that wherever he traveled, God would be with him and would eventually bring him back home—a completely foreign concept in this culture. The pagan gods of the time never moved but instead were believed to reside in religious places, places where gods were expected to be—temples, holy sites, altars, etc. But this God was showing something different. This God could apparently speak to anybody, anywhere, anytime, and Jacob seems to acknowledge this: "Then Jacob woke from his sleep and said, *'Surely the* LORD *is in this place—and I did not know it!'*" (Genesis 28:16 NRSV, italics ours).

Jacob—like Isaiah, Ezekiel, Paul, John, and many others after him—had his "perceptions cleansed" in the midst of a shadowy existence. Having seen "thro' narrow chinks of his cavern," he became aware of a reality that had been there all along. When he lay down that night and put his head on the stone pillow, life itself, in the material, was simply all that he knew, all that he experienced. But then he was shown a deeper awareness, an awareness of something/Someone that had always been there, but Jacob had never noticed. This unveiling reoriented his life. His world was expanded. Ours no less.

ALL I KNOW IS ALL THERE IS

In the 1998 film *The Truman Show*, Jim Carrey plays Truman Burbank, who stars in a twenty-four-hour-a-day television reality show, unbeknownst to him.[27] "In Truman's world, everything is phony, from the sun in the sky to the traffic reports on the radio to his relationship with his best friend." All the characters except Truman are professional actors "giving us phony emotions."[28] He's a real person, but in a totally plastic world; his reality is relative. Gradually, Truman's perception changes. Little by little he gets hints that the world he has grown up in is not the whole story. Cracks appear in the facade of his reality. He becomes dissatisfied with his life in Seahaven (the fictitious town). He begins to realize he no longer has a sense of what is real and that it is possible there is a bigger reality than he ever imagined he could experience.

The Truman Show is a story about how one man living a counterfeit life discovers the truth, and once he does, he has to decide whether to be honest about his situation or to go on living an artificial sham of an existence.

We are all confronted with this same dilemma. Once we become aware of the counterfeit life we have invested in, will we continue to live as we always have, or will we seek to walk in Truth? If we are locked in to a certain predetermined way of perceiving, if we are deeply committed to a given way of seeing things (and who isn't?), if we have taken up residence in Seahaven, all this talk about unveiling and reorienting and having your world expanded could be experienced as a threat. To grow and develop in our experience of God, we need to reconsider our approach to reality and be willing to view things differently. We need to make the move to widen and cleanse the doors of perception to a better comprehension of the reality that is infinite.

The seminal psychologist William James tussled with the idea of a "fixed mind-set" in his *Varieties of Religious Experience*.[29] He lamented the fact that the vast majority of humans lock themselves up in static ideas and notions that are obsolete, or just plain wrong. However, most of us continue to insist these are true because we are just too lazy or fearful (or both) to reconsider. It turns out that the biggest blockage to the next experience of God is the last experience of him because it is the one in which our perceptions find themselves deeply rooted.

Along with the Hebrew prophets, Jesus and the New Testament writers affirm that selfishness, rebellion, and an entrenched refusal to step toward the relentless pursuit of God fundamentally affect a person's abilities to perceive him.[30] This *entrenchment* clouds the possibility of revelation; the world is interpreted by constructing a narrative that *a priori* excludes God from the equation. Any attempt to cleanse the doors of perception is blocked, and so the poisoned, reduced narrative is passed down through the generations and considered normal. In other words, this kind of unbelief is a self-generating and self-sustaining endeavor, built on the refusal to acknowledge God or his claims on our lives and that there is possibly *more than we already know*.

The sad reality is that, although most of us are open to new concepts early on in life and often into young adulthood, this tends to stop once we move beyond college. By the way, if you are interested in finding the most enlightened of all individuals on the planet, you can no doubt find them in any university freshmen dorm room, late at night, learning to play guitar as they sit around "illuminating" each other. But it seems that once this formal season of learning is complete, our minds are made up, and our decisions and utterances are an endless repetition of views that have in the meantime become obsolete, outworn, and unsound. This applies to politics, scholarship, and the arts as well as social service. Views, just like leaves, are bound to wither, because the world is in flux. But so many of us would rather be faithful to outworn views than undergo the strain of re-examination and revision. Indeed, intellectual senility sets in long before physical infirmity.[31]

We tend to have an overdependence on the waning intellect of our twentysomething selves. Perhaps instead of this, we ought to learn to assess the authenticity of our lives by how many times we are able to see the world from a new perspective.

Our point is, yes, we have to move beyond the idea that "we only see what we believe is possible." But even further, we have to move to a place of being able to grasp the truth of "all I know is *not* all there is." As we look closer at a culture in desperate need of widening its doors of perception, we should note that those who refuse to leave their narrowed existence are actually stating the exact opposite: "All I know *really is* all there is." Consider the absurd nature of this statement: "You know, now that I've thought about it … Yes, I truly believe that all that I know, all that I have been able to comprehend is truly all that there is. Regardless of evidence to the contrary, I am positive that my breadth of knowledge and experience encompasses all that has ever been or ever will be."

It is hard to imagine any person in their right mind making such a bold and arrogant statement. Yet, when we take a step back and observe a culture of people (not just those on the Camino or at Burning Man, but those in the supermarket or at church), we realize that most of us, whether we articulate it or not, believe that, "all we know is all there is." We might never utter those words, but a truth does not have to be stated to be a reality.

Consider discussions surrounding politics, economics, and social perspectives; even more superficially, think about those with locked-in opinions on such things as entertainment, sports, or even our favorite foods or restaurants. A perspective of life that deep down buys into an "all I know is all there is" ideology is missing out on so much, and is probably fairly miserable to be around too.[32]

"All I know is all there is. My experience must be the sum total of human existence."

How very prehistoric of us to even consider these statements to be true.

If we go back into Blake's concept of "the doors of perception," we realize he is diagnosing a universal longing for things to be made right, a longing that is limited by a profoundly incomplete perception of reality. How ridiculous to believe that the limit of all that is just and true and beautiful in our world is within our grasp when all we have seen and experienced is a darkened cave. The belief that "shadows" constitute reality, simply because one has never seen or known anything else, explains so much about our world.

Take for example the "worldly" (disenchanted) experience of beauty. This view of beauty is divorced from its total context—such a beauty still captivates to some extent but fails to point beyond itself, and so it ensnares the viewer in an idolatrous hold. *Real* beauty on the other hand goes well beyond the appreciation of some perceived loveliness of an image in a magazine or in the magnificence of nature, and leads to an enchanted encounter with a transcendent beauty that captivates and "transports" the beholder into an immediate experience of it, not just the aesthetic appreciation. This is what the Bible calls the splendor/glory of the Lord. In the darkened experience of the cave, people readily accept a false measure of beauty and self-image—eating disorders, depression, breakdowns of relationships all stem from this hollow perception.

We have allowed our cave-dwelling existences to lead us down some illusionary paths.

We have set up a reality that no one actually believes. Even though we know it's not real and true, we don't change it. We ignore the points of friction. We choose to ignore the lies we've come to accept while using all the numbing agents possible to keep us from reality. Use the death of pop icon Michael Jackson as an example of irony. *He died of an overdose of anesthesia.* Isn't that a metaphor for our culture?[33]

We have become an anesthetized society, believing that what we see are actual existing truths, instead of what they really are ... firelit shadows on the wall of a captive-filled cave. Too many of us live our lives as if we are chained up in a cave while being forced to watch shadowy imposters flitting across a stone surface. Sadly, we become convinced there is no way out of that darkness. It is tragic that the "chains" that we believe are keeping us in the cave are, in actuality, of our own making and we choose to simply do nothing. "We need no urging to choose what it is that will destroy us because again and again we choose it without urging. We are more than half in love with our own destruction. All of us are."[34]

In order to avoid getting imprisoned in obsolete ideas—our own or ones we have inherited from our culture or religious tradition—we simply must continue to struggle with life's most important and vexing questions: what does it mean to exist?; how does one come to know the Truth?; can it be true that God has drawn near to us in Jesus Christ?; how then should we live?

These are existential questions all humans must grapple with if we are to be honest about what it means to be human.

> These questions cannot be resolved by their being incorporated into a system, cannot be understood except that understanding arise[s] out of one's own existence before God, and cannot be drawn to a conclusion only to be left behind. No propositional resolution of these questions is available. We are invited instead to an understanding of the Truth through faith, which is to say that we are invited to embark upon a life in relationship with God. The understanding of Truth is not a matter of formulating a proposition but of trusting one's life to the Lordship of Jesus Christ.[35]

Theologian Murray Rae rightly reminds us that authentic Christian faith, real discipleship, must always be characterized by a "transformation of the individual under the impact of revelation."[36] This means constant and direct response to God. The Bible cautions us that if this kind of living faith is scorned, then any understanding of God will be lost.

METANOIA: THE CLEANSING OF PERCEPTION

Owen Barfield, one of the Inklings, wisely alerts us that our way out of any mental prison is to realize the limitations of our current mode of consciousness.[37] The "first step of all is to realize that mental habit is a prison. [...] But one way or another, what matters is our coming to realize that the way we habitually think and perceive is *not the only possible way*, not even a way that has been going on very long. *It is the way we have come to think, the way we have come to perceive*" (italics ours).[38]

Clearly, in order to reframe our understanding of God and the world, we have much un/learning to do. The Scriptures are absolutely clear on this—in fact, the first recorded words of Jesus initiate his ministry with this call: "After John was put in prison, Jesus went into Galilee, proclaiming the good news of God. 'The time has come,' he said. 'The kingdom of God has come near. Repent and believe the good news!'" (Mark 1:14–15).

This is directed at the people of God; as Danielle noted in the foreword, "the first calling [to repentance] is not to sinners but to saints." And perhaps this calling is especially aimed at the religious leaders (those most certain about their beliefs). Israel too needed a cleansing of its collective perception before the people could truly see and comprehend who it was they were dealing with in Jesus. We learn from Jesus that those who have eyes to see and ears to hear are those who, by God's grace, have been able to let go of such limited frameworks and to perceive the world anew under the condition called *faith*. It's no different for us today. We need to have our perceptions cleansed and transformed if we are to be able to see and understand the truth. And yet "despite how often and how beautifully openness as a concept is held up and celebrated in our postmodern context, real change is just plain difficult."[39]

In the New Testament, this transformation is brought about by a process called *metanoia* and at its core entails the ongoing renewal of our paradigms and perceptions (*nous*). *Metanoia* is necessary for the ability to hear the Word and follow it. It involves a "turning"—a person's radical decentering in favor of God. Certainly, a genuine conversion to Christian faith involves a fundamental transformation of our understanding. Without this, we will remain alienated from God, and his appearance in the form of a servant will remain a scandal and an offence. *Metanoia* therefore represents a real challenge to the persistent attempts of those who propose that we can discover the truth on quite different terms.

Anna Robinson, our beloved editor, reminded us that:

- repentance is standing on the desk in order to look at the world in a different way
- repentance is offered to and refused by the residents of Grey Town. They make hell for themselves by closing themselves off to *metanoia*
- repentance is part of the transformation of Harold Crick
- repentance is the right response to any reductionism, to our heresies, and to our idolatrous tendencies to try to control and limit God
- repentance is the way to renew and re/enchant our darkened *nous*[40]
- repentance is a prerequisite to the art of seeing again (as we shall explore in chapter six).

Communicating the bigger picture of God (through theology, story, and our lives) draws people to repentance because:

> God replaces our desire for worldly things by luring us away from them by showing us Himself, which is infinitely more lovely, infinitely more valuable, and infinitely sweeter than all our other lusts and desires. This is the Christian's experience of Romans 2:4—when God shows us His kindness, it is an irresistible beauty that compels us to repentance.[41]

The Scriptures teach us that no spiritual progress is possible without humility. Humility requires us to admit that *all we know is NOT all there is*. "This is not a conversion of the mind; it is a conversion of the heart. Without it, we are stuck, certainly in this life, and perhaps in the next."[42] *Metanoia* is therefore crucial to cleansing the doors of perception, the key to transformation, and the pathway to true knowledge of God.

Engaging with true repentance has always been a challenge for the stubborn human mind, but even more so in our twenty-first-century "echo chambers," in which our beliefs are amplified and reinforced within our closed networks. We must recognize that the shift required for a person to come to a place of repentance is monumental. It can only truly happen when the Holy Spirit opens our hearts and minds to "see" another way: "when he, the Spirit of truth, comes, he will guide you into all the truth" (John 16:13). One of the sacred roles of the Holy Spirit is to illumine us, to make us sensitive to the form of Christ in the world, to help us understand Scripture, and appropriate the truth and live into it. The Spirit will guide us out of the dungeon. Or, as Paul says in 1 Corinthians 2:9–16:

> "What no eye has seen,
> what no ear has heard,

and what no human mind has conceived"—
the things God has prepared for those who love him—

these are the things God has revealed to us by his Spirit.

The Spirit searches all things, even the deep things of God. For who knows a person's thoughts except their own spirit within them? In the same way no one knows the thoughts of God except the Spirit of God. What we have received is not the spirit of the world, but the Spirit who is from God, so that we may understand what God has freely given us. This is what we speak, not in words taught us by human wisdom but in words taught by the Spirit, explaining spiritual realities with Spirit-taught words. The person without the Spirit does not accept the things that come from the Spirit of God but considers them foolishness, and cannot understand them because they are discerned only through the Spirit. The person with the Spirit makes judgments about all things, but such a person is not subject to merely human judgments, for,

"Who has known the mind of the Lord
so as to instruct him?"

But we have the mind of Christ.

To overcome the problem of limiting perception and illusion, we must learn how to truly pray, both for ourselves and those around us. For in prayer (before God and in Christ and by the Spirit) we can no longer live in fantasy, but must engage Truth and allow ourselves to be judged by it. "Prayer is the atmosphere of all conversion; other discourse leaves in shadow what the self does not wish to see."[43]

LOOKING "AT" OR "THROUGH" A WINDOW

I (Mark) lived for ten years in a beautiful, one-hundred-year-old home in a small, rural midwestern town. Among its many unique features was the front corner window. Because of the age of the home and our lack of funds, the windows were not the efficient, newer windows, but instead were the original windows (i.e., old). In comparison to more modern windows, these were huge, each one measuring five feet tall and five feet wide. There were multiple similar-sized windows throughout the house, but this was my favorite ... because of the view.

Our house was positioned on the corner of the main street in town, and by turning off all the lights in the house and peering out of that corner window, there was a rather picturesque view of the main street … especially when it snowed. Looking through the window at the falling snow, with a corner streetlight magnifying each flake a hundred times, was, or at least was close to, a holy experience.

But when I stopped and examined a small crack that had appeared in the bottom right corner, I saw that this was also the window that had paint flecks on it due to sloppy trim work; and a layer of dust, dirt, and grime in between the actual window and the screen window; not to mention enough ladybug corpses to fill an insect graveyard. It was not nearly the same euphoric, holy experience from this perspective.

Here's what I learned: there is a huge difference between looking *at* a window and looking *through* a window. When I looked *at* that front corner window, I saw the cracked glass and the need for a thorough cleaning. When I looked *through* the window, I saw, among other things, the beautiful snow-covered streets of my very own personal Narnia. How I saw the world depended upon how I approached the window.

We need to see the world differently. We need to see the pilgrims on the Camino and Playa with a different set of eyes. We can look *at* the window and only see the overwhelming brokenness in front of us, a world that is wandering the deserts and trails of life with no sense of the divine. Or we can look *through* the window, beyond what we think we already know, beyond what we have perceived to be true of our culture, and understand that perhaps it is *all of us*, those who believe and those who do not, who have been peering through these "narrow chinks of the cavern."

LIFT UP YOUR GATES, YOU ANCIENT DOORS!

Blake's poetry suggests that instead of going ever deeper into the cave, we should step closer to the opening, and eventually extend our heads through the aperture where we are able to see things as they really are … seemingly vast and unbounded.

And it is to our collective condition of reductionism, idolatry, irresponsibility, withdrawal, fear, self-protection, rebellion, and unreality, that the psalmist calls us to cleanse our perception, and fling open the ancient doors.

The earth is the LORD's, and everything in it,
the world, and all who live in it;
for he founded it on the seas
and established it on the waters.

Who may ascend the mountain of the LORD?
Who may stand in his holy place?
The one who has clean hands and a pure heart,
  who does not trust in an idol
  or swear by a false god.

They will receive blessing from the LORD
  and vindication from God their Savior.
Such is the generation of those who seek him,
  who seek your face, God of Jacob.

Lift up your heads, you gates;
  lift them up, you ancient doors,
  that the King of glory may come in.
Who is he, this King of glory?
The LORD Almighty—
  he is the King of glory.

PSALM 24:1–7, 9–10

We surely have some kind of role in bringing people to a place of deeper awareness, don't we? To tell a story where the reality of God is experienced, an experience much richer and deeper than any of us have ever believed to be possible? But how do we begin amongst a generation that seemingly doesn't want to hear the story of a reality that has been there all along? Philosopher Martin Buber answered this way:

> This generation must be made receptive [...] to the voice of the mystery which speaks in those utterances. And we should not do all this with the purpose of preparing them to repeat the teachings and perform rites, but so that they may acquire the power to make the original choice, that—listening to the voice with that power—they may hear the message it has for their hour and their work that they may learn to trust the voice, and through this trust, come to faith, to a faith of their own.[44]

Can we really make this generation receptive to a reality that has been obscured? Can we help cleanse these doors of perception and open wide these ancient doors?

SECTION 3
A RE/ENCHANTING

In section one, we explored the nature of the eclipse of God and of the reduction of our knowledge and experience of him, which has resulted in a much smaller, diminished, heretical grasp of the faith. We have consequently reduced the story of God to dry doctrine and tasteless tofu, resulting in a reduced life that simply settles for a narrow (hellish) existence.

Section two examined the idea of cultural and missional anthropology and asked questions surrounding the idea of longing and desire. Our lack of understanding of culture and our reluctance to admit that *all we know is not all there is,* has resulted in a cave-dwelling existence from which all of us should be rescued. There simply must be a turning away from a confined and narrow way of perceiving and receiving truth, both about God and this broken world.

In this third section, we want to introduce ways to reimagine our view of God and the world. We propose that to correct the reduction in our theology—our understanding of God—we will first need to recover the art of seeing God in larger and wi[l]der frames. To move from *ossified doctrines, wooden proclamations, empty doxologies*, and *legalistic ethics* toward a great reframation, there must be a re/enchanting of all that has been extracted and siphoned from the story. As we begin to enlarge our frames, we propose we'll not only begin to see a "bigger" God, but we'll also live and tell a bigger, more beautiful story.

THE ART
OF SEEING

(A RE[FRAMED] VISION OF
GOD AND GOSPEL)

The real voyage of discovery consists not in seeking new
landscapes, but in having new eyes.

— **MARCEL PROUST**

Design. Story. Symphony. Empathy. Play. Meaning. These six
senses increasingly will guide our lives and shape our world.

— **DANIEL H. PINK**

Lacking a systematic framework for understanding the clash
of forces in today's world, we are like a ship's crew, trapped
in a storm and trying to navigate between dangerous reefs
without compass or chart. In a culture of warring specialisms,
drowned in fragmented data and fine-toothed analysis,
synthesis is not merely useful—it is crucial.

— **ALVIN TOFFLER**

In *The Art of Seeing*, the influential philosopher and thinker Aldous Huxley
recounts how, at the age of sixteen, he "had a violent attack of *keratitis
punctata*" (the inflammation of the upper layers of the cornea).[1] This, he
writes, "left me (after eighteen months of near-blindness, during which I
had to depend on Braille for my reading and a guide for my walking) with
one eye just capable of light perception, and the other with enough vision
to permit my detecting the two-hundred foot letter on the Snellen chart at
ten feet." For the next few years, doctors advised Huxley to read with the
aid of a powerful handheld magnifying glass—before later promoting him
to spectacles—which allowed him "to read tolerably well," provided that
he kept his "better pupil dilated with atropine, so that [he] might see round
a particularly heavy patch of opacity at the center of the cornea."

The task of reading caused Huxley considerable strain and fatigue, and when he finally acknowledged that his "capacity to see was steadily and quite rapidly failing," he discovered a method of teaching oneself to see again called "visual re-education." Within a few months of attempting this relearning, he was reading without spectacles—and without strain or fatigue. At last, the opacity in the cornea, "which had remained unchanged for upwards of twenty-five years, was beginning to clear up." Although his vision was far from normal, Huxley had succeeded in teaching himself to see by *re-educating his vision*, and with a clarity of sight that was "about twice as good as it used to be" when he wore spectacles.[2]

Huxley's ability to re-educate his failing vision caused him to question how and why previous ophthalmological treatments had been so unsuccessful. His conclusion was that ophthalmology has "been obsessively preoccupied with only one aspect of the total, complex process of seeing—the physiological. Ophthalmologists have paid attention exclusively to eyes, not at all to the mind which makes use of the eyes to see with."[3] In other words, to perceive and comprehend something requires the engagement of the mind (*nous*) synthesized with the senses.

Sensing is not the same as perceiving. The eyes and nervous system do the sensing; the mind does the perceiving. Any improvement in the power of perceiving tends to be accompanied by an improvement in the power of sensing. The natural consequence of this is an improvement in seeing—the product of both sensing and perceiving.[4]

This Huxley calls "the art of seeing," and it involves adopting an active, disciplined approach to re-educating oneself in order to see/perceive again. Interestingly, this "art of seeing" is very similar to the psychophysical skills and habits that are typically acquired in early infancy or childhood by a process of mainly unconscious self-instruction. In other words, it is discovering how to see with and through the (humble and enchanted) eyes of a child. Before we can explore this childlike re-education, we first have to break the tyranny of our all-too-adult eyes.

THE GENIUS OF BOTH/AND

A number of years ago, organization and leadership guru Jim Collins caused something of a revolution in the uber-pragmatic corporate world. Collins suggested that most of our problems arise when we see the world in increasingly analytical (reduced) formulas and then allow these now reduced ideas to monopolize our thinking. To break out of this "tyranny" and to bring lasting, system-wide change (or to create a "great company"), leaders had to learn to see things much more in terms of wholeness, synthesis, and possibility. We believe he is absolutely right.

Reductionist thinking—what he calls the "Tyranny of the OR"—is the type of analytical rationality that cannot readily accept mystery or paradox, one that is unable to live with two seemingly contradictory ideas at the same time. Under the tyranny of the OR, people believe that things must be either A *or* B, but they cannot be *both*. And because the either/or answer is inevitably a form of reduction, one becomes a victim of his/her own ever-reductive analysis. The net result of this process—to use those perceptive words of William Blake—is that "man has closed himself up, till he sees all things thro' narrow chinks of his cavern."

Just consider how this either/or way of seeing has played out in our history: theological controversies and denominational splits are always built on ever-reducing understandings of God and the church. (By the way, the very word *de-nom-*ination means defining ourselves over against others—it is inherently sectarian.)

The alternative to reductionist thinking, to use Collins' term again, is to embrace the "Genius of the AND." That is, we are to cultivate an ability to embrace multiple possibilities at the same time. Instead of choosing between A *or* B, we are to figure out a way to have both A *and* B.[5] In other words, we resolve our problems not by more analysis but by synthesis. We need to always think bigger ... never smaller.[6] We must acknowledge that truth is always mysterious and we should allow that mystery to work its magic and provoke us to corresponding awe and wonder. It is this symphonic way of thinking—as we shall see—that connects the dots, opens doors, and cleanses perceptions to enables us to really see again.

Michael Heiser suggests that the Bible, and revelation itself, presents us with something of a theological and literary mosaic. In any mosaic, we gain a perspective that is both broader and deeper only if we allow ourselves to see the various pieces in their own wider context. The pattern in a mosaic often isn't clear up close, appearing to be just a random assemblage of pieces. Only when you step back can you see the wondrous whole. Sure, the individual pieces are essential; without them there would be no mosaic. But the meaning of all the pieces is found in the completed whole. The picture in the mosaic isn't imposed on the pieces; it is derived from them.[7] It is this skill of perceiving wholeness that has often characterized our greatest thinkers and theologians ... people who use godly imagination to enable them to put seemingly disparate things into meaningful relationship in order to form unified wholes.

The "Genius of the AND" is not at all new. In fact Collins simply rediscovered an insight that is latent in universal truth: in order to heal any form of brokenness, whether it is in people or organizations, one has to always attempt to re-situate the broken pieces in the context of the whole in order to make sense of it. To heal something one must restore it. There is always renovation in real wholeness. This is why restoration and healing lie at the heart of Jesus' atoning work in the world.

> It is in Jesus, of course, and in the people whose lives have been deeply touched by Jesus, and in ourselves at those moments when we also are deeply touched by him, that we see another way of being human in this world, which is the way of wholeness. When we glimpse that wholeness in others, we recognize it immediately for what it is, and the reason we recognize it, I believe, is that no matter how much the world shatters us to pieces, we carry inside us a vision of wholeness.[8]

If we wish to avoid the cloying seductions of heresy, and reframe our sense of God and the world, we need to allow ourselves to be led by the Spirit in a search to experience the *pleroma* (the fullness) of God; to pursue a type of wholeness that leads us beyond our settled convictions and toward a wholeness we may have never imagined existed.[9]

We suggest therefore that the main clue to escaping this heresy of reduction is to recognize that the answer is always bigger than we tend to think it is. Any selective truth must always be evaluated on the basis of its relationship to the totality from which it is derived. The only way back from this broken way of thinking is to be able to reset the "little" truth or belief once again within its "greater" and true ecological context.[10] As we explored in chapter one, YHWH cannot be pinned down. He is always much bigger than we tend to think he is. Let us not think *either/or* but *both/and*—it's truth *and* goodness *and* beauty; it's faith *and* hope *and* grace; it's love *and* truth *and* obedience that are needed to know God. In the second half of this chapter, we will also suggest an application of the "Genius of the AND" to our understanding of the gospel. The good news is forgiveness *and* reconciliation *and* adoption into the family, *and* restoration *and* mission *and* ... wholeness.

PARADOXOLOGY

Certainly, one way to engage with reframation is to recognize that, in the end, all the most foundational truths of the Christian faith are paradoxical.

In a paradox, what seems at first to be absurd or self-contradictory, in fact proves to be true by holding the irreconcilable poles in tension.

Reductionist thinking is problematic when dealing with living systems, whether they be organizations or people, but it is super-problematic when dealing with the greatest truths or mysteries of the faith, which are always paradoxical in nature—for example, the Trinity (how can God be One and yet be Three?); the Incarnation and the two natures of Christ (how can a man, who is by definition limited, also be God, who is by definition unlimited?); predestination and free will (how can freedom be understood in the context of God's overwhelming sovereignty?).

All the central, defining truths of the Christian faith only reveal themselves to those with adoring eyes of faith, a love for the sheer in/comprehensibility of mystery, and a respect for the integrity of paradoxical truth. By invalidating these *a priori*, either/or thinking inevitably ends in theological heresy, reductionism, and cramped religion.

These truths can only be known by holding diametric aspects to be true—in paradoxical tension. The paradox *is* the truth ... To attempt to resolve it is to lose its dynamic. For instance, consider that we live in two worlds at the same time: one where the past is the cause of all that is present and future (first things/protology), and the other in which the future constructs both the present and the past (last things/eschatology). You will never understand any of these foundational truths if you cannot learn to live and love both mystery and paradox.

> What if the tension between apparently opposing doctrines is exactly where faith comes alive? What if this ancient faith we call Christianity has survived so long not in spite of but precisely because of its apparent contradictions? What if we have settled for neatly packaged, simplistic answers, instead of seeking out the deep and rich realities of our faith? What if it is in the difficult parts of the Bible that God is most clearly revealed? What if it is in and through our doubts that we learn the meaning of true relationship with the God who created us—of true worship? What if Christianity was never meant to be simple?[11]

Krish Kandiah's book *Paradoxology* makes a bold claim: that the paradoxes that at first sight appear to undermine belief are actually vital to a vibrant faith, and that it is only by continually wrestling with them—rather than trying to pin them down or resolve them one way or another—that we can really worship God, individually and corporately. When paradox is surrendered, then we end up with the unbelieving doubt of a person who cannot permit his or her mind to be blown, or the sloppy sentimentality of liberal ideology and religion, or just the plain old grumpy fundamentalism of conservatives who like things to be black *or* white.

JUST WIGGLE YOUR SHOULDERS LIKE THIS

I (Alan) was recently in an art gallery exhibiting a number of the twentieth-century artist Wassily Kandinsky's paintings. I love Kandinsky's art because in many of his paintings he claims he was actually trying to paint music, to visualize what he was hearing. Think about that for a moment. In a recording of an interview with the artist, he advised that, in order to understand his paintings (and in fact all abstract art), one has to take Jesus' advice to become like children very seriously indeed. One has to look at the paintings with the simple and innocent eyes of a child and, in doing so, re-educate one's eyes in the art of seeing.[12] Children are naturally humble (as well as playful) when it comes to acquiring knowledge; they are always deep in learning mode, always accepting they have more to learn. This is why Jesus says we must change and become like children to be able to enter the kingdom of God (Matthew 18:3–4).

J. M. Barrie, famous for writing *Peter Pan* in 1904, encouraged adults to see the world through the eyes of the child, and, in doing so, brought about a re-education of sight. The 2004 movie *Finding Neverland* depicts Barrie bringing *Peter Pan* to life on the stage of the West End in London.[13] Before the premiere, conflict arises as the producer (i.e., "the money" behind the show) is extremely skeptical that the story will appeal to his upper-class theatre patrons.

On opening night, Barrie reserves twenty-five seats, scattered around the theatre, for children from a nearby orphanage. Of course, the children are instantly drawn in to the show, regardless of the elegant surroundings and the stodgy theatre goers on either side of them. As the appropriate amount of pixie dust is sprinkled on the actors, and as the instructions are given to "just wiggle your shoulders like *this* and let go," even the most curmudgeonly of adults, when seated next to a child, begin to see with new eyes, and so enter into the world of Neverland.

The obvious question for each of us to consider is, *can we approach God with a similar innocence and joy?* For it will be the playful, unprejudiced, humble, and curious who will be able to make sense of the God who is beyond our wildest imagination, and who will begin to pursue wholeness in ways that bring about meaning and purpose.

It was the childlike eyes of the early church Fathers and Mothers that meant they were able to plumb the depths of beauty, goodness, and truth of God in the way that they did. Like children, they had unprejudiced, humble, and curious eyes of wonder.[14] And this childlike reverence and awe is a prerequisite for grasping mysterious truth. The quantum physicist Max Planck eulogizes childlike thinking in contributing to advances in the area of science:

> The feeling of wonderment is the source and inexhaustible fountainhead of [the child's] desire for knowledge. It drives the child irresistibly on to solve the mystery, and if in his attempt he encounters a causal relationship, he will not tire of repeating the same experiment ten times, a hundred times, in order to taste the thrill of discovery over and over again. The reason why the adult no longer wonders is not because he has solved the riddle of life, but because he has grown accustomed to the laws governing his world picture [...] He who does not comprehend this situation, misconstrues its profound significance, and he who has reached the stage where he no longer wonders about anything, merely demonstrates that he has lost the art of reflective reasoning.[15]

As we noted in chapter two, God is both above and beyond all things (transcendent), and yet as Creator he is also within all things (immanent). We therefore need to widen the doors of our perception in an attempt to take it all in. In doing so, we are able to discern the presence of God in everything that he has made. We will thereby discover that "the whole universe is a cosmic Burning Bush filled with the divine Fire yet not consumed."[16] Or, as poet Elizabeth Barrett Browning noted,

> Earth's crammed with heaven,
> And every common bush afire with God;
> But only he who sees, takes off his shoes,
> The rest sit round it and pluck blackberries,
> And daub their natural faces unaware.[17]

Blake hints that a way forward is:

> To see a World in a Grain of Sand
> And a Heaven in a Wild Flower
> Hold Infinity in the palm of your hand
> And Eternity in an hour[18]

Here we are back in the enchanted world where God is understood to be everywhere ... infinite. It's all in the *seeing*! William Blake (echoing Proverbs 23:7 and Jesus in Mark 7:14–23) yet again: "The tree which moves some to tears of joy is in the eyes of others only a green thing which stands in the way ... As a man is, so he sees."[19]

To live in God's world is to have a willingness to see and experience the world through the spiritual eyes of faith. This requires a paradigm shift in our primary vision.[20] Episcopalian priest Barbara Brown Taylor recounts one such paradigm shift after listening to a sermon on wonder:

> I could no longer see myself or the least detail of my life in the same way again. When the service was over that day I walked out of it into a God-enchanted world, where I could not wait to find further clues to heaven on earth. Every leaf, every ant, every shiny rock called out to me— begging to be watched, to be listened to, to be handled and examined. I became a detective of divinity, collecting evidence of God's genius and admiring the tracks left for me to follow: locusts shedding their hard bodies for soft, new, winged ones; prickly pods of milkweed spilling silky white hair; lightning spinning webs of cold fire in the sky, as intricate as the veins in my own wrist. My friend taught me to believe that these were all words in the language of God, hieroglyphs given to puzzle and I could no longer see myself or the least detail of my life in the same way again.[21]

Ben (a friend of Alan's) once had a teaching role where he had to play a mad scientist in order to introduce kindergarten children to the wonders of science. At one point he was trying to explain to a group of children how magnets worked. One child kept saying that Ben was all wrong, insisting instead that they worked by "magic." Ben again attempted to explain the scientific nature of magnetic fields and their intricacies, to which the young girl responded, "Yeah, that's magic!" Ben had to agree. Sometimes you just have to wiggle your shoulders like *this* and let go ...

ALWAYS YEARNING, ALWAYS LEARNING

In his 1952 groundbreaking book, *Your God Is Too Small*, J. B. Phillips calls on Christians to reframe their understanding of God by embarking on a personal search for a more meaningful concept of him.[22] Phillips felt then, as we do now: the trouble facing us today is that we do not have a god big enough to help us make any real sense of our world, a world where our experience of life has grown in myriad directions and our mental horizons have been expanded to the point of utter bewilderment by world events and scientific discoveries. Our inherited maps no longer fit the territories. In fact, although we live in this incredibly complex, ever-evolving world, our ideas of God have remained largely static and formulaic for many centuries. Phillips wrote from a deep conviction that if it is really true—that there *is* a God who is in charge of the whole cosmos, of human history, as well as the mysteries of life and death—then we can hardly escape a sense of futility and frustration until we begin to see what he is like and what his purposes are. We all need to expand our vision of who God is.

The very fact that it is *God* with whom we engage means that we should always expect to be expanded while being reframed—in other words, it means that we should expect to have our minds blown every time. Think about the inconceivable size and scale of the universe itself; then consider that the Being we call "God" is the Being who created this infinite space with words. He spoke everything into existence ... from nothing to something ... just like that! How do you get your mind around that?!

If we were to similarly recast God's love and grace in a wi[l]der frame, then it's worth contemplating how, in the Incarnation, the eternal, all-knowing, mind-blowing God emptied himself and entered fully into the very limited human experience of a servant, enduring the depths of darkness and sin on our behalf in and through the cross (Philippians 2). We must ask ourselves, *why would this eternal Being do this for me/us?* And the only possible answer to this is ... inconceivable love and grace, the kind which, once again, blows any normal sense of ratio and scale that we might possess. This is the grace of God in a wi[l]der frame.

Consider Nicodemus in John 3. He seemed to be similarly overwhelmed during his interactions with Jesus, late one evening in the dark of night. "How can this be?" he responds, when Jesus tells him he must be born again if he is to see the kingdom of God. Perhaps Nicodemus was beginning to realize that the very small world he had been inhabiting was not the reality he had always believed it was. Jesus was blowing the doors off his small-minded religious tendency to tweak a few laws here and there, and instead was calling him to new birth. Any encounter with Jesus requires the same. Any time we truly contemplate who Jesus is must surely blow our minds. His call to us is always to more. To a bigger God. A bigger story. A bigger life. It really doesn't matter if all this feels somewhat overwhelming. Actually, the point is that one *ought* to feel overwhelmed when dealing with the Infinite and the Eternal.[23]

The unquenchable sense of yearning for God does not come to a halt even at the end of all things, when all creatures are brought face-to-face with

God. Genuine longing can never tire of looking at the beloved. Augustine uses the term "insatiable satisfaction" to express this "ever-moreness."[24] In seeing the Face that surpasses all desire, "we will be insatiably satisfied, without growing weary. We will always be hungering and always being filled."[25] "We will have attuned the ear for that Voice," which, once heard, leaves one forever listening.[26]

> When God sends his own living Word to his creatures, he does so not to inform them about the mysteries of the world, nor primarily to fulfill their deepest needs and yearnings. Rather he communicates and actively demonstrates such un-heard of things that man feels not satisfied but awestruck by a love which he could never have hoped to experience.[27]

LEARN MORE, UNDERSTAND LESS

One of the things we lament in contemporary expressions of Christianity is that we have failed to really inculcate a love of learning, a culture of deep and searching theology, especially one that rests comfortably in the ineffable mysteries of God. Where in our faith communities are we providing opportunities for this to happen, alongside each other? Where are we allowing the "Jacobs" in our churches to cross the Jabbok River and wrestle their faith out with God? Where does one come across groups like the Inklings (those who regularly share their creative works with one another) in the typical church? It seems we prefer our truths to be laid out in three-point sermons addressing the most recent "felt need," delivered in an entertaining monologue, with no room for dialogue at an elementary level. We are still existing on milk when we should be eloquent in truth, as the New Testament writers lament.[28] How do we account for that?

The call we are making is a call to learn. A call to feed yourself and then feed others. Stop chewing on tofu-flavored theological bubblegum; read "the greats," the very best in the field. And read beyond your narrow traditions. Read books, listen to podcasts ... anything that forces you to think for yourself. Stop complaining about the big words; it is really worth learning what "the greats" have to say; get a dictionary; learn their language if you have to. Learn together in community, and not just a community filled with people like you—find others, from different environments, backgrounds, ethnicities, experiences, and perspectives, and create communities where all might be re-educated in seeing again. David Bentley Hart, himself one of our great contemporary theologians, writes:

Wisdom is the recovery of innocence at the far end of experience; it is the ability to see again what most of us have forgotten how to see [...] God is not only the ultimate reality that the intellect and the will seek but is also the primordial reality with which all of us are always engaged in every moment of existence and consciousness, apart from which we have no experience of anything whatsoever. Or, to borrow the language of Augustine, God is not only *superior summo meo*—beyond my utmost heights—but also *interior intimo meo*—more inward to me than my inmost depths. Only when one understands what such a claim means does one know what the word "God" really means.[29]

FROM A ONE-DIMENSIONAL TO A THREE-DIMENSIONAL GOSPEL

Re-educating our vision and practicing the art of seeing not only applies to our understanding of God, but is relevant to our understanding of the gospel as well. Our severely diminished and reduced explanations of the good news similarly need reframing.

Consider for a moment the questions universal to a search for God (whether the search is intentional or not). Questions at the core of existence for all humanity include:

- Who am I and how is my identity formed and defined?
- Where do I find a sense of justice in a broken world?
- How do I find a people to belong to, to be with?
- How do I approach work, calling, and purpose?
- What do I do with my sadness, brokenness, and sin?
- Who is worth following and where should my allegiance lie?

It is important for us to wrestle with how the answers to these questions inform and form a culture's response to God and Jesus. We so often miss how different contexts and cultural narratives determine how this good news is received. For there are largely three ways in which these questions are approached and their answers are subsequently found:[30]

THE WESTERN FRAME

A *Western* approach to the gospel is one that is founded in "true and false," "right and wrong," and "guilt and innocence" (much of what we described earlier in chapter one). Such views tend toward the "forensic" and "clinical."

The emphasis is consistently on the individual and the "personal" nature of salvation, and is crafted into a logical argument to explain who fits into which category (guilty or innocent) and what remedy is needed to save souls (what transaction needs to occur to rescue them).

We may say in general that in Western Christianity, especially Protestantism (remember Luther's panic attacks), salvation is understood primarily in terms of real, objective human guilt of sin before a holy and righteous God who cannot abide sin. Salvation is therefore viewed through the metaphor of legal standing before holy God. Guilty human beings are made or declared righteous by God on the basis of the work of substitutionary atonement in the cross of Jesus. This is known as *forensic* or *imputed righteousness*, whereby sinful humans are entirely dependent on the grace of God and the forgiveness of sin that comes through the shed blood of Jesus.

This Western Christian worldview is reflected in the way most Western Christians proclaim the gospel, focusing on how God forgives our sins on the basis of Christ's atonement, in which the Innocent pays for the guilty and releases them from guilt and sin. Think of the Four Spiritual Laws, the Two Ways and other similar tracts.

And just to once again be clear here, we *do* believe that forgiveness of real sin and guilt is a critical dimension of good news. The problem, as in all reductionism, is what is missing. Taken in isolation from the other dimensions of the gospel, assuming one cultural perspective, Westerners end up with what the theologian Dallas Willard called a reduced "gospel of sin-management" and then, like Procrustes (he of chapter one), everything else is subsequently forced to fit.[31]

THE EASTERN FRAME

In contrast to a predominantly Western approach, an *Eastern* way of understanding the good news has tended to experience and comprehend the world not through the lenses of guilt/innocence or right/wrong but rather through honor/shame, grace/disgrace. In an honor/shame culture, the primary perceived consequence of sin is dishonor, loss of face or esteem, a relational distancing or being shunned, and an experience of disgrace. "Shame is the fear, pain, or state of being regarded unworthy of acceptance in social relationships."[32]

The concept of honor/shame has been called "the pivotal cultural value" of the Bible.[33]

Beginning from Genesis 1, honor and shame run through the entire story of the Bible. "The term guilt and its various derivatives occur 145 times in the Old Testament and 10 times in the New Testament, whereas the term shame and its derivatives occur nearly 300 times in the Old Testament and 45 times in the New Testament." Yet leading theology books continue to emphasize guilt and courtroom motifs over shame and community motifs.[34]

Furthermore, it is important for Western Christians to realize that honor and shame is the "operating system for 65% of the world and 80% of the unreached."[35] The majority of people therefore don't experience the world through the familiar Western registers of the gospel.

Because many confuse guilt with shame, it is worth highlighting how they differ: guilt is usually tied to some *event* or *action*: I *did* something bad. Objective guilt (different to subjective Freudian "guilt feelings") happens when a person infringes a rule or law, for example in committing a crime, or, theologically, in sinning against God's holiness. In doing so, a person becomes objectively guilty. Alternatively, shame is tied to a *person* and to *relationships*: I *am* bad. It is largely experienced as an internal or subjective register ... a hemorrhaging of the soul. Shame is a feeling of not measuring up, which in turn creates an inner sense of unworthiness, reproach, dishonor, humiliation, and disgrace—a constant feeling of falling short of what one thinks is expected. Guilt is about *what* I've done. Shame is about *who* I am.[36]

Guilt is normally limited to individual actions. Shame is more social and contagious.

No one can share in your guilt, but many can share in your shame. The child whose father is imprisoned, the wife whose husband is unfaithful, the daughter whose mother is abusive—they all share the shame. They feel their self-worth is lessened. Shame wraps its arms around their ankles tightly, allowing them to walk but never to run. Shame is a focus on self, guilt is a focus on behavior. In this way, shame is far less logical than guilt. Guilt is connected to events that can be defined in objective forensic categories: who, what, where, when, and why. But shame is far less concerned with details.[37]

And so, for example, in a guilt culture, God's power is about "forgiveness of transgressors," whereas in a shame culture, God honors the lowly and humbles the proud. In a guilt culture, God's righteousness is about providing justice; in a shame culture, God's righteousness is about maintaining covenant faithfulness.[38] The question that scholars of honor/

shame are asking is whether those with a Western mind-set will ever be able to view the Scriptures through any lenses other than their own. "We assume that our own historical theology is comprehensive and flawless, without recognizing that it too has been contextualized within our own Western culture."[39] The result is a disregarded and ignored theology of honor/shame, with volumes written on guilt/innocence. Again, this is not an argument "for or against" either of these perspectives, but rather a plea to see our blind spots, and to appreciate just how much our interpretation of Scripture, and therefore the message we convey to others, is culturally biased. We must learn to embrace both/and. We must try and understand the gospel outside our Western paradigm/*nous*.

THE SOUTHERN FRAME

In addition to the Western and the Eastern way of gospel thinking, we must also appreciate the worldview held in the Southern hemisphere, especially perhaps Africa and South America. Southerners, who are traditionally very open to the spiritual dimension of life, have tended to experience the world through the lenses of power and powerlessness, fear and freedom from it, possession and dispossession, bondage and freedom. A proclamation of the gospel that disregards these issues will therefore carry very little impact in a Southern cultural context. In order for us to widen our lens of the gospel, we need to have a greater understanding of how it is being heard. In order to resonate in the hearts of the Southern peoples, the gospel must include a way to deal with, and explain, the dark motives of so many would-be leaders (the so-called "tin-pot dictators") and the willingness of people to be so readily enslaved by them. The gospel narrative must therefore intersect with both politics and community. How does the good news free people from bondage to such powers? What does it mean to live a life free from poverty, enslavement, and fear? How does the Lordship of Jesus fundamentally change the equation of power?

Another important aspect of majority Southern cultures is the awareness of the supernatural and thus also of fallen spiritual powers and their role in binding humans up; spiritual warfare is understood as part of life. African Christianity in particular sits within a much more enchanted view of the world, one which Westerners (who live in the demystified and demythologized worldview) must learn from. Westerners can also learn from the Southern perspective how the work of Jesus annuls the oppression of the principalities and powers that dominate a fallen world (e.g., Romans 8:37–39; Ephesians 1:21; 3:10–11; Colossians 1:16; 2:14–15).

THE "GLOCAL" GOSPEL

Hopefully it's clear that each of these different contexts necessitates a different appropriation of the gospel. Dimensions of the gospel that address our guilt must not be misappropriated and force-fitted to somehow address a sense of shame or to still our fears. Forgiveness is needed for guilt; unconditional love and acceptance is needed to address issues of shame; and the idea of redemption or rescue is needed for those needing liberation from enslaving powers.

Missionaries have known this, and have adopted these different approaches for decades. What is becoming evident is that in our globalized culture, all these issues can now be readily identified throughout the West. People in your everyday context, people on the Playa or the Camino, now commonly experience and express existential issues that register in all three dimensions. This is not a new or different version of good news; rather, it's recognizing the multifaceted nature of the gospel and acknowledging our limited and reduced understanding of it. If we are truly to consider what is "good news" to those around us, it's essential we embrace a larger understanding. We have to expand our proclamation of the gospel to suit, not make it smaller.

We live in a "glocal" world, characterized by both local and global considerations, and accordingly we need to embrace a "glocal gospel." Missiologists now believe that the overlap of these three dominant ways of understanding the gospel is increasing.[40] There is no longer a distinct separation of one from another, and those commonalities of good news perspectives, the middle part of the following chart, are only going to continue to grow.

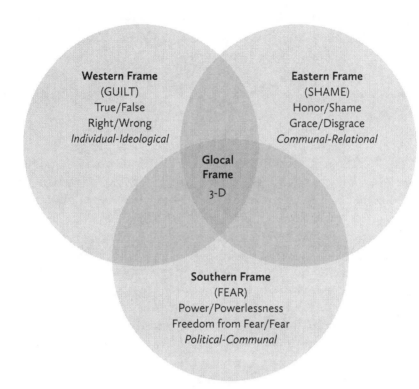

For instance, the issue of shame is permeating more than ever into a Western context. This shame and dishonor occurs through multiple contributing factors.

Consider the fact that America is an extremely competitive culture: from childhood playgrounds, to sport, to stock markets, gambling, business deals, and the pursuit of fame, everything is built upon the idea of winning. To be sure, this has created a high-achieving culture where people strive to be better than the next person. However, the problem with a competitive culture is that by celebrating the achievement of the celebrity-winner, the culture produces a whole lot of people who are considered "losers" by comparison. And it is here that people are shamed, because with losing comes the shame of not winning.

Another very significant example comes from the idealized celebrity-beauty: by idealizing what it means to be "beautiful," and in giving that beauty disproportionate worth, we create by implication a standard of ugliness by which everyone else is measured—let's face it, we are all "ugly" (read *unacceptable*) by comparison. This beauty myth contributes to a culture of honor and shame.

Rather than judging the drivenness and competitiveness evident throughout American culture, we would do well to consider that it might simply be symptomatic of the real human need to feel significant, to stand out, to be recognized. The forgiveness of sins (addressing objective guilt for having violated a standard) simply does not address the experience of shame. It's not meant to. God's love, grace, and acceptance do. The gospel here must rather proclaim that there is nothing anyone can do to increase how much God eternally loves each and every individual, regardless of strength or beauty, winning or losing. No one needs to prove themselves before *this* God. It is *this* God who also restores personal dignity by giving believers a new status and identity. The Scriptures constantly tell us that God opposes the proud (another major register of honor/shame) and raises up the downcast. He eternally "sees" us (foresight and election), and in choosing us he honors each one of us with a new identity as a fully legitimate member of his family. God has dealt with the roots of all shame and dishonor. God is the waiting Father who runs to the returning son, who embraces the one who has squandered everything and so dishonored the family name. This speaks volumes in an honor/shame culture in which fathers must always retain face and respect ... They do not run to greet people, let alone toward sons who have shamed the family.[41]

In terms of the register of power/powerlessness, in the West we have recently experienced mass social movements that are birthed from a sense of powerlessness. Take for instance Black Lives Matter. Those involved in this movement are communicating real experiences of real people who feel utterly powerless to change their destiny. This powerlessness was birthed out of the wrongful appropriation of their ancestors as slaves in what was later to become the United States of America. Because this is an issue of power, a more effective way to connect the gospel with those who have been affected by these issues is often through the gospel of liberation from slavery and oppression. This is why the Exodus narrative resonates in most civil rights movements. God is a Redeemer; he sets the captive free; he creates a community based on justice, equity, and the dignity of all concerned. He defeats and humiliates the powers and principalities that oppress and demean them. Once again, God's forgiveness of personal sins, although necessary in the healing of the human soul, will not address the problems raised by the forceful misuse of power. The #MeToo movement is likewise motivated by power/powerlessness motifs (as well as shame/dishonor) in its opposition to sexual harassment and assault of women.

And in terms of universal human guilt and culpability, God in his mercy declares the believer as righteous through the death of Christ on our behalf, thereby establishing a right relationship and ongoing access to God without fear of judgment. He forgives us our all too real sins in response to the fact that we are objectively guilty before God (we have all fallen short). God requires that we too learn to forgive others in response to our self-righteousness and judgmentalism.[42]

The integration of all three dimensions is required to bring a more comprehensive proclamation that addresses the different existential issues raised by all three major orientations. We must simply overcome the Western assumption that the legal framework of the gospel is the *only* biblical framework of salvation.[43] Salvation extends beyond our need for forgiveness to include our need for unconditional love, liberation from bondage, raising up the outcast and brokenhearted, and so much more. All three frameworks of the gospel are now current in every Western context. We need a whole lot more of both/and, and less of the either/or, in our register of the gospel. We need it bigger, not smaller! A gospel that can heal every human ill.

A reframed and expanded gospel never stops addressing our guilt, shame, and fear. But human beings experience an even broader range of existential and religious issues that arise from sin and brokenness: these symptomatic issues include depression, despair, loneliness, isolation, anger, immaturity, and rootlessness. They originate from the denial of death, meaninglessness, anxiety, alienation, unhappiness, etc., and these too are effectively dealt with by God. And so we can see that the gospel tackles our root issues:

- Human loneliness is addressed by us being placed by the Spirit into God's covenant family, a family built on love, grace, and acceptance. We *really belong.*

- Our deepest regrets are transformed by the God who redeems and repurposes the broken elements of our lives. *Nothing is lost in God's economy.*

- A false or fragmented identity is healed by the gift of *knowing who we truly are in Christ.*

- A meaningless life overcome with boredom and despair is reinvigorated by being commissioned into *a movement that is destined to change a broken and hurting world.*

- The human capacity to be enslaved through addiction and misdirected passion is addressed by freedom in discipleship and the power of the Holy Spirit. *Our once misdirected desires find their fulfillment and completion in God.*

- Fear of death is annulled through being granted eternal life that is experienced both *here and now, and forever.*

- A sense of lostness is dealt with by being "found" … God sees us, pursues us, saves us. *He is relentless.*

Why would we settle for a one-dimensional gospel when there is so much more good news to experience?

SO MANY MORE ROOMS

In 5Q, which exposes disastrous reductions in ministry, I (Alan) wrote that in order to learn and grow in God, we will first need to unlearn.

> But the desire, as well as the ability, to see things in their original wholeness exacts a price on those who find themselves captive to reductionisms of various sorts and varieties. The price of admission to the symphony [of fullness] is first and foremost repentance. Actually, repentance is the price required for any new learning in any domain— it's just that outside the church it's called unlearning, whereas inside the church it's called repentance. No one can learn who is not first prepared to unlearn. Likewise, no one can grow in God unless they are willing to repent regularly.[44]

This is the *metanoia* we explored in chapter five—unlearning, repentance— and it changes everything. It reframes how you see and experience God, people, the world, and mission. After conversion, and after any experience of real *metanoia*, you don't just look out *at* reality; you look out *from* reality. In other words, God is not "out there"; you find out that in fact you are in God and God is in you. "After his conversion experience, Paul is obsessed with the idea that 'I'm participating in something that's bigger than me.'"[45] In fact, Paul uses the phrase "in Christ" around 160 times to describe this sense of connection with and in Christ. Paul has the best one-liner of all to describe himself after conversion: "I no longer live, but Christ lives in me" (Galatians 2:20). Jesus living inside of me—now that's a transformed person!

This is a completely different experience of life. I don't have to fully write my private story. It's being written with me and in me. I am already a character on the stage. I am being used, I am being chosen, I am being led. You will know that after conversion. You will know that your life is not about you [...] You are about God.[46]

Adjusting our view to make room for a bigger picture of reality, and repenting of reductionisms, like all true encounters with God, will require change. To be able to learn something new, whether it is related to God or the good news or other forms of learning, we need to be prepared to let go of obsolete ideas and open our eyes and our hearts to being willing to grow, mature, and learn again. The learner needs to venture out of fixed paths into the unknown, and not allow their heart and head to be stunted by mere routine—this is especially true of religious routine. In fact, we would suggest that new breakthroughs are only gained by those who break out of the arbitrary boundaries that have been set by mere convention—that's why they are called breakthroughs.[47]

In remaining open to the mysterious wonder of God, and to prevent us from settling in a one-dimensional perspective, we are wise to pay attention to the words of Adrienne von Speyr:

God's will is *mystery* and remains so as well. God introduces us into this mystery, but not in such a way that it simply stops being mysterious. It cannot be exhausted by being revealed; just as in God the unveiling of a part of his being is always the opening of unlimited horizons in other directions, and at the same time to be drawn into God's mystery is a secret of intimacy. [...] Every aspect of God's mystery that he gives us to understand is surrounded by mystery and opens into greater mystery.[48]

Have we fallen into the trap of seeing God one-dimensionally—as if entering into one singular room in the vastness of a beautiful palace means we have arrived, and that we now know all we need to know about the unknowable God? What seems strange is that when most of us find that one room—that singular frame of God and the gospel—it just happens to be the one that contains our already established system of belief, and our already finalized way of making sense of the world.

There is so much more to God. There is so much left to explore.

To be able to think of God and the world in a much more expansive and "roomier" way should bring some movement and reshaping to our own lives. Beginning to accept the idea that there are more rooms than those we alone know, allows us to consider the need to repent of our one-room narrative. For it is in this turning away from a limited view, in the re-education of our vision, that we realize we need to unlearn all of what we have imagined we knew of God, and experience the struggle to believe and see afresh and anew. When we dare to keep nothing assumed or self-devised, we are plunged, sometimes in great fear and trembling, through a door we have never had the courage to open and into a room we had never imagined existed.

THE GREAT RE[FRAMATION]

(STEALING PAST THE WATCHFUL DRAGONS)

God is the perfect poet
Who in his person acts his own creations
— **ROBERT BROWNING**

Awe is the finest portion of mankind:
However scarce the world may make this sense
—In awe one feels profoundly the immense.
— **GOETHE**

"In our world," said Eustace, "a star is a huge ball of
flaming gas."
"Even in your world, my son, that is not what a star is but
only what it is made of."
— **C. S. LEWIS**

The Chronicles of Narnia, the classic children's literature books written by C. S. Lewis, are probably Lewis' best-known works, having sold over 100 million copies. Set in the fictional world of Narnia, a fantasy world of talking animals, mythical beasts, and "a deeper magic still,"[1] these seven books narrate the adventures of four siblings as they navigate the world of Narnia and its unfolding history.

Lewis, an Oxford scholar, literary critic, lay theologian, and Christian apologist, was often asked why he would bother to write a series of children's books. He responded by bemoaning how the parochial moralism of Sunday School religion effectively snuffed out his faith by teaching rational ideas about God and prescribing how exactly one *ought* to feel about, and how one *ought* to respond to, God.[2] This doctrinaire religion and clichéd reverence quenched any natural desire for God he'd once had as a child and therefore did much more harm than good. He likened these obstacles to living faith as fearsome dragons that stand guard at the door of every human heart, securing it against any real apprehension of God or any authentic faith. They have to be bypassed to find a true knowledge of God. Lewis suggested that stories, because of their indirection and appeal to the imagination, allow us to sneak past these spiritual inhibitions (the dragons). The Narnia stories were Lewis' attempt to do this:

> But supposing that by casting all these things into an imaginary world, stripping them of their stained-glass and Sunday School associations, one could make them for the first time appear in their real potency? Could one not thus steal past those watchful dragons? I thought one could.[3]

Stories steal past the watchful dragons because they require what Lewis referred to as a "willing suspension of disbelief" in the mind of the reader or listener; this openness on the part of the reader or listener is what makes narrative so powerful. So, for instance, when we sit before a lecturer, we are prone to arm ourselves by subconsciously locking the gates and setting a guard against any words or ideas that may cause unwanted emotions or affections. In some cases, we numb ourselves to a fresh reality because our minds are already settled on whatever content is being communicated; the gates of our perceptions are closed.

Contrast that with listening to a story. When we gather around the fire to hear a great story, we suspend our watchfulness. The guards are removed and the gates are left open. Things do not seem as suspicious when communicated in a narrative. But as we've already seen, stories are also brimming with realities and truths that can be incredibly potent, even life changing. We nod our heads in agreement, laugh out loud, and silently empathize with the characters. Good, beautiful stories plunge the reader into a fictional world in such a way that when they return to reality, they perceive the world with more clarity and joy than before.[4] Not only does story enliven and enrich the familiar, it is also one of the fastest and most effective ways to penetrate the human heart. This is simply how we are wired, and no one knew it better than Jesus.[5]

Lewis' Narnia was therefore not an escape from reality. Far from it; like all good stories it stimulated the (re)discovery of what is more real. Through story, Lewis brought true things to light that were either previously undiscovered, or that had been veiled by the familiarity of the everyday. Narnia helps both child and adult find new joy and delight in God and his story. It teaches about God's great sacrifice, friendship, courage, and faithfulness in ways that mere facts about them never could. Story activates the light in our minds and imaginations that illuminates reality, enabling us to see more clearly the things that were already there.

Narrative, with its elements of myth, drama, and poetry, offers us an indirect way of communicating truth—one that requires the listener to engage their imagination and fill in the blanks. This is precisely the power of the parable and the stories that Jesus relied on to communicate the Word. Stories are not just telling truth "straight," but "slant," as Emily Dickinson suggested we must:

Tell all the Truth but tell it slant—
Success in Circuit lies
Too bright for our infirm Delight
The Truth's superb surprise
[...]
The Truth must dazzle gradually
Or every man be blind[6]

Dickinson's appeal to tell the truth "slant" and for it to "dazzle gradually" are ways of getting past preconceptions, prejudices, defenses, stereotypes, and fact-dominated literalism, all of which prevent relational receptivity to God.[7] Interestingly, there came a time when the great Lewis himself would no longer write "straight theology." Writing to Carl Henry, who was inviting him to write for *Christianity Today,* he declined the opportunity by saying:

I wish your project heartily well, but can't write you articles. My thought and talent (such as they are) now flow in different, though I trust not less Christian, channels, and I do not think I am at all likely to write more directly theological pieces [...] If I am now good for anything it is for catching the reader unawares—thro' fiction and symbol. I have done what I could in the way of frontal attacks, but I now feel quite sure those days are over.[8]

Lewis' reason was strategic—the times had changed and, for his part, a new approach was required. He would no longer pursue the "frontal attack" of his previous books and essays.

TELLING THE BETTER STORY

We hope you now realize that our desire in this book is to wrestle with the same questions Lewis sought to address in writing *The Chronicles of*

Narnia. How might *we* steal past those watchful dragons in the hearts of people around us in order to proclaim a story of God that makes sense to the pilgrims on the Camino, the Playa, and everywhere in between? How might *we* bring about a great reframation so that this story of God can be communicated to others in its real potency?

In this path forward, past these watchful dragons, we hope you now can appreciate the challenges we face: the twenty-first-century church is lacking in method and language in its articulation of God to pilgrims throughout the world. We may well have the desire and passion to eliminate the reductions, as well as the biblical knowledge needed to engage others. We may even have the grace and compassion required to converse with anyone from anywhere. Yet for all our desire, knowledge, and compassion, something in our approach is still woefully lacking; something is desperately missing. We seem powerless to communicate a story of God in its real potency.

Where might we finally turn? (This is the place where that "go-to" Sunday School answer for every question comes into play.) Of course, the answer is Jesus: Jesus told a better story. Jesus told a beautiful story. A story not "destitute of poetry and barren of imagination," but rather rich with both. He did not eclipse or dilute or flatten or trivialize. There was no reduction of truth, story, or life.

In *Telling the Truth: The Gospel as Tragedy, Comedy and Fairy Tale,* Frederick Buechner says that when Jesus spoke, he spoke "not in the incendiary rhetoric of the revolutionary or the systematic abstractions of the theologian but in the language of images and metaphor, which is finally the only language you can use if you want not just to elucidate the hidden thing but to make it come alive." Buechner goes on to say:

> What is the kingdom of God? He [Jesus] does not speak of a reorganization of society as a political possibility or of the doctrine of salvation as a doctrine. He speaks of what it is like to find a diamond ring that you thought you'd lost forever. He speaks of what it is like to win the Irish Sweepstakes. He suggests rather than spells out. He evokes rather than explains. He catches by surprise. He doesn't let the homiletic seams show. He is sometimes cryptic, sometimes obscure, sometimes irreverent, always provocative. He tells stories. He speaks in parables.[9]

In Mark's Gospel, Jesus explains to his disciples why he uses stories:

> "You've been given insight into God's kingdom—you know how it works. But to those who can't see it yet, everything comes in stories, creating readiness, nudging them toward receptive insight. These are people—

Whose eyes are open but don't see a thing,
Whose ears are open but don't understand a word,
Who avoid making an about-face and getting forgiven."

[...] With many stories like these, he presented his message to them,
fitting the stories to their experience and maturity. He was never without
a story when he spoke. When he was alone with his disciples, he went
over everything, sorting out the tangles, untying the knots.

MARK 4:11–12, 33–34 MSG

Jesus spoke and tangles were sorted, knots were untied. Jesus spoke and
things unraveled.[10] In telling parables, Jesus unraveled a tradition and a
culture founded in the Abrahamic covenant and which was disseminated
through a people who could generally not find a way to keep their part of
the covenant. He came *not* to abolish, overturn, or do away with any part of
the covenant God had made with his people. Instead, Jesus sought to fulfill,
accomplish, complete, and bring to fruition the putting of the world back
together.[11] Jesus brought to his hearers a new perspective of the story of God:
"I am going to put it all together, pull it all together in a vast panorama"
(Matthew 5:18 MSG). Jesus reframed the story and it changed everything.

An essential part of our theological and missional task today is
to participate in a similar reframing and to "tell this story as clearly as
possible, and to allow it to subvert other ways of telling the story of the
world."[12] We are to tell a subversive story. The philosopher Ivan Illich was
once asked about the most effective way to change society. He responded
brilliantly by saying,

Neither revolution nor reformation can ultimately change a society,
rather you must tell a new powerful tale, one so persuasive that it sweeps
away the old myths and becomes the preferred story, one so inclusive that
it gathers all the bits of our past and our present into a coherent whole,
one that even shines some light into the future so that we can take the
next step forward. If you want to change a society, then you have to tell
an alternative story.[13]

Jesus brought about a reframation by telling a subversive, alternative story.
He told a story that is more than science, more than history, more than
philosophy, more than anthropology, and more than morality. A story that
not only happened once, but is happening still. "Like every truly great
story, its truth may lie not so much in its historical or even philosophical
veracity as in its effect on the soul of the reader."[14]

Ah, the soul. Yes, the great power is seen in its effect upon the soul. Reframing the story is more than communicating cute little quips or using tools to disseminate a poorly explained exegetical hypothesis. This reframing is not simply about finding a new remedy to help the medicine go down. This is about communicating a soul-shaping paradigm to the twenty-eight-year-old social studies teacher on the trail in Melide, Spain, and the forty-eight-year-old mostly naked artist on the desert plain in Black Rock City ... and everyone in between.

To do this, the current approach to our articulation of the sacred needs a few primary alterations. We need some new frames.

LOOKING THROUGH RE/ENCHANTED FRAMES

Throughout the previous chapters, we have contended that our culture has experienced a move away from an openness to all things divine, to a more closed, rationalistic, technique-based approach. As we have reiterated, this has brought about a hollow disenchantment and a crisis of interpretation, resulting in a non-participatory and non-transformative encounter with the God of creation and his purposes for the world.

For the sake of review, we believe this disenchantment has been brought about by:

- *demystifying*—by eliminating mystery, wonder, love, and awe from the equation of how humans can rightly approach and know God
- *depoeticizing*—through dangerously narrowing our perceptive range and linguistic capacity to talk about God, and subsequently reducing theology to rational code and religious formula, and
- *demythologizing*—through shrinking revelation to reduced-to-fit, anti-supernatural, atheistic presuppositions about life.

We want to propose a re/enchantment in how we articulate our faith in God. To recover that which has been lost, there needs to be a *re*mystifying, a *re*poeticizing, and a *re*mythologizing, which will result, with apologies to the Protestant Reformers of the sixteenth century, in a "Great Reframation."

REMYSTIFY

It is because of the desire to name, categorize, and control God that the plague of demystification has crept into our faith dialogues. As we stated in chapter two, the premodern world was mindful of enchantment and of mystery. However, we have now transitioned to a faith culture rarely open to the mysteries of the divine. Many hold the belief that if they cannot catalog and systemize their encounters with the divine, they must not be real.

So how might we steal past these watchful dragons and bring forth a sense of mystery, awe, and wonder, and an openness to the sacred elements of life once again? How do we nudge awake a world that seems to have overslept? How do we move a culture, which participates in the numbing of the senses, toward a state of wonderment? How do we move them closer to what Abraham Heschel refers to as radical amazement?

> Radical amazement has a wider scope than any other human act; it refers to the whole of reality, not only to what we see, but to the very fact that we do see and to the very self that sees. We must strive to keep this radical amazement alive within us. Beyond all our scientific theories and explanations lies the profound experience of radical amazement.[15]

Part of the issue affecting our capacity to remystify can be traced back to our inability to ask or engage with the questions that lead us to a deeper sense of mystery. Many of us approach the divine in the same way we would a recipe, with a dash of this and a pinch of that, leading us toward formulating a faith in Jesus. Instead, a life given over to the mystery that is Jesus looks "more like falling in love than baking cookies."[16] The consistent call of God upon his people is a mysterious encounter of the Creator and his creation, rather than following prescribed cooking instructions once you've preheated the oven to 350°F.

I Asked for Wonder

The starting place for this remystification is the recovery of wonder. This moves us away from the oversimplified "spiritual v religious" discussion and into a different depth of conversation. Anthropologist Dr. Mary Catherine Bateson says, "Wonder can take you into science. It can take you into art. Other human beings are amazing and beautiful. The natural world around us; the more we study it, the more fascinating and intricate and elegant it turns out to be. Which is my interpretation of the Book of Job, incidentally."[17]

To Bateson's point, the character of Job, in what is called "the greatest poem of ancient and modern times," suffers unspeakable pain and loss.[18] His cries of "Why?" fall upon deaf ears (both his friends' and God's) until chapters 38–41, when God gives the most curious of responses:

Where were you when I laid the foundation of the earth?

Tell me, if you have understanding.
Who determined its measurements—surely you know!
    Or who stretched the line upon it?

Have you comprehended the expanse of the earth?
    Declare, if you know all this.

Who has cut a channel for the torrents of rain,
    and a way for the thunderbolt,
to bring rain on a land where no one lives,
    on the desert, which is empty of human life,

to satisfy the waste and desolate land,
    and to make the ground put forth grass?

Do you observe the calving of the deer?
Can you number the months that they fulfill,
    and do you know the time when they give birth,
when they crouch to give birth to their offspring,
    and are delivered of their young?

JOB 38:4–5, 18, 25–27; 39:1–3 NRSV

These chapters give the impression that God is preparing Job for a natural history exam. But, as Bateson says, "That's not really what it is. I think the point about the Book of Job is that Job is a virtuous member of an institution. He's respectable, he obeys all the rules, he's complacent, he goes through the appropriate rituals that were required in his community at that time. But he has lost his sense of wonder. And then God says, 'Look. Just look. Realize how incredibly amazing it is. How incredibly complex it all is.'"[19]

Beautiful and complicated; awe-inspiring and overwhelming. Job asked God 210 questions and in return God asks Job seventy-eight. In fact, in the entire book, Job received no answers. Just question after question from God, enabling Job to recognize his "appropriate size," which then prompted an "appropriate response":

I'm speechless, in awe—words fail me

JOB 40:4 MSG

I'll cover my mouth with my hand, *for I've already said too much*

JOB 40:4 THE VOICE

And now I see that I spoke of—but did not comprehend—*great* wonders that are beyond me. I didn't know

JOB 42:3 THE VOICE

This sense of mystery and awe in the presence of the sheer majesty of God needs to be cultivated if we are to see something of the glory of the Lord. Von Balthasar notes that, unless a person is acquainted with trembling awe that reaches down to the very ground of one's being—what the Bible calls the "fear of God"—they are not yet ready for the contemplation of Jesus Christ.

> Contemplation [of God] starts at the point where the believing mind begins to perceive a dawning light in the abyss of the mystery, where the mystery begins to reveal itself in all its vast proportions. Not in the sense of doubt, of loosening the tautness of the faith's affirmation, but in an astonishment which reaches to the very roots of our being. For we must be aware, at every moment, that the mystery of Jesus Christ transcends all the experience of God accessible to natural man and man as he is in history.[20]

Anyone contemplating the life of Jesus needs to be more deeply aware every day that something impossible, something inconceivable has occurred: that God, in his absolute Otherness, chose to manifest himself in a very specific human life.

When we come before *this* God, revealed in Jesus, we ought to feel scandalized; we must feel our minds reeling, the very ground giving way beneath our feet. We must at least experience that "ecstasy" of noncomprehension that transported Jesus' contemporaries (Mark 2:12; 6:51). They were amazed, beside themselves, stupefied, overwhelmed; their sense of normal reason abandoned them (literally). And this happened again and again (e.g., Matthew 7:28; 12:23; 13:54; Luke 2:48; 4:32; 8:56; 9:43, etc.). "In the gospel, anyone who encounters Christ is impelled either to worship him or to pick up stones with which to stone him. Evidently, the gospel does not foresee any other kind of response."[21]

We need to learn to present a God that none of us expect or anticipate. A God that takes our breath away, whether in awe, astonishment, or surprise. How many of us are simply telling a story about connecting the dots with three understandable homiletical points formed acrostically, followed by a nice, neat conclusion? Instead, a true articulation of the good news should leave us breathless. Our goal should not be that people walk away from an encounter with the gospel with all their questions answered. Instead, we should be learning to ask the right questions and to enter into an ever-deeper, awe-inspiring mystery.

If we tell a remystified story of God, it should impact others in such a way that they do not know what to do with this unexplainable and astonishing God who offers such good news. In his brilliant little book *Jesus with Dirty Feet*, Don Everts seeks to explore "a real basic description of Jesus, simply from His words, for the curious and skeptical."[22] Everts portrays a Jesus who people are seriously impressed with, but are not sure what to do with; a person who raises far more dangerous and mysterious questions than gives safe and comforting answers. He does this by telling simple stories of Jesus from the Gospels. Everts recounts the story of a friend of a friend, someone with absolutely no faith, church background, or any real concept of God or Jesus, reading the final draft of this little book about Jesus. After reading the draft, the reader queried whether the book was actually going to be published. When answered affirmatively, this person with no real knowledge of Jesus, in awe of this provocative, counter-cultural story, looked around, and in a somewhat hushed tone asked, "Did he, uh, ... did he get in trouble?" The reader had assumed a Jesus resembling a dish made from tofu. Instead he got Warheads. He read of a Jesus who was simultaneously offensive, impressive, and awe-inspiring, and because of this he assumed something must be wrong with the book.[23] Are we encouraging the same kind of astonishing, mysterious, and awe-inspiring encounters with a God who is beyond our scientific explanations, logical arguments, and assumed knowledge?

It is critical that we recover wonder and astonishment at the sheer truth of God and the gospel if we are to reframe our sense of God and the world. It is by acknowledging the ever-greatness of God that we gain more insight into him. We need to remystify the Truth so that it reveals itself, yet again, to wonder.

Abraham Heschel believed that wonder and awe are "an intuition for the dignity and preciousness of all things," "a way of understanding into a meaning greater than ourselves," and "an opening to transcendence" ... all things for which pilgrims trying to find their way are searching.[24] Can followers of Jesus wake up to the concept of mystery, and communicate a God that is not a result of accumulated knowledge but instead is the source of our wonder?

REPOETICIZE

It is a great tragedy that much of the articulations of the sacred have been labeled, at times proudly, "destitute of poetry and barren of imagination" (again, see chapter two). Part of the purpose of this book is to plead with those of us who tell the sacred story to a better use of words, a deeper use of language, a resurrection of imagination, and a reinvigoration of poetry. Even though the majority of biblical text is composed of narrative and poetry, today's faith conversations have largely been closed to a deeper experience of the divine by the exclusion of both. This in turn has meant that our vocabulary, the language we use to share meaning, has been stripped of any hints of divine *Eros*, or of passionate yearning for God. We can no longer hear, see, recognize, or experience the depth of God and his good news.

How might we overcome the prosaic nature of our current framing of the sacred? And can we communicate a theology that is open to voices, expressions, and language that fall outside the range of our present, reduced reality?

In the 1950s, Amos Wilder, a theology professor, minister, and poet, wrote a work called *Theopoetic: Theology and the Religious Imagination*, which wasn't published until 1974. Wilder served in World War I and, upon his return, attempted to continue a similar kind of theological work and practice to the one he had engaged with prior to going away. Yet, the world, his friends, his community, and he himself, had changed so much that he was unable to continue as he had done before; the current theological understanding and practice was not connecting with the longings and desires of those he was meeting day after day. In response, Wilder began to explore what kind of theology might make sense to someone who had just experienced World War I.

In his attempt to address what was missing, he began writing about this need to pay more attention to the role of imagination and language—what he called the *theopoetic*. He wrote:

> It is at the level of the imagination that the fateful issues of our new world-experience must first be mastered. It is here that culture and history are broken, and here that the church is polarized. Old words do not reach across the new gulfs, and it is only in vision and oracle that we can chart the unknown and new-name the creatures. Before the message there must be the vision, before the sermon the hymn, before the prose the poem.[25]

Wilder called for a renewal of our deep religious imaginations as we reflect on the story of God and on the longings and desires of contemporary culture. "Religious communication generally must overcome a long addiction to the discursive, the rationalistic, and the prosaic."[26]

The poet Samuel Taylor Coleridge wrote that "imagination is the living power and prime agent of all perception." He took the view that, collectively, all human beings at all times are imaginatively shaping the world they see; not just shaping their own little self-expressive world, but all of perception. In a book about reframing our perceptions, this should alert us to the fact that how we use language affects the very way we are capable of seeing the world. So, the more we can expand our language and deepen our metaphor, the more of the world we are actually capable of perceiving. And consequently, the more success we will have at cleansing the doors of perception.

Theologian Walter Brueggemann exhorts the church to make use of poetry, rather than flattening out all the images and metaphors to make the story of God fit into a nice but lifeless formulation.

> This is why the poetry is so important; because the poetry just keeps opening and opening and opening whereas the doctrinal practice of the church is always to close and close and close until you're left with nothing that has transformative power. So we have to communicate to people, that if you want an experience of God that is healthier than that, you're going to have to take time to sit with the biblical metaphors and poetic images, to relish them and allow them to become a part of your prayer life and to seep into your very vocabulary and your conceptual frame.[27]

Wakening the Mind

It has been an assumption of the disenchanted modern worldview (scientism) of the last few hundred years that, by setting aside things like art, metaphor, and imagination, humanity would finally be able to get to a logical, mathematical simplicity that is the truth. Because we live within this cultural milieu, our theology—our capacity to talk and think about God—has been similarly disenchanted. The Western church, by opting for a supposedly scientific-critical technique, has likewise ended up with a notion of objective truth that is by definition free of poetry and imagination—the kind of theology that is developed by using the same type of technical process required to make computers or washing powder. We have spent decades searching for meaning, looking for new information, new arguments, or new procedures in order to create the latest in theological technology. We have lost the capacity to read and understand both the world and the Word poetically—through the power of entering in and living the metaphor.

Eugene Peterson suggested that poets offer a reframing, a new way of seeing, a new way of experiencing. They awaken us from what has become familiar, dragging us "into the depth of reality itself." Poets don't simply tell us *about* something; they force us "into the middle of it. Poetry grabs for the jugular. Far from being cosmetic language, it is intestinal. It is root language. Poetry doesn't so much tell us something we never knew as bring into recognition what is latent, forgotten, overlooked, or suppressed."[28] Repoeticizing therefore is not about new ways to collect and disseminate information but instead about putting *a new frame around a picture*. We need to recover poetry instead of just the prosaic; imagination instead of mere information. In adopting the language of poetry and imagination, we recapture the language of intimacy and experience. Poetic speech is not intended to be an explanation, it is not a fanciful way to illustrate; rather, it invokes imagination. It makes an image of reality in such a way as to invite our participation in it. We are not necessarily more informed by it, but we will have more experience.

> Poets are extravagant and bold, scorning both the caution of the religious philosopher and the earnestness of the ethical moralist. [In Revelation] St. John is a poet, using words to intensify our relationship with God. He is not trying to get us to think more accurately or to train us into better behavior, but to get us to believe more recklessly, behave more playfully—the faith-recklessness and hope-playfulness of children entering into the kingdom of God. He will jar us out of our lethargy, get us to live on the alert, open our eyes to the burning bush and fiery chariots, open our ears to the hard-steel promises and commands of Christ, banish boredom from the gospel, lift up our heads, enlarge our hearts.[29]

Walter Brueggemann even goes so far as to say, "Poetic speech is the only proclamation worth doing in a situation of reductionism."[30] Spot on. This is because metaphors open up new ways of seeing and perceiving God. Poetry is the language that is used throughout the biblical narrative, especially among the prophets. Those wild-eyed Hebrew prophets spoke the word of God to a people who no longer understood the presence of God or his relentless pursuit. They came with very little experience, even fewer credentials, but having listened to God and studied culture, they spoke to the people. With poetic rhetoric, the prophets spoke a subversive and alternative story. They spoke with a prophetic imagination, taking what they knew about the world in front of them and envisioning a completely different story being lived out. This is the task of those called to speak about the sacred, to articulate the alternative world God has promised, and that he is in fact birthing at any given time.

Consider Martin Luther King's "I have a dream" speech as an example of prophetic poetics. This was a history-making speech, calling its hearers to an alternative way of life. Yet King didn't employ the technical language of civil rights legislation, though it had everything to do with that. He didn't give his hearers information—he awakened a yearning in their hearts for justice.[31]

Again, the solution is not a simple change in aesthetic. It is not decorative. It is not frivolous. It is not simply reading or speaking more poetry. It is a radical shift in our rhetoric that includes a language that is deeper, richer, more steeped in metaphor, and more dynamic; speech that touches heart and soul, as well as the mind. This is not a call to simply create a new and improved doctrinal statement. It is instead a call to embrace a theological language that fully engages the current world as it is—not a new revelation but a new frame, which offers an opportunity for a new response. Because, as Shelley said, "Poetry lifts the veil from the hidden beauty of the world, and makes familiar objects be as if they were not familiar."[32] Theological poetry even more so.

C. S. Lewis' advice to would-be interpreters of the Bible is to let the figurative speech of the Bible speak for itself and not try to reduce it to theological formulas or to literalize it. He recommended two basic rules for exegesis: first, never take the metaphors literally. Second, when the significance of the poetic images—what they say to our fear, hope, will, and affections—seems to conflict with any theological abstractions we might adhere to, trust the essence and intention of the images *every time*. Lewis suggested that whatever revelatory information the poetic language in the Scriptures has to confer can be received only if the interpreter is ready to meet it halfway. Abstract theology, he proposed, is not likely to be more adequate than the sensuous, organic, and personal images of Scripture—light and darkness, river and well, seed and harvest, master and servant, hen and chickens, father and child. Lewis also claimed that it is an act of intellectual impertinence to ask a text to deliver assurances in the propositional language of theologians when it is written in the evocative language of poetry. Besides, Lewis rightly maintained that abstract thinking is itself simply a tissue of analogies and metaphors: an abstract reframing of spiritual reality in legal, chemical, or mechanical terms.[33]

The willingness to repoeticize opens us up to a deepening and wi[l]dening of God and gospel that leaves us vulnerable and receptive to a truth we have all sought to avoid time and again.

REMYTHOLOGIZE

Remythologization essentially involves a reinsertion of what, we believe, is a way of making sense in a senseless world. It is more like tasting than thinking; something that transcends a finite understanding of this world and miraculously gives vision to see the entire world beyond a limited reality.

Again, as a review from chapter two, we are not using the term *myth* in its pop/vernacular definition—to describe a false belief, a legend, or a baseless superstition. Neither is our use of the term about simply using some clever and engaging tale, told to entertain or distract, but rather it's a way of wrapping truth in a narrative in order to convey primal truths to its readers.

We use the term in exactly the same way C. S. Lewis did, who himself wrote material that had huge mythic resonance. Lewis understood *myth* as a descriptive term to identify the dimension of literature that is "extra-literary," a dimension that contains something derived from beyond the written words themselves. A work that contains mythological elements will draw a reader out of himself or herself and into something greater.[34] Lewis claimed that to say a story is mythic is not to say it is mere fantasy. Quite the opposite. By appealing to the power of myth, we give ordinary, everyday things new life and meaning. This is because myth reaches into the innermost levels of human consciousness. It resonates with us because of its universal and fundamental truth.[35]

In our search for meaning in a somewhat confused and despairing world, myths are indispensable in giving us a "reframed" language, full of meaning, beauty, and hope. Myth is a way of thinking and speaking that gives us truth about the world and ourselves. Mythic language can help us wrestle with questions of self-identity, and tribe-identity, while giving us a road to walk as we sort through the unfathomable mysteries of the world.

A Unifying Vision of Reality

It was the nature of myth that was at the center of a now renowned discussion between friends on a late-night stroll on September 19, 1931. On the picturesque path known as Addison's Walk on the grounds of Oxford's Magdalen College, C. S. Lewis, J. R. R. Tolkien, and Hugo Dyson took a transformative walk that included an exploration into the nature of myth.

Lewis, having professed atheism since a teenager, had become a theist in the years leading up to 1931. Naturally a skeptic, he had come to believe in a God of sorts, but:

> Lewis explained that his difficulty had been that he could not see "how the life and death of Someone Else (whoever he was) 2000 years ago could help us here and now." He could admit that Christ might provide a good example, but that was about as far as it went. Lewis realized that the New Testament took a very different view, using terms such as *propitiation*, or *sacrifice* to refer to the true meaning of the cross. But these expressions, Lewis declared, seemed to him to be "either silly or shocking."[36]

Lewis and Tolkien shared a love of mythology, but up to this point, it had not helped Lewis come to terms with the story of the gospel. Years before, he had concluded that Christianity was simply "one mythology among many" and was as false as all other religions. But that short walk that night in 1931 seemed to play a crucial part in the story of Lewis, the self-described "most reluctant convert."[37]

Alister McGrath, in his extraordinary biography of Lewis, writes:

> Tolkien helped Lewis to realize that the problem lay not in Lewis' *rational* failure to understand the theory, but in his *imaginative* failure to grasp its significance. The issue was not primarily about *truth*, but about *meaning*. When engaging the Christian narrative, Lewis was limiting himself to his reason when he ought to be opening himself to the deepest intuitions of his imagination.[38]

Tolkien argued and reasoned, and Lewis came to the following understanding: "The story of Christ is simply a true myth: a myth working on us in the same way as the others, but with this tremendous difference that *it really happened*."[39] "To put it another way, just as Christ came not to abolish the Law but to fulfill it, so he came not to put an end to myth but to take all that is most essential in the myth up into himself and make it real."[40]

McGrath continues:

> For Tolkien [...] Myths offer a fragment of that truth, not its totality. They are like splintered fragments of the true light. Yet when the full and true story is told, it is able to bring to fulfillment all that was right and wise in those fragmentary visions of things. For Tolkien, grasping Christianity's meaningfulness took precedence over its truth. It provided the total picture, unifying and transcending these fragmentary and imperfect insights. For Tolkien, a myth awakens in its readers a longing for something that lies beyond their grasp. Myths possess an innate capacity to expand the consciousness of their readers, allowing them to transcend themselves. At their best, myths offer what Lewis later termed "a real though unfocused gleam of divine truth falling on human imagination." Christianity, rather than being one myth alongside many others, is thus the fulfillment of all previous mythological religions. Christianity tells a true story about humanity, which makes sense of all the stories that humanity tells about itself.[41]

Lewis was thus radically reframed. No longer to just be understood in its technical literary sense, myth now opened a door for him, one that God seemed to chase him through. He wrote just days after this conversation with Tolkien and Dyson: "I have just passed on from believing in God to definitely believing in Christ—in Christianity."[42]

Suddenly, there was a way of integrating the desires and longings that Lewis felt with the reasonable reality of this "true myth." This reframing of myth and of faith allowed Lewis to understand the potential for the merging of the world of reason and imagination.

> For this is the marriage of heaven and earth: Perfect Myth and Perfect Fact: claiming not only our love and obedience, but also our wonder and delight, addressed to the savage, the child, and the poet in each one of us no less than to the moralist, the scholar, and the philosopher.[43]

Is it possible for us to do the same thing in our telling of the story of God? To spend our time less in confirming the veracity of Christianity and more in exhibiting its unifying vision of reality? This would mean a merging of the world of reason and imagination, a synthesizing of science with arts that would bring to fruition something of an *imaginative apologetics*. It is the imagination that opens our capacity to apprehend meaning and it is this larger view of reality that eliminates the reduced, flattened, and trivial telling of the gospel.

LIFE IS A CABARET

If all this talk about poetry and the imagination seems foreign to evangelical ears, then we need only listen to Paul as he encourages the Ephesian saints to "be filled with the Spirit, speaking to one another with psalms, hymns, and songs from the Spirit. Sing and make music from your heart to the Lord, always giving thanks to God the Father for everything, in the name of our Lord Jesus Christ" (Ephesians 5:18–20).

I (Alan) was recently pondering what "speaking to one another in hymns and spiritual songs" could possibly mean? Was Paul really suggesting that we live our lives like a Broadway musical? (I hope not, as musicals are by no means my favorite art form!) But it certainly sounds like it. Paul does seem to be suggesting that we are not to just sing songs in congregational worship, but rather we are to converse as if we were singing to each other. This requires cultivating a hymnic form of speech that derives its sensibilities from the Old Testament Psalms as well as the New Testament hymns (e.g., Colossians 1; Ephesians 1:1–10; Philippians 2:5–11, etc.). By urging them to live their lives inside the metaphor of a spiritual song, Paul is encouraging the saints to live *within* the enchanted world where the Spirit-inspired mystery and awe inspires a life of thanksgiving.

The always-insightful Adrienne von Speyr agrees:

> If Paul expresses the wish that we might live in the fullness of the Spirit so that he rules in a living way our whole life [...] we must make a personal effort to converse with one another in the language of the Spirit [...] It is from this source that we are to draw our thoughts and mental occupations, so that what we communicate to others may be, not of us, but of God. The words we use to converse with God must also give their characteristic stamp to the words we use in our Christian conversation with one another. In this way both we ourselves as well as our interlocutors are placed in an atmosphere of God [...] But if psalms and hymns give their imprint to our everyday speech, the words we have at our disposal to explain ourselves become ever more lively and appropriate. Not, as it were, by imposing from above a sort of foreign vocabulary on our everyday speech, but by impressing on our entire daily life the sense of the psalms and hymns and thus accustoming our quotidian reality to the supernatural world in virtue of the word of God that is contained in these spiritual songs. Our human intercourse is thereby blown wide open.[44]

The language of the Psalms (and hymns) is theopoetic speech laden with a sense of mystery and wonder, dread and love, suffering and joy, desire and longing—in a word, *pathos*. When we speak to one another with this kind of speech, it opens one up to the presence of God and gospel in fresh and new ways. This is why we are encouraging the reader to repoeticize, remystify, and remythologize our ways of speaking about God.

And if anyone is given to think that this piece of Pauline advice is a tad too poetical for Paul, we suggest simply reading the first chapters of Ephesians and Colossians to experience Paul's own poetic worldview at play. Our standard readings of Paul are captive to the scholastics and rationalists who use him to do their theological accounting. But this is a reduction of the Pauline gospel by particular theological interest groups. Paul is way too mystical to be a rationalist (see 2 Corinthians 12:1–4, for instance), and he knows full well that the only way one can really express the in/credible things God has done is through poetic language and songs![45]

RE-DIG THE WELLS

In Genesis 26, a very obscure story is told of Isaac. Isaac, of course, is the son of Abraham, whom God covenanted with to make a great nation. After Abraham's death, and during the time of a famine in the land, Isaac settled in the Valley of Gerar. God blessed Isaac, like his father before him, with "flocks and herds and a great household" (Genesis 26:14 NASB). As would be expected, with so many to provide for, the need for water was great. But his nation's adversary, the Philistines, had filled all the wells with earth.[46] God's people had no access to a major necessity of life.

In response to this great need, Isaac "had to re-dig all of the water wells that his father had installed" (Genesis 26:18 The Voice). In order for the people to live, Isaac had to clear the ground and cart off the debris, so that all that had cluttered and obstructed the flow of water from the wells was removed and the water could stream through once more.

He dug the wells again so that the people could drink deeply from that which gave life. So much of the story of Jesus we tell similarly needs to be dug again. And all the clutter and debris removed. So that people can drink deeply of that which gives them life.

We can see examples of this "re-digging" of stories all across the cultural landscape. Stories and narratives that had grown "cluttered and obstructed" have been brought to life by, at times, a radical and far-reaching re-digging. Consider the 2015 Broadway musical *Hamilton* as a quintessential display of re-digging. Hamilton was a "founding father," the creator of the nation's financial system, and the first Secretary of the Treasury. Creator of the musical, Lin-Manuel Miranda, has taken Hamilton's story and turned it into a musical phenomenon, endearing itself to the theatre community, and receiving a Grammy Award, a Pulitzer Prize, and eleven Tony Awards. Incorporating hip hop, R&B, pop, and soul, and casting non-white actors as the founding fathers, the show has also appealed to broader culture. "I'm just doing what everyone else that's writing musicals is doing," says Miranda. "I'm finding a musical vocabulary to tell this story. For me, hip hop seems to be the only way to tell Alexander Hamilton's story because it's a story about words and it's a story about using words to save your life and destroy your life."[47] Miranda did not change the story of Alexander Hamilton; he simply put a new frame around it.

But the church? *Oi vey!* The church thinks the answer is more puppet shows and nativity pageants ("we even have live animals this year") that will proclaim the gospel and win the world to faith in God. Or perhaps a teaching series on NASCAR racing because it will appeal to men, the lost demographic. Please, *please* hear our cry. No more tawdry Jesus puppet shows! No more Bible dramas with bathrobes as costumes! And no more equating the death of Dale Earnhardt with the death of Jesus. Please! No more inferior art; no more dreadful attempts to tell such a magnificent story with such low-quality and artless craft. We must tell a better story as well as tell the story better; a story that brings about healing, transformation, societal change, and restoration. A re/enchanted story that surprises its hearers, both by uncovering brokenness and in giving hope.

This re/enchanting is what C. S. Lewis was attempting in the creation of *The Chronicles of Narnia*. It has been called an attempt at "rearranging reality." "For Lewis, the narrative of Narnia has the capacity to re-enchant a disenchanted world. It helps us to imagine our world differently. This is not escapism, but is about discerning deeper levels of meaning and value in what we already know."[48]

Walter Hooper tells a fascinating story about the illustrations created for *The Lion, The Witch and The Wardrobe*, the first published book in the Narnia series. Pauline Baynes, the illustrator hired by Lewis, had not discussed the content of the book with Lewis before beginning work on it, so she was not familiar with the story. Hooper recalls Baynes' account:

> When she was drawing all those pictures of Aslan being tormented by the White Witch and others [...] she had to rip up her paper again and again because she was weeping on the pages over the fate of Aslan. It just broke her heart. So, finally, she finished the illustrations and then sent them

off to the publisher but even a week later still bothered by all that had happened to Aslan she found herself surprised when it suddenly broke on her: "Oh, I know who he is! He is Jesus Christ!"

Just as Emily Dickinson advised, Lewis told the truth but told it "slant," and the effect on Pauline Baynes was that it "dazzled gradually."[49] Hooper rightly states, "This is the way you get past the watchful dragons. You don't want a person to be told 'This is Jesus Christ and I want you to see this before you begin the book.' No. Let it happen to you as it did to her. So when she actually takes in what Jesus has done for humanity then it will break up on her, 'this really happened in a real world. And I am one of the beneficiaries of it.'"[50]

The real power seen in the effects of re/enchantment is not in the creative stories that are told, nor in the moralizing allegories that are revealed. The thing that gives the frames of re/enchantment their real power and meaning is the world they evoke, the transformation of life they demonstrate, and the hope they give. And if ever there was a time we needed a richer, broader, deeper story, it has to be now.

The question we are asking every follower of Jesus to wrestle with is this: is the story we are telling big enough, mysterious enough, poetic enough, and mythical enough to allow us to once again experience the reality of God beyond the clutter and debris of this world that gets in the way? Is it able to move the moon so we can experience God beyond the eclipse, a God infinitely bigger than the small and insignificant being our hearts and minds have reduced him to?

It is the same story, about this same Jesus, that just a few dozen people began to tell 2,000 years ago. This story reframed the love of God, and it literally changed the world. In/credible! And there at the beginning, they allowed nothing to get in the way. No clutter, no debris filling up the well. They simply told the story, lived the story, and drank deeply from its well.

I'LL HAVE WHAT
SHE'S HAVING

(THE PARABLE OF THE IN/CREDIBLE
WITNESS)

Every time you live an attribute of Jesus you create a
metaphor through which you can share the gospel.

— JEFF VANDERSTELT

Jesus refuses to allow us to abstract our knowing from our
living. The gospel is not information; it is a way of life.

— STANLEY HAUERWAS

What we are teaches the child far more than what we say, so
we must be what we want our children to become.

— JOSEPH CHILTON PEARCE

So how might we then live? How does entering into a repoeticized,
remythologized, and remystified story impact how we live our lives? In
stark contrast to Harold Crick (he of chapter three), how might we combat
the tendency to live small lives of mediocrity and to settle for less than the
ultimate?

Well, consider the example of Clarence Jordan. In his own unique way,
Jordan lived an in/credible life.

Jordan didn't set out to be anybody special. He didn't set out to be the
kind of person people would write books about, or plays about, or
television documentaries about. He didn't set out to lay the foundations
for a project to build houses for poor people that would extend around
the world. He didn't set out to get people riled up and angry at him.
He started out as a simple small-town boy, born the middle child in a
large family in Talbotton, Georgia, in 1912. It was just that Clarence just
always saw things differently.[1]

Jordan is probably best known for his *Cotton Patch Gospel*, a translation of the New Testament into southern vernacular, as well as being a preacher/storyteller who was in high demand during the 1950s and 1960s, some time before civil rights became a mainstream issue in the States.[2] But it wasn't Jordan's public proclamations about Jesus, his homiletical prowess, or his hermeneutical expertise that set him up as the antithesis to Harold Crick. Clarence Jordan lived a beautiful life, countering the fundamentalist evangelical culture of the time, which had bought deeply into a reduced truth, a reduced story, and a subsequently reduced life.

Growing up white and privileged in a divided and fractured part of the world, from a young age Jordan observed the racial injustice in the deep south—everything was separate, from schools to churches to neighborhoods. Jordan could not find a way to reconcile the Jesus of the Gospels with evangelical practices, which chose the way of culture over the alternative, subversive story of the gospel. "During and after his seminary career Jordan became involved in the then-radical work of racial reconciliation."[3]

Jordan dreamed of forming a community where people lived the story of Jesus, unreduced and whole. In 1942, he purchased a 400-acre farm just outside the town of Americus, Georgia in order to create an "incarnate community of the New Testament." With an undergraduate degree in agriculture, Jordan wanted to be a scientific farmer, bringing the best agricultural practices to his home state in order to improve the lot of poor farmers, both black and white. He taught locals how to improve farming, rotate their crops, and fertilize their lands. He paid everyone equal wages and welcomed black people and white people around his table (both extremely subversive acts in this era). His community, aptly named *Koinonia* (the Greek word for fellowship/communion), began to provide the entire community with eggs and produce, and it even established a "cow library" (yes, it's what it sounds like).

Eventually, as word slowly got around about Jordan's radical way of life, he was asked to stop preaching at conferences around the country, as well as those close to home. He and his family were excommunicated from their local Baptist church for bringing a young man from India to church with them one day (the congregation didn't believe he wasn't African American). The local community turned on Jordan and *Koinonia* by boycotting their roadside market, peppering their homes and businesses with gunfire, letting loose their farm animals, and chopping down their pecan trees. Local store owners refused to sell them supplies, their insurance was canceled, and no bank would do business with them.

It got worse: in 1957, the clandestine hate group Ku Klux Klan held a rally in Americus, Georgia, driving seventy automobiles around *Koinonia*, brandishing weapons and threatening acts of violence and death. *Life Magazine* obtained a picture of this Klan rally and published the photo on their front cover. This increased publicity led to a growing awareness of the work of *Koinonia*, and is generally considered to have saved the lives of many on the farm. One New York paper wrote: "It seems to me [...] the *Koinonia* story down there in Georgia has as much meaning for us as the non-violent bus strikes in Montgomery, Alabama. In Montgomery, if you recall, it was Negroes who stood their ground [...] in Americus, Georgia it's southern white people and some negroes, trying to live peacefully in a community that has turned against them."[4]

Clarence Jordan called his way of life and his *Koinonia* venture "a demonstration plot for the kingdom of God." He didn't live his life intending to be an activist. He lived his life to be like Jesus. Jordan was a champion of the poor and a pioneer of civil rights, but very few have ever heard of him.

Millard and Linda Fuller, the founders of Habitat for Humanity (an organization that has built more than 500,000 homes and has provided housing for more than 2.5 million people), birthed their radical idea of transforming housing while living at Jordan's demonstration plot. The Fullers were mentored by Jordan before he died in 1969, at the age of fifty-seven. Linda Fuller writes, "We had never met a man with such deep understanding of what it means to be a Christian nor anyone who was as much like Jesus as Clarence Jordan. [...] He believed the essence of Christianity was incarnation; a spoken word without it being acted upon was absolutely meaningless."[5]

BECOMING A THEOLOGICAL PERSON: LET YOUR LIFE SPEAK

This book is not simply a call to have a better grasp on theology or to be able to tell a better story; it's more a call for us to take Paul's description of being "living letters" (2 Corinthians 3:1–3) very seriously indeed. We are certainly not wanting to add to the clutter of reductionist rhetoric by producing better or more precise definitions, nor are we attempting to encourage followers of Jesus to just be a bit more creative in sharing the gospel. We are calling for a new demonstration of *the way* of Jesus as well. It is not just speaking prophetically; it involves living prophetically, living heroically ... just like Clarence Jordan. Not just *studying* theology but *being* theology.

If we are to develop a gospel proclamation that actually reframes the prevailing understanding of God and the world, then we will have to scrap our historical penchant for simply investing in scholastic study while disregarding the visible demonstration of theological doctrine in life itself. We must adopt the posture of both/and. We must expand beyond mere study and verbal articulation to include an incarnational way of living.

This is why discipleship is so vital to the credibility of our proclamation. The genuine disciple's beliefs must come from a living, tangible relationship with God. In the Scriptures, knowing God (or the Truth) is less about being able to control and name the experience. To "know" God is more like the kind of knowing described when Adam *knew* (*yâda*) Eve and she conceived.[6] This form of knowing involves a kind of union, a dialogical participation with the other. One must have at least a readiness to love God if one is going to have any chance of understanding him. In this light then, knowledge of God is less of an attempt to *intellectually grasp God* than it is an attempt to *touch God*. If we make it all about information about God then, "we allow ourselves to lose God behind some prop cardboard cut-out of God, mistaking the menu for the meal, and forgetting that music is the stuff of sound and motion, not marks of ink on paper."[7]

The true disciple allows this relationship with God to transform them, incarnating their beliefs in his or her life—they live the truth they seek to proclaim. Theological truth cannot be divorced from life itself. It's not enough to claim to know the truth as if it can be contained in a mere idea. It was Søren Kierkegaard who rightly asserted that all truth means subjective change.[8] If I want to claim something to be true (in the religious sense particularly) then it must have changed my life, or my life itself will be communicating that I don't really believe it to be true. Without tangible change, the medium of my life thus cancels out the message I claim to believe. There is nothing saintly about that. Demons believe that God is One, and they shudder at this truth (James 2:19), but it does not change them! Truth must impact and change us or, in the end, it will simply judge us. Or as theologian David Tracy says, "there is never an authentic disclosure of truth which is not also transformative."[9]

Jesus, the Word made flesh, is the one example where the medium of a person's life was most perfectly the message. Jesus was *the* definitive theological person in that he perfectly presented the will of the Father to the world. Discipleship must follow in this way of Jesus, for "everyone who is fully trained will be like their teacher" (Luke 6:40). Authentic truth has to be incarnated in an act or in some action; the way of incarnation is the criterion of all real truth (1 John 2:22; 4:2), and "walking in the truth" is the way the believer possesses the truth (2 John 1–4; 3 John 3–4, etc.).[10] We can therefore say that while Jesus is the (sole) incarnation of God, we all must in a real sense become incarnations of Jesus. In some analogical way, disciples of Jesus are meant to be living embodiments of Christ in the world.

The decisive factor for the spiritual greatness of a person is therefore not found in their logical teaching, but rather in their mode of life. It is for this reason that von Balthasar speaks about the exemplary disciple of Jesus (the "saint") as *a theological person*.[11] We like this term; it suggests that our life bespeaks theology, and people are reading it all the time. It has been said that the definition of a saint is someone who makes it easier to believe in God.[12] "Every person, by living authentically, shall become a Torah, an instruction."[13] Authentic disciples—people who really *live* their messages and so beautify truth—enrich the church in marvelous ways because they restore the balance between theory and practice, a balance that every new generation of Christians must strive to attain.[14]

THE DISCIPLE AS ORDINARY HERO

It is *love* that is the final defense of the faith. Jesus himself actually expected no other kind of apologetic when he said that it is by our love that the world will know we are his disciples (John 13:34–35). Love is therefore the defining mark of authenticity.[15]

It is not the theological manuals (full as these may be of unquestionable truths) that can plausibly express to the world the truth of the gospel, but rather, the existence of the authentic, faithful, heroic disciples who have been grasped by Christ and his gospel.[16] For instance, we can look at the work of Mother Teresa and observe someone who allowed God to "say" with her life the same kind of message he communicated through the life of his Son, Christ Jesus.[17] Claiming to have doctrine down pat and to believe in all the right things (as important as these are) will never provide an adequate defense for Christianity. Because we are expected to express the beliefs we hold to be true, only the living embodiment of theology in and through the very life of the authentic disciple can serve as a viable defense (apology) of the Christian faith.

Let's face it, we all know that the in/credible witness of a true disciple is a far more effective way of reframing people's understanding of God, church, and world than almost any other form of witness. When people encounter and observe someone who really lives the message, they are confronted with what Jesus looks like through the particular and unique form of the witness. The holiness of any authentic follower of Jesus displays something of the captivating beauty of God's revelation in Christ, drawing those around them closer to God and to consider who Jesus is. This type of powerful witness is seen in the biblical heroes and disciples (e.g., Mary, Paul, John, Peter), in history (e.g., Augustine, Francis, Corrie ten Boom), but also in the Clarence Jordans of the world. It is equally true for all of us who claim to follow and love Jesus. J. V. Taylor, the British missiologist, once remarked, "How secondary, indeed how futile, are all the means of communication unless they are actually born out of the very truth they are meant to convey."[18]

The authentic witness of a faithful believer enables others to be sympathetic to the Christian message and to receive the intellectual content of theology. The appeal of the theology being espoused is therefore somehow inextricably linked to the credibility and integrity of the believer in question. This also explains why a bad (or false) witness, or the apparent hypocrisy of believers, gives people and society a good excuse to reject the claims of Christ on their lives.

And it is important to note here that we are not referring simply to the role of individual witnesses in reframing God and gospel, but also to the irreplaceable role of the faith community. Lesslie Newbigin, probably the premier missiologist of our times, was convinced that "the primary reality of which we have to take account in seeking for a Christian impact on public life is the Christian congregation." He pondered how it is possible that the gospel would be taken seriously in the West where the claims of Christ have been undermined by the false witness of historical Christendom. How indeed would the gospel be rendered credible again? He ends up claiming that "the only [believable] hermeneutic of the gospel is a congregation of men and women who believe it and live by it." To be clear, in saying this he does not deny the importance of the many activities we employ to challenge public life with the gospel—evangelistic campaigns, distribution of Bibles and Christian literature, conferences, etc. But he does say that these are all secondary, and that they have power to accomplish their purpose only as they are rooted in and lead back to a believing community.[19]

Hugh Halter, one of our dear friends and a brilliant practitioner of incarnational mission, says it like this:

The incarnational big-story gospel will require a place of discovery, where people will be able to see the truth before they hear about it. This place will not be a location but a community of people who are inclusive of everyone. These people will be making eternity attractive by how they live such selfless lives now, and will be modeling life in a New Kingdom in ways that will make it easy for other people to give it a try. People like this aren't desperate to convert everyone; they are desperate to be like Jesus and to be where Jesus is.[20]

ADDING BEAUTY TO HOLINESS

Judaism has a name for the idea of making life and spirituality *beautiful*; it's called *hiddur mitzvah—hiddur* meaning "to make beautiful" and *mitzvah* meaning "commandment, or good deed."[21] This ancient teaching is intended to communicate that one is not just to live in a way that merely obeys the commandments, but life is to be lived in a way that also beautifies them, and that life itself is thereby beautified in return. In the rabbis' understanding, every opportunity to obey God is also an opportunity to "adorn" or "beautify" God.[22] To reframe both God and the world in ways that make the gospel accessible and appealing, we suggest that we need to adopt some of this thinking, adding beauty to holiness.

To understand this call to *hiddur mitzvah* is to understand that life is not to be reduced to obeying the rules in order to satisfy a code of morality. Instead, it is an invitation to live a life that adorns the ways of God with mind-blowing beauty, not as a means to earn the love of God, but in response to the love of God.

This concept is very likely what Paul and Peter mean when they encourage disciples to "adorn" the gospel (Titus 2:10 and 1 Peter 2:12; 4:11); good works and holy lives, lived beautifully, glorify God and serve as credible witness. A person pleases God when he or she decorates their lives with good works, and the gospel itself is rendered beautiful in the eyes of those who behold it.

Paul has a similar idea in mind when he encourages the Ephesian believers to live "to the praise of his glorious grace" (Ephesians 1:6, 12, 14). Markus Barth, in his brilliant commentary on the epistle, says that God has for so long and intensively showered grace on his people that finally they cannot help but sing paeans to his splendid grace. According to 1 Corinthians 10:31 and Romans 15:5–6, eating, drinking, and all other human actions, including abstention, are to serve the praise of God's glory. "By its singing, shouting, dancing, moaning, in the face of the pitfalls of sin or misery, but equally under the shower of the mercies of God, God's people are appointed to be a witness to God and a light among the nations, 'my chosen people, the people whom I formed for myself that they might declare my praise.'"[23]

Perhaps that great twentieth-century prophet, that voice crying out in the wilderness, can help us understand what it means to live beautifully—the one and only Fred Rogers. Aka "Mister Rogers," this sweater-wearing, ordained Presbyterian minister was host of *Mister Rogers' Neighborhood*, a U.S. children's television show, for thirty-three years. He taught children (and adults) how to live in a way that told a different story. In 2002, a few months before his death, Mister Rogers gave a prophetic commencement address at Dartmouth College, an Ivy League school. In his characteristic childlike simplicity, Rogers reminded us all to:

> Be true to the best within you. Not just true to yourself, but to the best within you. I'm talking about that part of you that knows that life is far more than anything you can ever see or hear or touch. That deep part of you that allows you to stand for those things, without which humankind cannot survive. Love that conquers hate. Peace that rises triumphant over war. And justice that proves more powerful than greed.[24]

In this address, Rogers summed up what he believed would be the mission of a new millennium in four simple words: "Make goodness attractive again."[25] A story personified by goodness; a life that embodies beauty—very few things would be more attractive to those engaged in an existential quest for meaning and purpose.

Again, the proposal we are making in this chapter is that living an unreduced life calls for a new demonstration—a new way of approaching the world, which interposes the whole in contrast to the broken.

Compare the following two choices of how to live in the midst of a broken world:

In July of AD 64, a great fire burned throughout Rome for over a week, destroying almost three quarters of the city. Rome's emperor at the time, the unpopular and incredibly cruel Nero, "played his fiddle while Rome burned to the ground," leaving over half the city homeless. The fiddle playing of Nero is probably more folktale than actual event (considering that fiddles did not come into existence until around the eleventh century). However, "his gleeful indifference to the plight of his people is fact [...] People suffered and Nero didn't care. His city burned and Nero reveled in his well-protected life of luxury. His cold-heartedness in the tragedy was proven when he built his 'Golden Palace' and 'pleasure gardens' on the ruins of the fire."[26]

In stark contrast, consider Vedran Smailović. On May 27, 1992, during the Bosnian War, Smailović stood less than one hundred yards away from where twenty-two people were killed by a shell falling directly on them as they were waiting in line at a bakery. In response to this horrific event, Smailović, the principal cellist of the Sarajevo Opera Company at the time, did all he knew to do. In protest at the chaos, hatred, and stupidity of war, Smailović brought his cello out and sat in a chair in the middle of the crater left by the deadly explosion. Every day for twenty-two days (one day for each person killed on that spot) Smailović filled the air with beautiful music. As explosions and sniper fire rang throughout the street, this lone cellist risked his own life, protesting against the ugliness and brokenness of his city by holding up beauty in its face.

We live in an ugly and broken world, the pieces of which are far from being reassembled. But the ideal, the way God intended the world to be, still matters, even when reality does not reflect it. Showing up and living beautifully in an otherwise reduced world is still important. It reminds us there is something more, something higher, something better.

Can we tell a story of good news into a broken world by giving it a glimpse of a more beautiful way to live? Can we make goodness attractive again? Blaise Pascal chose this approach in the seventeenth century:

> For Pascal, there was little point in trying to persuade anyone of the truth of religious belief. The important thing, he argued, was to make people wish it were true, having caught sight of the rich and satisfying vision of reality it offered. Once such desire was implanted within the human heart, the human mind would eventually catch up with its deeper intuitions.[27]

LIVING A QUESTIONABLE LIFE

Michael Frost, our zany and prophetic friend, talks about Christians needing to *live a questionable life*. He says that the life of those who believe in Jesus ought to arouse curiosity among those who do not believe, leading to questions and faith sharing. In other words, authentic followers of Jesus should live lives that cry out for an explanation that will inevitably involve recounting the impact of the gospel on their lives.

Behind this idea of living a life that evokes questions lies an axiom of communication theory that says that *when predictability is high, impact is low.* In other words, when the audience thinks they know what you're going to say, and you go ahead and say it, your words will have very little impact. On the other hand, when an audience is surprised or intrigued, they will think long and hard about what they've heard. The point is that we should always try to live in a way that surprises if we want to really be heard and noticed.

Can we live lives that are so surprising (questionable) that people want to ask "Why?" when it comes to how we raise our families, how we approach career/money/stuff, how we invite others in, how we are willing to speak truth to power, or how we are committed to a just world? We ought to live lives that are counter-cultural in the same way Jesus did.

In many ways, this is precisely what was going on throughout the book of Acts—they shared their possessions, fed the poor, supported the widow, embraced the outcast, honored slaves, and empowered women whom society had left voiceless.

Move ahead a couple of hundred years or so from Acts and you will discover that Christians were living questionable lives ... so much so that the Roman emperor Julian became concerned that Christians might actually take over the empire! These "atheists" (referred to as such because they denied the pagan gods) had devoted themselves to sacrificial acts of kindness and to "love feasts" that fed the hungry and the poor. What were Julian's big concerns?[28]

· These people actually feed others who are not a part of their church.
· These people tend the graves of those who are not a part of their religion.
· These people actually absolve others of their debts and forgive their persecutors.
· These people practice hospitality and take people into their homes.
· These people treat slaves as family.

In contrast to the brutality of life under Roman rule, "these people" were markedly different. They changed their world by surprising it. Is it possible that, at times, our best presentation of the gospel is simply living such a beautiful life that these pilgrims in Spain and Burners in Nevada begin to wonder if there might be, after all, something to this God we believe in?

In contrast, it is not hard for any reader to consider how the impact of the always-surprising good news of Jesus is diminished when we persist in our oh-so-tired and predictable ways of talking about God and gospel.

Ponder the prevalent "John 3:16" signs at the Super Bowl; the guerrilla street evangelist who doesn't bother to ask your name or your story in the rush to tell you that you are going to hell; the endless altar-calls with the repeated choral refrain of "Just as I am"; our tracts and flyers; our moral rants on how ungodly America is becoming; and so on. It's all so predictable and unsurprising.

In a now-famous scene from the 1989 romantic comedy *When Harry Met Sally ...* , the two title characters are having lunch at Katz's Delicatessen in Manhattan. The couple are arguing about a man's ability to recognize when a woman is faking an orgasm. Sally claims that men cannot tell the difference and that women do it all the time. Harry, his insecure male ego now offended, claims he would always know if a woman was faking it. And so, to prove her point, Sally vividly (and we should add fully clothed) fakes a very loud orgasm while other diners watch on somewhat incredulously. At the end, the whole café is quiet. The scene ends with Sally casually returning to her meal as a nearby patron places her order with the now famous words: "I'll have what she's having."[29] (By the way, Katz's Deli still hangs a sign above the table that says, "Where Harry met Sally ... hope you have what she had!")

This then is how we should live our lives ... *orgasmically*. We should out-serve, out-suffer, out-party, out-work, out-love, out-give, out-live, and out-everything everyone else. We should live our lives in such a way that those observing us want to say, "I'll have what they're having."

AN ANTIDOTE FOR THE EMPTINESS OF EXISTENCE

Throughout this book, we are pursuing an openness to the mere possibility that there is a bigger story to live into. The emptiness of existence that so many experience is not the way it *has* to be. Is there a way to live, to contribute, to create beauty that could move us toward an antidote for this emptiness of existence? We propose there is, and we believe that living a questionable and surprising life is a strong start toward inviting others into an alternative reality; an alternative life to that of the mundane *Grey Town*, *Harold-Crick-like* existence; a life filled with beauty brought about by those who feel called to play cellos in broken places and to make goodness attractive again.

The role of art, and of living an artful life, is significant in a world in search of meaning and beauty. Novelist and sci-fi writer Ursula K. Le Guin suggests that art is one of the ways we break routine thinking and allow our perceptions to be cleansed:

> The daily routine of most adults is so heavy and artificial that we are closed off to much of the world. We have to do this in order to get our work done. I think one purpose of art is to get us out of those routines. When we hear music or poetry or stories, the world opens up again.[30]

Similarly, James K. A. Smith gives us more than a clue to one of the keys of reframation: "If you want to change how the world thinks, you first have to change how they imagine. That's why, today, artists are our apologists."[31]

> The arts speak to aspects of human nature ignored or denied by a culture captivated by brutal notions of "efficiency" or quasi-scientific narratives that reduce us to animality. It's in literature, poetry, film, and so many other art forms that we hear echoes of a biblical understanding of humanity—that we are created in God's image, animated by hungers and hopes, made to delight and play. In other words, the arts are evidence of what I've called "cracks in the secular"—the recalcitrant mystery at the heart of the human that refuses to be eviscerated. Art continues to shout *Nein!* to our disenchantment.[32]

THE POET/PRIEST

Have we ever considered that it is possible we do not always have the "right" people, in the right places, with the right abilities communicating the story of God?

Is it possible that we have underestimated who actually has the greater influence in reframing the story of God? Or perhaps it is simply that we have a limited view of who is to have a voice in this reframing. G. K. Chesterton wrote, "I don't deny that there should be priests to remind men that they will one day die. I only say that at certain strange epochs it is necessary to have another kind of priests, called poets, actually to remind men that they are not dead yet."[33] We are living today at a "certain strange epoch" where we believe it is imperative to have other "kinds of priests." Not by eliminating all others, but by encouraging a broader range of those who live and create a better, more beautiful story.

The universal search for hope and meaning is ever present and at times filled with overwhelming despair. It is into this existential search that the artist is called to enter, not succumbing to the hopelessness but instead offering solace and remedy to this sensation of emptiness. This emptiness of existence is what we have partially unpacked in chapters four and five. We believe "other kinds of priests" are one way out of the despair of longing and desire, and such priests would include those in the arts, in its broadest definition—the poets, the writers, the dancers, the actors, the painters, the musicians, the producers, the directors, the preachers (of course preaching is an art), the storytellers, the photographers, the teachers, and the _____ (insert any and all we have left out). The bringing about of the beauty of God is not just for clergy, the so-called *professionals*. Living a better story is not just the domain of the theologian or pastor, those trained in the "correct" systems or methods. Instead, it is demonstrated through the expression of art, in which the common search for meaning and truth is acknowledged and entered into. The arts will never convince anyone to believe in God—they are simply the frames. They lead people to consider the way the world works and to subsequently speak with a raw intensity and honesty about life both with and without God.

Eugene Peterson gives us good reason to explore an artful response, in that, "Artists make us insiders to the complexity and beauty of what we deal with every day but so often miss. They bring to our attention what is right before our eyes, within reach of our touch, help us hear sounds and combinations of sounds that our noise-deafened ears have never heard."[34]

Art itself is inherently a great and surprising witness. It's like throwing a banquet for hungry people, being hospitable to strangers, disclosing fascinating possibilities to people who are worn out or bored.

> Artistry is integral to human life, and [...] art is meant to hint at minor marvels, hurts, and mysteries that we may have missed. When a visual artist brightens up a neighbor's perception with wonder, empathy, or a smidgen of hope, it becomes a thank-offering to build up the city of God.[35]

This is because the true artist seeks to engage the world, experiencing its cruel pain, but also at the same time its infinite possibility, and its inordinate beauty. In other words, true art is *prophetic*, and allows the outlines of a form or idea to slowly dawn according to its own terms. To borrow Emily Dickinson's phrase again, it's allowing an idea to "dazzle gradually," rather than trying to shoehorn concepts into neatly packaged formulae.[36] And the Christian artist is the person who opens him or herself to the Spirit, not in a passive way, but with all their senses keyed and alert, seeking to listen to and obey what is revealed by the Spirit in that process. In so doing, they harness all their ability and the materials available to them in order to faithfully fulfill the vision given by God.[37] We are similarly called to live our lives, open to encounter with God on his own terms.[38]

REPAIRING THE UNIVERSE

In a world fractured by copious reductionisms and heresies, it is this calling to live a broadly defined artistic life of beauty that allows us to find a way forward toward meaning, toward recognizing a role in living a story that reshapes our sense of God and the world.

In Jewish spirituality, many consider the most important task in life is to find what is broken in the world and to repair or heal it. This is the meaning of the phrase *tikkun olam*—to repair the world/universe. The faithful Jew assists God in the restoration and healing of the world through the *mitzvah*, the various acts of goodness and kindness that are done in accordance with the *Torah*, with God's instruction. Faithful disciples therefore bear a responsibility not only for their own moral, spiritual, and material welfare, but also for the welfare of society at large, for the establishment of godly qualities throughout the world—they are healers of a broken world and restorers of a lost glory.

Although a distinctly Jewish phrase, followers of Jesus can readily identify aspects of Jesus' mission in the idea of *tikkun olam*. It is in and through Jesus that God is bringing all things together (Ephesians 1:9–10). Jesus spoke of this "renewal of all things" (Matthew 19:28); Peter described the time when God would "restore everything" (Acts 3:19–21); and Paul tells us that, through Jesus, God has "reconcile[d] to himself all things" (Colossians 1:19–20). Paul also gives us a commissioning of sorts to participate in this renewal and restoration, "For we are the product of His hand, *heaven's poetry etched on lives [poema]*, created in the Anointed, Jesus, to accomplish the good works God arranged long ago" (Ephesians 2:10 The Voice). This participation in healing the world "gives concrete expression to our identity and community in Christ for the world. They are not the means to our salvation, not even our own idea. They are the embodiment of what 'we are,' of what God 'has made us.'"[39]

Repairing the world is a fantastic metaphor that helps us articulate the mission of the church in light of the mission of Jesus. Just imagine! In his earthly ministry, Jesus repaired the breach between God and the human race, restoring right relationships between people, and modeling a life of love and service before all. In his redemptive work on the cross, Jesus atones for the world; he restores, heals, reconciles, and justifies the lost and broken world. In his resurrection and ascension, Jesus (and all of us in him) brings all things back together again, restoring and repairing the universe and helping put the broken pieces back together once more (Colossians 1:15–20; Ephesians 1:15–23; 1 Corinthians 15:20–28). Christians in the way/pattern of Christ therefore work to apply and extend Jesus' mission through the medium of their lives and actions. In all this, Jesus blazes the trail for those of us who follow in his way.

Repairing, healing, and restoring the world in Jesus' name and cause is a wonderful way to live a surprising life that has a positive impact. For one, it forces us to take ownership of the story we are living, as well as the story we tell—a story that can either contribute to or repair the brokenness of the world. We have a choice as to which story we adhere to and which story we are known by. But there is no way to avoid telling a story of some sort with our lives—the way we live our lives is going to tell a story, whether we want it to or not.

"There is no such thing as an unwritten life, only a badly written one."[40] Our lives will either tell stories of individualism and self-reliance or stories of restoration and redemption—stories of ugliness or stories of beauty. We choose our way.

THEO-DRAMA: PLAYING OUR PART IN THE PLAY AS IT UNFOLDS

We have been given a role to play in this grand story of God, and to miss out on this contributes to a reduced life. N. T. Wright often writes about a theology of living, centered around the idea of an unfinished Shakespearean play. Wright asks us to imagine that we have been given a five-act play written by William Shakespeare. This play involves the very fate of the universe … so it is fraught. There's just one problem, however: only four of the five acts have been written. And it is *we* who have now been invited to participate in the play that is missing its one crucial and final act. What would we do? What would be our strategy? How would we perform our role in finishing this play?[41]

Well … we have to assume we would study the first four acts pretty thoroughly. We would want to determine the pattern and the plot, to get inside the minds of the characters and their developmental arc in the narrative that has been going somewhere for the four previous acts. We would then attempt to enter into this fifth act and play the parts and assume the roles we have been given, according to the story as it has developed thus far. In doing so, we would bring Act V to life, attempting to perform the play as best we can, with the hope of fulfilling the author's original intention.

In Wright's understanding, we are now living in the fifth act of this story of God. The first four acts have played themselves out thus far in the story of Scripture—from creation, to brokenness, to promises and covenants, to the climactic point of the story found in the humanity and the divinity of Jesus. The first followers of Jesus we read about in Acts and the ensuing pages of the New Testament have given us a start. We are now called, and have been given the vocation (which actually mirrors the vocation given to man and woman in the garden) to pursue this way of God. We join him on mission as he continues to repair this broken mess of a world in the image of the final act—the act he has had in mind since the beginning of the story.

We understand and tell this beautiful story well when we discover our ultimate vocation is to play our role as best and as faithfully as we can in this grand and godly unfinished story. In the timeless words of the inimitable Walt Whitman, "The powerful play goes on and you may contribute a verse."[42]

SECTION 4
A RE/LEARNING

We have now explored the depth of our many reductions (section one), noted the nature of our all too human limitations and longings (section two), and proposed a way toward rediscovering a more re/enchanted way of understanding our world (section three). We now want to offer here two final chapters that will hopefully reorient the reader to see what God is doing in our world and to join him, as well as providing practical next steps in applying the process of reframation.

Because we are so fixed to a formulaic understanding of God and gospel, we are guilty of a failure to notice the details, intricacies, and nuances of those around us. We therefore squander the opportunity to connect people with God in ways that really resonate with who they are, or with their longings for the beyond ... for the sacred.

We believe that because, as Christians, our spiritual radar is tuned to the frequencies of different eras, we have become ignorant of the contemporary interests and concerns of the world in which we are called to witness to Jesus. There is a great need to reset this so-called radar to the very particular issues we are facing at the current moment. We need to be able to name what we are seeing and hearing, and help provide pathways to the life-giving connections between people and their God.

Over the next two chapters, we want to consider how these frequency adjustments might be approached, as we explore some basic rhythms of life, and how we might begin to see the sacredness of the image of God buried deep in the souls of all people.

SHARDS OF HEAVEN'S KALEIDOSCOPE

(AN ARCHEOLOGY OF THE HUMAN SOUL)

Lying deep within myself I seized a most worthy souvenir, a shard of heaven's kaleidoscope.

— PATTI SMITH

The Lord is closer to us than we are to ourselves: higher than my highest and more inward than my innermost self.

— ST. AUGUSTINE

There is something that can only be found in one place. It is a great treasure, which may be called the fulfillment of existence. The place where this treasure can be found is the place on which one stands.

— MARTIN BUBER

The 1927 novel *Death Comes for the Archbishop*, set in the New Mexico territories at the turn of the twentieth century, is a story of Roman Catholic missionaries attempting to establish a diocese and bring the gospel to a melting pot of frontier families, Mexican settlers, and Native Americans. At one point, one of the priests, Father Vaillant, describes an experience that gives him a clue to his missionary vocation:

Down near Tucson, a Pima Indian convert once asked me to go off into the desert with him, as he had something to show me. He took me into a place so wild that a man less accustomed to these things might have mistrusted and feared for his life. We descended into a terrifying canyon of black rock, and there in the depths of a cave, he showed me a golden chalice, vestments and cruets, all the paraphernalia for celebrating Mass.

His ancestors had hidden these sacred objects there when the mission was sacked by Apaches, he did not know how many generations ago. The secret had been handed down in his family, and I was the first priest who had ever come to restore to God his own. To me, that is the situation in a parable. The Faith, in that wild frontier, is like a buried treasure; they guard it, but they do not know how to use it to their soul's salvation. A word, a prayer, a service, is all that is needed to free these souls in bondage. I confess I am covetous of that mission. I desire to be the man who restores these lost children to God. It will be the greatest happiness of my life.[1]

This narrative of discovered artifacts would come to represent a calling for Father Vaillant: the buried sacred objects were symbolic of the traces of God buried deep in the souls of all people. The missionary task was not to bring God *to* them but to uncover these relics of faith and assist people to use this knowledge and understanding to pursue the restoration found in the gospel of Jesus. Father Vaillant's divinely appointed vocation, he discerned, was to unearth this treasure and "restore to God his own."

MISSING THE KEY

I (Alan) rediscovered this idea of buried artifacts the hard way. About four years ago, my dad passed away. He had not been in good health for over a decade, and as Deb and I have been living in the U.S., we would often receive phone calls from my brother and sister informing us of another hospital visit or some new treatment plan. Eventually that dreaded call came asking us to instantly return to Australia, as Dad had just a few days left. We immediately flew home to be with my family and share the last few days together with my father.

Now a bit of backstory: Dad could not by any stretch of the imagination be considered a spiritual or religious man, or a seeker of truth—quite the opposite. And he also was not given to reading much at all. The one book I am aware of him reading in his adult life was *Chariots of the Gods*, in which Swiss author Erich von Däniken makes claims about extraterrestrial influences on early human culture.[2] For some reason, this captured my dad's imagination and, from his perspective, it offered a plausible rationale for the origins of human life and civilization. It also, in my mind at least, gave him a way to dodge responsibility for the moral and existential claims of the biblical God.

Oddly, during the last few days of his life, Dad kept asking the believers in our family about the rod and the staff mentioned in Psalm 23. Many of my Christian family members began to think Dad was now all of a sudden interested in the Bible, and proceeded to share with him devotionals about the Lord being the Shepherd of our lives, and how he leads us through the valley of the shadow of death, etc. I knew better. I'd had numerous previous conversations with him about how he believed the rod and the staff were in fact secret weapons given to Moses by aliens—weapons that could split waters, allow his armies to win, and draw water from a rock. These were the secrets to Israel's apparent success. So, far from being curious about the spiritual meaning of Psalm 23, I felt that Dad was in fact "sticking it" to those of us who believed the Bible. I must admit to being somewhat angry with him for mocking us, even as he lay on his deathbed. I thought, "Inappropriate, Dad!"

On the night he died, we were all gathered around his bed. (It was not pretty, as he was really struggling for breath.) Deb noticed a Gideon Bible by the bedside and suggested we should read Psalm 23 to him, given he had been inquiring about it over the last few days. I was too emotional for this, and so my brother read the psalm while I concentrated on praying for Dad and watching his face. Almost unbelievably, as we came to the verse mentioning the rod and the staff, my father died. I mean, *right on that verse*! He entered eternity with those particular words resounding in his ears.

I have to admit this shook me up. What could that possibly mean? I don't believe this was a sign of his salvation (although of course I would not exclude that), but I do think it is significant for me and for the purposes of this book. I have come to believe that through those interminable arguments about aliens and pyramids, disagreements I dismissed as a cheap substitute for real faith dialogue, Dad was actually giving me a key to his soul ... and I had missed it. This drove me back to the rediscovery of what I had previously understood about the artifacts of faith that lie buried in every human soul. A moment of reframation if ever there was one.

Recall how, in chapter four, we discussed various ways in which God might reach into this world, and how the world around us and our own experiences are full of "clues," the signals of transcendence, that point us to a world beyond ... to the meaning of the universe. We observed how these clues present themselves to us in innumerable ways if only we would pay attention. We also looked at how there is an innate longing in us all for something else, as mysterious as it might be. Now consider von Balthasar's brilliant insight into the fundamentally religious human condition:

Man is the creature with a mystery in his heart that is bigger than himself. He is built like a tabernacle around a most sacred mystery [...] It is already there, its very nature is readiness, receptivity, the will to surrender to what is greater, to acknowledge the deeper truth, to cease hostilities in the face of the more constant love. Certainly, in the sinner, this sanctuary is neglected and forgotten, like an overgrown tomb or an attic choked with rubbish, and it needs an effort to clean it up and make it habitable for the divine Guest. But the room itself does not need to be built: it is already there and always has been, at the very center of man.[3]

"The room itself does not need to be built: it is already there." What if my dad's obsession with aliens was the clue to opening his heart to God? What if I had simply followed the clues to my dad's belief system (something inherent to us all), which might have disclosed the existential roots in my father's particular search for meaning in the possibility of aliens? Why was this idea of aliens and UFOs so important to him? What religious need was it addressing? What existential/religious questions was he attempting to resolve? Don't all humans seek to know where they came from, to know the purpose of their lives, and to know where it is all heading? My dad's belief might well have been misdirected, but it was belief nonetheless, and as one of God's good news people, I ought to have taken it more seriously.

This personal story exemplifies our belief that every individual person, in fact every corporate culture, is similarly offering to us the keys to their souls. But because we are so fixed to a formulaic understanding of God and gospel, we are not listening. We therefore fail to even notice these keys, squandering the opportunity to connect people with God in ways that really resonate with their sacred longings as they experience them. Our missionary calling, one similar to Father Vaillant's, is to uncover the traces of God that can be found in each and every person. The keys to the soul have been misplaced and it is going to take some hard work, looking in places we have never considered before, to find what has been lost.

BECOME A DETECTIVE OF DIVINITY

As proclaimers of Jesus and his story, as people who live in an enchanted universe filled with rumors of God and of angels, it is important we learn how to recognize the myriad ways that God touches us outside the realm of what is explicitly "religious." Once we begin to see this, we can then bring the meaning and context to what people are experiencing. God touches us through painful growth experiences of loss and grief, through moments of creative and athletic excellence, through times of victory over our problems, through the tenderness of relationships, and through encounters with the exquisite nature of creation. God's grace falls on the just and the unjust alike; all humanity experiences God's hand. These moments when we touch something eternal and noble and good are God's footprints in our lives—his prevenient grace (see chapter ten). People need to realize that the God they feel they do not know has, in fact, already been at work in their lives in many ways.[4]

The Canadian theologian and preacher Bruxy Cavey once posted this enticing tweet, inviting believers to become detectives of divinity: "God leaves a trail of breadcrumbs in nature, art, science, religion, and every individual life—all leading toward Jesus. Today, let's be alert, stay curious, ask questions, and share the Gospel so we can partner with God and help people complete the journey."[5] Missionally speaking, this is what the Jesuits mean in their motto of "finding God in all things." The metaphor of being a detective, following clues in people's lives and in culture, is a very useful one.

We can take a cue from James Reece (a character in the TV series *Criminal Minds*) regarding the kind of clues we are looking for. "There are certain clues at a crime scene which by their very nature do not lend themselves to being collected or examined. How does one collect love, rage, hatred, fear? Yet, these are the things that we're trained to look for."[6]

SHOW ME YOUR IDOLS AND I'LL SHOW YOU WHO YOU ARE

If you love to travel, then you know when the opportunity comes to visit a new city, there is the temptation to take the road most traveled, going from tourist trap to tourist trap. It's easy to follow the Frommer's Travel Guides, signing up for the double-decker bus tour, and filling a visit with so much frenetic activity that the true essence of the city is neither seen nor experienced. However, probably the best way to see and experience a city is to *walk it*, paying attention as you go to the culture, the people, the customs, the sights, and the sounds. One can enter into the heart of a place by walking a neighborhood or two.

In the book of Acts, we read of Paul attuning his radar to the metropolis of Athens, a city famous for philosophy, architecture, politics, and literature. While exploring the streets, we get the impression he is paying attention and taking note of the spiritual environment of the people God has called him to. We are told, "he was deeply distressed to see that the city was full of idols"(Acts 17:16 NRSV).

The idols of a people say a lot about a city. Just to recap, an idol is anything we try to use to fill what only God can fill, and is therefore anything we use to replace God. Idols are those dimensions of our lives to which we have ascribed ultimate value. When an object, person, or ideology becomes the means by which we try to fill our innermost need for unconditional love, unsurpassable worth, and absolute security, it becomes an idol. Idols often become the quicker, alternative route as we unsuccessfully attempt to fulfill our insatiable longings—longings that will not rest until they find their place in God. As we have seen, humans have an inbuilt homing device that, if allowed to operate according to its original design, will inevitably lead them to God. Idolatry jams up what ought to be an innate instinct for God. Idols are embodiments of misdirected worship, allowing people to falsely satisfy their innate God-hunger.

In the secular West, we typically try to find meaning through what we achieve, what we possess, or whom we impress. It is because of the existential weight invested in them that idols serve as significant pointers to what we think is important in life. This, in turn, forces us to ask: what *really* is being valued/worshipped? What existential issues are being addressed? Why is *this* so important? A people's idols are huge clues to the hearts of both individuals and culture. Show me your idols, and I'll show you who you are.

To be honest, the description we read of Athens (being "full of idols") sounds like any other city or town any of us have ever known, whether it be big or small, urban or country. Tim Keller therefore rightly advises would-be missionaries to contemporary Western culture that engaging people through the lens of idolatry is a more appropriate, more profoundly biblical key to unlocking the souls of the people than justification by faith now is.[7] He is in good company ... Paul thought so too.

PAUL FOUND HIS KEYS

Engaging his hearers through the lens of idolatry is exactly Paul's approach in his speech on Mars Hill (Acts 17). The fact that he was "deeply distressed" indicates he was sensitive to the spirituality of the place. Grieved in his spirit, he empathetically attuned himself to the context. He began to search for the soul keys among the religious artifacts of the city. He did this in at least three ways:[8]

First, "People of Athens! I see that in every way you are very religious" (Acts 17:22). Paul immersed himself in their culture, studying their religions and their idols, in an attempt to uncover the dynamics of their religious quest and to understand how the Athenians resolved the existential dilemmas that all humans face. As we have already noted, idols almost always represent some aspect of human need and desire: the need for protection from the perils of nature, the need for approval, the need for significance, the need for love. Belief systems, whether they be those of Athens or ours today, are sustained by the various dominant stories that shape identity and give meaning. As such, they provide undeniable insights into the human heart.

Decoding a people's religion(s) inevitably involves identifying the defining meaning-narratives of the city/people. This means sorting through those narratives and stories that endure and support a specific line of belief. For instance, when Paul references an idol to "an unknown god," it is highly likely this was a reference to the Corn King, the god Ceres—from where we get our term cereal; this god was seen to die every year (in the form of a seed) and rise again (in the form of the harvest). From this narrative/metaphor of the Corn King, Paul is able to draw a direct line to the death and resurrection of Jesus as the basis of cosmic renewal and salvation.[9] The natural forces of renewal reflected in the idol and the associated belief system, are fulfilled by Jesus.

What are the dominant narratives in our world today and what elements within each of them support a particular way of believing? What kind of morality and ethics are actually present in these stories? What beliefs are being expressed? Why do they capture our attention again and again in an endless cycle? Those are the questions Paul had to ask in Athens and the same ones we need to ask today. Why is the political climate in America at a ridiculously fevered pitch? Is it because we have made being "right" and in control an idol? Why do comfort and financial security drive us to the unhealthiest of places? Is it because the idol of materialism has overtaken us? What has brought about the phenomenon of "helicopter parents"? Is it the idol of safety and control, and the constant element of living in fear?

Second, "A group of Epicurean and Stoic philosophers began to debate with him. Some of them asked, 'What is this babbler trying to say?'" (Acts 17:18). Interestingly, the term "babbler" translates as a "scavenger of thoughts." These sophisticated thinkers saw Paul as someone digging around for bits and pieces of philosophy and theology, scavenging for the "shards of heaven's kaleidoscope" in the collective Athenian soul.

Here we are told that Paul engaged with that quintessentially Greek phenomenon, the philosophers. If Paul was to have any chance of unlocking the Athenian cultural code—or anywhere in the Greco-Roman world for that matter—he would have to grasp the significance of the Hellenist's drive to express what is *real* through philosophy. As detectives searching for clues, it's important to understand that philosophy, at its best, is an honest human quest to make sense of the world.

The questions we must therefore wrestle through include: can we engage and involve ourselves in philosophical thinking, discussions, and debate (without drawing the lines of separation and raining judgment down on the "wrong" side)? As we pay attention to the culture within which we are immersed—who is being read, what are the current bestsellers, who are the influential authors (both academic and pop culture) ... and why? Author Brené Brown provides a pertinent example. What nerve has she struck that her TED Talk on "The Power of Vulnerability" has been watched over 38 million times?[10] What is it about her books that has intrigued individuals across a broad spectrum? Or what is it about the British philosopher Alain de Botton's writing that resonates so deeply with so many? Or why the fascination with psychology professor Jordan Peterson, an incredibly polarizing author and speaker? Or you can go more technical and ask the same questions about the thinking of Slavoj Žižek or Friedrich Nietzsche? What is it about their messages that connects with today's society? We cannot be afraid to ask those questions and have those conversations.

And third, in Paul's approach to the Athenians, "As some of your own poets have said"(Acts 17:28). We can affirm that all true art involves some search for meaning, the love of beauty, and the struggle with the tragic. For the Greeks, artists functioned in a similar way to the prophets of the Bible, and poets were often referred to as such. Prophets speak more than they know—their words (or drama, or paintings) hint at a surplus of meaning (a thousand words in one line) that is significant for the society of which they are a part. Paul the missionary intuitively knew this, and so in Athens he studied their artistic expressions, seeking keys to understand and unlock their ultimate desires.

To help us understand our own twenty-first-century culture, we need to be aware of the artists, poets, and writers who are currently attempting to unlock our ultimate desires. We need to consider why some succeed greatly and others fail miserably. Why is it that superhero movies seem to have endless appeal, and millions of people cannot wait to see what Iron Man will do next? Is it because our culture severely lacks anything resembling heroism and we are desperate to find someone we can believe in? Or consider the brilliant 2017 movie *Get Out*. Director Jordan Peele's film isn't just entertainment—it is a commentary on race and prejudice, with prophetic undertones. What are the movies that have connected with the zeitgeist of culture, and why exactly?

Some of the most powerful poets/prophets of our day are the comedians who have struck a cultural chord in uncertain times. The Dave Chappelles, Hannah Gadsbys, and the Trevor Noahs of our world are speaking words that contain a portion of the angst so many people feel but do not know how to articulate. And they are being recognized for their presence in the cultural discourse—Noah, as a satirist, was named one of *Time Magazine*'s Top 100 Most Influential People in the World in 2018. Are we working hard enough to get a pulse on a world so desperate for so many things to be put in their right place? If not, it is most likely because we are either too lazy to put the work in or because we are simply afraid of something being too "unclean" for our sanctified sensibilities.

Obviously, you can make the same observations about the power of music and the influence of songwriters. In the 1960s, Bob Dylan's songs had a gravitational pull to a generation desperately seeking something they were not experiencing anywhere else. Today, Kendrick Lamar and Donald Glover seem to communicate messages that unlock the ultimate desires in people who often feel on the edges of culture. Donald Glover's "This is America" video, released under his musical moniker Childish Gambino (and now viewed over 500 million times), is packed with cultural metaphors and symbolism, clearly resonating with many living in the middle of racial conflict.[11] Following Paul's example, we *must* be aware of the messages our musicians are conveying, as key voices in our culture.

We must be active in all dimensions of human life, especially at the cultural level, because culture is the sphere where people and societies share common meaning. As part of the redemption of all aspects of life, we should be actively interpreting movies, literature, pop culture, experiences, new religious movements, and the like. It is precisely these things that have the elements of human searching and yearning in them that must be correlated to the mind and heart of God if they are to be redeemed.

In answering a call to mission, we need to grapple with the heart resonance, the desires, the griefs, of our "city," our "Athens," and the way those longings are expressed through any and all artistic expressions. We need to pay attention to the songs that grab a generation, the movies that seem to have high resonance and impact, the literature that captures portions of cultures. What are they ultimately communicating? Are they despairing or hopeful? What are they alerting us to? What symbols carry most meaning? What are the primary metaphors? What religious aspect or quest is being named?

Von Balthasar claims that "all great art is religious, an act of homage before the glory of what exists," and the greatness of that art—what in fact makes it religious—is its capacity to transmit that glory and to inspire a response, a transformation, in the subject.[12]

The gospel should always be restated in engagement with the dominant myths, dreams, and images of the age, that is, with the contemporary quest-patterns of a changing world. Therefore, we simply cannot avoid some understanding of the preeminent ideas that have informed, and continue to inform, our culture.

NOT SIMPLY "WHAT" BUT "WHY"

As we learn to be missional anthropologists, we need to not only have an understanding of "what" a culture engages in, but "why" as well. In the book *The Culture Code,* Clotaire Rapaille writes of his experience of being hired by the food and beverage company Nestlé to assist them in their attempt to sell instant coffee in Japan in the 1970s. (A reminder from chapter four—Rapaille is renowned for his research into the determining factors influencing an individual's particular ideas and behaviors.) Prior to hiring Rapaille, Nestlé's strategy was to simply convince the Japanese consumers to make the switch from tea to coffee. They believed they could persuade the Japanese culture to love coffee. They were sorely mistaken.

The narrative of tea was deeply embedded in the culture of the Japanese people. Still, to this day, tea is the most commonly consumed beverage in Japan and is an important part of their culture. "The Tea Ceremony" or "The Way of the Tea" is a ceremonial way of preparing and drinking tea, and there are informal tea gatherings (*chakai*) and formal tea gatherings (*chaji*). Some of these events can last up to four hours. These ceremonies represent the inner, or spiritual experiences of the Japanese people. They take their tea very seriously. If Nestlé was to bring instant coffee into a tea culture in Japan, they were going to have to understand the emotional attachment to tea as well as what attachments, if any, they had to coffee.

Rapaille describes how he gathered focus groups together to understand better how they each felt about coffee, in the hope of learning something that would benefit Nestlé. He tried various activities with the groups, all designed to bring participants back to their first imprint of coffee and the emotion attached to it. In most cases, though, the journey led nowhere. It was determined that their strategy to encourage consumers to switch from tea to coffee could only fail. Coffee could not compete with tea in the Japanese culture if it had such weak emotional resonance. To have any success, they must give the product meaning. They needed to create an imprint for coffee in Japanese culture.[13]

Every narrative of every culture is made up of imprints passed down in a multitude of ways, over many years, and which are deeply rooted, more deeply rooted than we are often willing to take the time to understand. Again, understanding a culture's beliefs and behaviors as a whole is not about the "what" as much as it is about the "why." This seemed to be the way of Jesus. Ever notice how Jesus never answers a question with a straight answer? There doesn't seem to be a single occasion where Jesus answers a question directly.[14] Almost always he puts his finger on the real issue—the subtext—of the matters of the heart, including motivation, sinful disposition, and will. In so doing, he speaks into the existential issue presenting itself—it is partly this that makes Jesus' appeal so mysteriously compelling and relevant.[15]

In Athens we see Paul—that archetypal apostle to the Gentiles—doing what Jesus did (and what Rapaille suggests we do) by going directly to the issue-behind-the-issue implied in the explicit cultural expressions of the Athenians. By engaging its art, poetry, philosophy, and religion, he is effectively deciphering the culture code of that ancient city. He is thus able to speak with resonance to the issues that had historically been the Hellenic people's concern. Ultimately, for Paul and for us, it is about learning to address the heart of the matter.

FOLLOW THE TRACES

So then, following Paul's example, go into your neighborhood, into the places of education, into people's lives, and look for the evidence, the signals of transcendence, the traces of God. Spot the clues of everyday love, rage, servanthood. Here is a short summary list, along with a few more suggestions, to help you in becoming a better detective of divinity:

- Start with prayerful attention: because you want to know what God is already doing in that context or that person's life, we suggest that you ask God, "Lord, what are you doing right now in this home, pub, workplace?" Go on prayer walks, asking the Spirit to reveal what God feels and thinks about what is going on.

- Look for the dominant metaphors in culture: for instance, the so called "digital natives" (those generations who are born into the digital world and feel completely at home in it) already have metaphors that correspond quite well to those of an invisible spiritual world ... the *internet* and *virtual reality*. Digital natives already believe in a world in which you can move back and forth, in the same way the wardrobe was an entrance into the enchanted world of Narnia. They don't have to talk about purely objective facts to know that things are *there*; in the same way they don't have to talk about location and spots on the compass to know that space is *there*.

- What is "the blink" you get of the neighborhood? Deb Hirsch (yes, *that* one) has developed an innovative approach to mission that she calls *incarnational reality*. This involves us learning how to engage our world with all our (spiritual) senses in an attempt to get a full picture of the context. What's the flavor of the neighborhood—does it leave a bad or good taste? Where are the smells—what draws you in and what repels you? What do you see if you look with the eyes of faith? What are you hearing—where are its cries of desperation or shouts of joy?[16]

- What are the people's values and activities telling you about themselves? Where do they spend time? What do they really value? What are their political affiliations and how invested are they in them ... and why?

- What are they (not) reading? If they don't read, where are they getting their information from? Who is defining them? If narrative gives us identity (as we've already noted), what narratives are defining them? What story do they tell themselves in order to make meaning and to negotiate their way in the world?

- Who are their heroes? Why? The logic here is "show me your heroes and I will show you who you are." This is because heroes are embodiments of what we value and believe. A people's heroes are often found in their comic books, literature, and on the sports field, etc.

- Listen to their music: if you've not already noticed, we believe that music is one of the most fertile areas for detective work. The lyrical content alone provides significant clues. Try reading the lyrics of great songs and gauge their poetic strength—be it U2, Bob Dylan,

Tupac, Hozier, Passenger, Joni Mitchell, or Stormzy. Beyond the lyrics themselves, ask yourself what is the mood of the music? What makes it resonate with the soul's search for beauty, justice, relationship, and spirituality?

- Watch the movies that seem to have resonance in the group. As we've already noted, movies give us multiple clues about our culture. What questions are they answering? What yearnings are they appealing to? Sense the drama in the narrative. Who is it that the viewer is bonding with, and why? Does the movie embody a cry for redemption? For rescue? For adventure, perhaps? Love or the despair of lovelessness? These are the existential questions that concern us all.

- Explore the nature of their religious pursuit—both implicit and explicit. Suspend your judgment as to whether you agree or not. Form an outline of their basic spiritual quest (the search for meaning, identity, purpose, and belonging) that is evident in their overt forms of religion but also in their art, poetry, and literature that reveal the soul. Remember, at root all people are spiritual. Humanity is haunted by divinity.

THE SCENT OF A FLOWER WE HAVE NOT FOUND

Taking our cues from Paul's example in Athens, and learning to consider both the "why" and the "what," gives us a way to better understand our world. We must also remember that no one's unbelief, no one's brokenness can turn off the humming; no amount of baggage and hurt from past experiences can wash away the restlessness of the heart because, as we have stated throughout, the search is on. That is the good news.

The bad news, however, is this: people are looking for the right thing in the wrong places. They are going door-to-door searching for that which is true in an attempt to make sense of our world. But what we see played out in front of us day after day might be best described in country musician Johnny Lee's words. In his classic song from that bull ridin', hard livin', country line dancin' cinematic masterpiece *Urban Cowboy*, Lee informs us, "We are looking for love in all the wrong places."[17] Or if you are less into country music and more into science fiction, the *Star Trek: Deep Space Nine* episode "Looking for par'Mach in All the Wrong Places" is titled in tribute to Lee's song. (*Par'Mach* is defined in the episode as "the

Klingon word for love, but with more aggressive overtones.")[18] While not considering ourselves fluent in Klingon *or* country music, both these examples illustrate the ubiquitous phenomenon of searching for the right things in all the wrong places.

According to James K. A. Smith, "The effect of the brokenness in the world is not that we stop being lovers, not that it turns off our love and desires. The effect of sin and brokenness and fallenness is that we start loving the *wrong* things."[19] Because our souls are restless, because there are deep longings within us all, because there is a desire to love and be known, the question is not "*will* we love?" but "*what* will we love?" And the idols we attach ourselves to, especially the besetting and oft repeated ones, provide a profound insight into our inner world and motivations. The French phenomenologist Jean-Luc Marion teaches about the nature of "saturated phenomena." These are signifying events in which something "more" is present. He especially points to idolatry as an example of this. The idol is a saturated phenomenon because it captures our attention more acutely and holds more meaning than other objects, and, as a result, it carries religious significance.[20] The difficulty comes in learning to strip back the overt idolatry in order to expose the inherent yearning for divinity, understanding that God is the fulfilment and completion of all human longing.

G. K. Chesterton reputedly said, "The man knocking on the door of a brothel is unconsciously looking for God." Or a more contemporary translation might be: the young man or woman who swipes right on Tinder is really looking for God. This behavior is clearly broken, and we are not condoning it. But to understand the significance of this, instead of judging the action, ask yourself what is *really* being sought when a person pays someone else for sex? Or what is going on in the innumerable fleeting sexual encounters happening today? Let's identify and name the subtext: the answer ought to highlight the existential quest motivating the action. So it could be an attempt to overcome loneliness in human connection. It could be a search for momentary relief from pain, drudgery, or boredom. It may be the desire to dominate or abuse—this in itself is caused by root issues that can be traced to the existential concerns of the heart.

While they may not overtly acknowledge it, the one ringing the bell of the brothel is covertly reaching for personal union with Beauty, Love, and Joy.

> The books or the music in which we thought the beauty was located will betray us if we trust to them; it was not in them, it only came through them, and what came through them was longing. These things—the beauty, the memory of our own past—are good images of what we really

desire; but if they are mistaken for the thing itself, they turn into dumb idols, breaking the hearts of their worshippers. For they are not the thing itself; *they are only the scent of a flower we have not found*, the echo of a tune we have not heard, news from a country we have never yet visited.[21] (Italics ours.)

Or, consider another possible example of misdirection: when a person goes to a clairvoyant, they are exposing themselves to the occult, but at least in so doing they have indicated they are really interested in the future and their particular role or fate within it. Yes, there is a confusion of means and ends. That we are not denying. But the missional challenge here is to suspend your judgment and try not to critique the overtly sinful behavior. Instead, look at the *person* and what is really being sought and why.

The same "looking for the right things in the wrong places" approach can be seen in one of the most prevalent phenomena in every human life ... the problem of addiction. There is something in the human condition that will substitute reality with false, idolatrous alternatives when it cannot, or will not, engage with real life; addiction is just one way humans attempt to deny reality.

Let's analyze drug addiction as an example: what is the existential subtext when people are taking drugs? There are probably two broad reasons—first, the need to medicate or alleviate a sense of anxiety or pain at facing life, and second, a desire to be lifted out of what is perceived to be a dull and boring life, to experience a form of ecstasy.[22] The addict's strategy is an attempt to short-circuit the hard work of real engagement with the issues at stake. He or she has instead taken to a counterfeit method of escaping pain or chosen a shortcut to gain real pleasure.

Drugs are inherently spiritual—that is part of their appeal. Sure, drugs are cheap alternatives to real prayer and spirituality, which require sacrifice and discipline, but that does not mean they don't fulfill something of a spirituality. My (Alan) own testimony confirms this; as a young man I can still recall how my friends and I used to get high, and we almost inevitably ended up talking about God, the cosmos, meaning/lessness, love, and of course, good and evil. In fact, when the leader of our circle had an encounter with the Holy Spirit at a local Pentecostal church one night, he brought the good news of Jesus right into our midst, and he ended up leading me to Jesus. I discovered that everything I was seeking for in drugs—a yearning for ecstatic experience and/or the escape from meaningless suffering—was perfectly fulfilled through Christ. There were no churches, evangelistic rallies, or any "Christians" involved at all—that all came later. In my ongoing involvement among people on the edge (Burning Man or the local city), I have seen time and again that God will be found by those who seek him, no matter which way they might come to him. That is true for all our stories, not just those of the drug-addicted.

Addictions are just symptoms of some deep brokenness at the core of human nature. They occur when the most basic of drives, yearnings, and desires that can only ultimately be fulfilled in God, are substituted with those things, people, ideas that promise everything, but deliver only bondage and death. Again, a prime example of looking for the right things in the wrong place.

Obviously, this thinking can be applied to any behavior. The issue is the direction or misdirection of our loves and desires. As we explored in chapter four, Augustine wrote of ordered and disordered loves and of evil being a perversion or negation of the good. C. S. Lewis similarly taught that all our vices are really virtues gone wrong—of looking for the right things in the wrong places.[23]

> It would seem that Our Lord finds our desires not too strong, but too weak. We are half-hearted creatures, fooling about with drink and sex and ambition when infinite joy is offered us, like an ignorant child who wants to go on making mud pies in a slum because he cannot imagine what is meant by the offer of a holiday at the sea. We are far too easily pleased.[24]

If we require proof of these misdirected desires, we simply need only search our own hearts to know the truth of this. What are we ourselves really looking for in the places our longings take us? Recognizing our own motivations, desires, and temptations will allow us to see in them a mirror of all human desire. It will allow us to see each other for who we all really are—souls with the image of God buried within, deeper in some than others. So the next time we feel unable to connect with people who party hard or who dress and act differently, consider our own desire for belonging, for joy, and our longing for something beautiful. We can at least affirm that in others. The next time we feel unable to connect with people who are just driven by money and prestige, think about our own desires for significance, meaning, and the desire to make a name for ourselves ... Just remember that our own vices are virtues gone wrong. At the end of the day we are all merely beggars pointing out to the other beggars where to get the bread. It is in this recognition of our common humanity that we must learn to meet others.

UNWRAPPING THE WOUNDS OF CULTURE

The good news is that, even in the midst of our common brokenness, Jesus has entered in and drawn close to us in a world full of division and hurt and has offered an opportunity to find the right thing in the right places. And we can look to him, as always, for an example of how exactly to go about this.

In a fascinating story in John's Gospel, the author tells us that Jesus *has* to go through Samaria on one of his journeys. He *has* to go through this land of division and animosity, a land with centuries of volatility based upon centuries of widespread scorn and deep hatred.

He arrives at a well at noon, in the heat of the day, thirsty. While there, a Samaritan woman comes to the well alone (a sign she is most likely ostracized from her own community). Jesus asks her for a drink, and, in doing so, breaks through two cultural barriers: one, she is a Samaritan and, two, she is a woman.

The woman is taken aback by this Jewish man speaking to her, but even more so when he tells her, "If you knew the generosity of God and who I am, you would be asking *me* for a drink, and I would give you fresh, living water" (John 4:10 MSG). The woman appears to be a combination of amused and dumbfounded. And then, almost out of the blue, Jesus gets personal:

> Jesus said to her, "Go, call your husband, and come back." The woman answered, "I have no husband." Jesus said to her, "You are right in saying, 'I have no husband'; for you have had five husbands, and the one you have now is not your husband. What you have said is true!"
>
> JOHN 4:16–18 NRSV

(Sometimes it doesn't seem fair to have a conversation with Jesus!)

Jesus speaks not only to a Samaritan, but a Samaritan woman, a Samaritan woman who had been married *five* times. But notice, in Jesus' voice there is no disqualification, no condemnation. Instead, Jesus appeals to the desire of her heart with great compassion, to the place she has looked for love for so long, and he points out the dehumanizing cycle she has become trapped in by going from relationship to relationship, none of which have brought her what she really wanted or needed. Jesus takes the cover off her life.

Her response? Religious talk—a discussion about which temple is the "right" temple. For her, as is the case for many today, engaging in "religious" talk is easier than being transparent about the brokenness of her life. Jesus does not fall for it. He paints a picture of God, not as a place to worship, but as a person to be experienced.

Jesus bridged the cultural distance. He entered into the division and hatred and moved in close, going against accepted cultural norms. Jesus offered her the very thing she had spent her life searching for but had been unable to find. Refusing to get caught up in a discussion about religion, he instead focused on the good news he was bringing. He didn't speak to her about morality or purity. Instead, Jesus spoke of her thirst, her longing. Without realizing it, the woman had long desired only that which Jesus could give, and here, at this well, she was just beginning to understand what that was.

Jesus gave this woman a picture of God that she and others had never seen before. You might even say he brought about a great reframation in her understanding of the divine. In our search for the keys to a culture, and in our quest to uncover the sacred artifacts embedded deeply in each person—if we are able to take seriously the example of Paul in Athens and Jesus in Samaria—we just might accomplish a similar reframing.

ROMANCING
THE CITY

(LIKE GETTING CAUGHT
IN THE RAIN)

If the signals of transcendence have become rumors in our time, then we can set out to explore these rumors—and perhaps to follow them up to their source.

— PETER L. BERGER

If you love each thing, you will perceive the mystery of God in things.

— FYODOR DOSTOEVSKY

Being incarnational is like getting married.
Being incarnational is like making love.
Being incarnational is like candlelit dinners.
Being incarnational is like Piña Coladas and getting caught in the rain.

— MICHAEL FROST

In quite possibly the most painfully excruciating eight minutes of film ever recorded, Prince Charles (Prince of Wales and heir apparent to the British throne) was interviewed in 1981 alongside his newly announced fiancée, Diana Spencer. In what is labeled their "engagement interview," Charles and Diana's attempt to describe their courtship and pending nuptials succeeds in making all who watch feel quite uncomfortable in *so* many different ways. When the interviewer asks the couple, "I suppose then that the two of you are in love?" the nineteen-year-old Diana responds immediately, "Of course." In contrast, the ever-starchy Charles, almost thirteen years her elder, pauses briefly, then responds in the most impersonal and dispassionate of ways, "Well, I suppose so ... whatever *being in love* means."[1] How romantic. History proceeds to confirm what anyone viewing would have immediately realized: poor Diana should have run away as fast as she could at that very instant.

This "Prince Charles way of thinking" is similar to the wife who asks the husband, "But, darling, do you love me?" to which the man replies, "Of course I love you. I married you, didn't I? I told you at the ceremony that I loved you, and if I changed my mind, I'd let you know. What more do you need from me? We had a ceremony, didn't we?" It effectively communicates that the grand gesture and declaration of a wedding says and does all that needs to be said and done.

As we grow in relationship with others, we must acknowledge that any proclamation in word and deed must go deeper than grand gestures and declarations. In helping people look for love in the right places, we must learn to *court* those we encounter. Ultimately, what we are trying to articulate is this: the church cannot continue proclaiming the good news of Jesus in the same way Prince Charles approached love and marriage.[2]

OF SPEED DATES AND ONE-NIGHT STANDS

As we have described in chapters four and five, we lack true understanding of our Camino and Burning Man pilgrims because we fail to get to know them; we tend to exegete Scripture pretty well while failing miserably at exegeting the culture/s in which we are immersed. This is like going on multiple first dates, all of which rarely make it past introductions and an appetizer, and should probably be described as "speed dating evangelism." Hardly the way of Jesus, who loved the world so much that he moved into the neighborhood for thirty years and no one noticed! Following this (incarnational) way of love, we simply have to find ways to *romance our culture*, to lovingly engage with the hearts of people who have no real idea how wide and deep an experience of God can be. We must move toward something deeper than a cursory announcement and proclamation of love, void of relationship.

Consider my (Mark) first date with my wife of thirty-one years, Monica. My attempt to woo her included all the extravagancies a twenty-two-year-old college senior could muster: I was clad in my best, and only, polo shirt which, by the way, I had ironed for the occasion (a grand gesture indeed for someone who had never used an iron before); I had packed a picnic basket replete with the only food I knew how to prepare on a grill (hamburgers and corn on the cob); and we spent the entire day in the beautiful Great Smoky Mountains National Park, including watching the sunset in the extraordinarily gorgeous Cades Cove. It was an unbelievable fifteen-hour start to a relationship with the greatest person I have ever known. And yet, as grand a gesture as that first date had been—including the monumental accomplishment of ironing not only my shirt but my plaid pastel shorts as well—it was just the beginning. I had to learn many other ways to win her heart. I had to learn the subtle and romantic art of *wooing*.

Similarly, we fear that too many depend upon grand evangelistic gestures to "win souls for Jesus." ("Of course we love you, we planted a church for you, didn't we? ... Yes, we are devoted to the community. We've built this multi-purpose building for you to come to. It even has a food court.") Many of us are unwilling to engage in the loving work of "wooing people to Jesus" that is necessary in our post-Christian world. The telling of the good news cannot simply be about the grand gesture, the ceremonial presentation. So, as we began the discussion in the last chapter, we continue to explore some basic practices that must occur if we are to move beyond the lip service of a prescriptive gospel story and into rhythms that will help us plumb the depths of the image of God buried deep within us all.

We want to suggest that the idea of *romancing your city*—a metaphor first suggested by Michael Frost—is an incredibly useful way of approaching incarnational mission with an eye to winning the love of the person/people we are seeking to reach. What will it take to romance a culture well? What has to happen for a relationship to be developed that could transform *both* parties? We propose it is the same thing it takes to go beyond a first date: we will need to find the keys to the beloved's heart, to attend, to court, to woo, with the intention of marriage, for better or worse, richer or poorer. It will require a willingness to learn about and to understand someone else, a willingness to consciously stop talking about yourself and what only *you* believe for a moment. And it will require stepping outside your own cultural box and learning to ask questions about the other—simple, genuinely curious questions, not ones designed to lead someone to your cleverly designed agenda for the relationship, but instead, questions that lead to a genuine understanding of the other. Those who are the worst at romance are those who have not learned how to simply pay attention, listen, and *interpathize* (we will explain this term later). We need to develop some rhythms and practices, which we will now explore.

THE ART OF PAYING ATTENTION

One of the most significant missional leaders in Australia (and a mentor and friend of Alan's) was a man named John Smith. A prolific activist, communicator, and missionary, John engaged in many schools, pubs, motorcycle gangs, Parliament, and anything in between. I (Alan) clearly remember John talking at a conference about prevenient grace and telling stories to a packed room full of young leaders (of which I was one)—stories about how he made it his practice to find out what God was doing in the odd and edgy places of our culture.

John told a story of how one day, after speaking at one such large event, a young woman approached him and told him she had been profoundly moved by what he had said and she very much needed to talk further about Jesus and his meaning for her life.[3] Unfortunately, the event had gone on too long and she, somewhat enthralled by his message, realized she was late for work, so she begged John to meet with her later that evening so they could talk further. Always a passionate evangelist, he of course agreed. She then thrust a piece of paper in his hand, asking him to meet her at that address, and then she ran off.

Later, when he checked the note, he realized he had just agreed to meet her at one of the city's most notorious strip clubs. He decided to go nonetheless. (And while he did go alone, there were some legitimate reasons for his choice, and so we ask that you suspend your judgment here.) At the strip club, he found a table, and asked the waitress to get Linda (not her real name). When the waitress returned, she brought him a drink but sans Linda. He told her that he had been asked to meet Linda there that night. The waitress, still not believing the story, asked for his name. When he told her his name was John Smith, she replied, "Oh yeah, *sure*, everyone is called 'John Smith' in this place." Eventually, however, he persuaded her to get Linda.

When Linda arrived, she thanked John profusely for coming to this risqué place and began to tell him the story of her life: She had always loved dancing and always wanted to be a performer. At seventeen she met a young Christian guy and fell in love. At some point he had taken her to hear John preach at his local church, and that day she became a Christian. However, things were not all well; her boyfriend came from an ultraconservative denomination that looked down on all types of activities as "worldliness," especially dancing in any form, and not long after, the parents forced the young man to end their relationship on those grounds. It was dancing *or* teenage love. Because of her deep sense of calling, Linda chose dancing, but having to make this choice devastated her. Believing all Christians to be soul-crushing legalists, she subsequently gave up on the church and on Christians, and devoted herself to a career in dancing.

Now, life is difficult for professional dancers and she, like many in the arts, struggled to find work in her chosen calling. But following her longing to dance, and against her better judgment, she ended up stripping for a living. It was not the best solution, but she explained adamantly that she was not a prostitute and that the leering men could not touch her, and well, at least here, she could dance ... and get paid for it.

She talked to John about her family, her dreams, Jesus, and the meaning of life, and that she felt it was time for her to come back to Jesus. When the time came for her to do her strip dance, she turned to John and, while acknowledging that it was a lot to ask, she asked him to stay and watch her performance because it had everything to do with the story of her life. John thought this was taking it a bit far, but again Linda prevailed, and he stayed for her performance. The choice of song was a beautifully mournful melody by Janis Ian called "At Seventeen." The song is all about rejection and being an "ugly duckling." Linda had actually woven the story of her loss of faith into her strip act ... her "art." Later that night, John had the privilege and joy of praying with Linda about a "coming home in the faith," right there in the strip club.

Now I (Alan) remember being in that room full of enthralled young leaders as John recounted this story. I still remember the stunned silence as John then asked a question, one that in a moment changed my entire perspective of mission: "Was Jesus in that strip club that night?" Can God be found in that place of tragedy and brokenness, and in others like them? There is no other biblical answer than, "Yes, of course." We now found ourselves on the horns of a dilemma: if this was so, that God really was in that place, wooing Linda to himself through Jesus Christ, is it all right for us as God's people to join him in his mission in these places? And again, I believe we are forced to affirm that it is not only possible, but that it is necessary that *some* of God's people join him in these so-called "godforsaken" places of the city.

Now be sure, the point we want to make here is not that all believers should go to strip clubs and evangelize strippers. That's incidental to the real (God) story going on in the narrative. The question that must drive us is whether we can join with God in his mission—learning to pay attention in whatever place we find ourselves.

FIND OUT WHAT GOD IS ALREADY DOING

Jesus said, "The truth is that the Son does nothing on His own; *all these actions are led by the Father.* The Son watches the Father closely and then mimics the work of the Father" (John 5:19 The Voice). In other words, when Jesus goes to the pub or to the market (or to the strip club, for that matter), he is always looking for what the Father is already doing, and he subsequently joins the Father in what he is *already* doing. And we believe this is exactly what we need to do when engaging in any and every context of life.

Finding God everywhere is at the core of a missional spirituality rooted in our growing awareness that God can be found in every person, in every place, and in all things. This means we must pay attention. We must learn to become aware of *what* it is God is doing and *where* it is that he is doing it. Again, in the words of Jesus, "I have not ever acted, and will not in the future act, on My own. I listen *to the directions of the One who sent Me* and act *on these divine instructions. For this reason*, My judgment is always fair and never self-serving. I'm committed to pursuing God's agenda and not My own" (John 5:30 The Voice).

Recognizing this pattern in the life of Jesus, Brad Brisco notes that we often wrongly assume the primary activity of God is in the church.[4] He says that the primary activity of God is in the world, and the church is the chief instrument created by God to be sent into the world to participate in what he is already doing. Therefore, instead of ministry being all about human ingenuity and what we can do for God, it is rather about discovering what God is already doing, and in light of our gifts and resources, discerning how he wants us to join him.[5] Brad is not alone in speaking like this. In fact, here he is drawing deeply from the wells of our greatest missional theology.

For instance, Lesslie Newbigin reiterated that, while the kingdom of God is always present in the church, God's sovereignty must never be allowed to become the domesticated possession of the church. "Mission is not simply the self-propagation of the church. On the contrary, the active agent of mission is a power that rules, guides, and goes before the church: the free, sovereign, living power of the Spirit of God." Speaking from forty or so years of experience as a missionary to India, he notes that:

> Mission is not just something that the church does; it is something that is done by the Spirit, who is himself the witness, who changes both the world and the church, who always goes before the church in its missionary journey. It is therefore not enough to speak of the proclamation of the kingdom and of the presence of the kingdom; we must also speak of the prevenience, the previousness of the kingdom.[6]

The kingdom of God is prior to, and also beyond, the church. It is God's rule and sovereignty over the entire universe. By definition it is not, and cannot be, limited to the church. This means that when we begin to articulate good news to someone who does not yet believe, we can be assured that God has concerned himself with this person long before the would-be evangelist ever arrived. In fact, contextualization of the gospel depends as much on finding out how Christ is *already* active in the culture as it does on bringing Christ to the culture. The Bible affirms throughout that God is constantly at work in the world in many ways, in every time, and in different places. "Evangelism is not about Christians working on God's behalf because God is powerless without them. Effective evangelism must start with recognizing where God is already at work, and getting alongside God in what is going on there. God's story, not ours, is the authentic starting point."[7] In fact, this theme of preparatory grace goes back to the early church in the teaching of the so-called *praeparatio evangelica*, that an anticipation of the Christian message can be found in all cultures and in every human heart.

The calling of those who follow Jesus is to lovingly attend to what God is doing and join in—bringing a little romance to those around them. Darrell Guder agrees:

> Missionaries, beginning with the New Testament apostles and continuing today, constantly encounter the preparatory work of God's Spirit when they enter into a new place. They do not bring the gospel: Christ, as Lord over heaven and earth, is already there. Christ brings his witnesses across frontiers into new areas of mission. They then witness to the reality of Christ as they find words, experiences, images, and metaphors in another language for the testimony of faith—we think of Paul's address on the Areopagus. At the same time, they translate the gospel into practices that demonstrate the meaning of God's love in Christ.[8]

One of the terrifying conclusions of the much-reduced heretical gospel (chapters one to three) that grips the church in the West, is that it has bequeathed to most evangelicals the concept that somehow we've got God in our back pocket. Many believe, either implicitly or explicitly, that somehow we transport him like a commodity, and we "take God" with us wherever we go. The assumption is that he just arrives on the scene when we get there and not before. We dialogue with people about God, assuming they have had no prior God experiences—theophanies, yearnings, religious experiences of the transcendent, and the like. We conclude they were entirely godless and unspiritual before we came along. As we have already seen, this is simply unbiblical; it cannot explain Paul's approach to the Greek people in Athens, let alone our own personal stories of experiencing the good news (which imply God came and "found" us where we were too … lost without Christ, just like Linda in the strip club).

Isn't God everywhere present? Surely by virtue of his immanence in all things, the creator God was/is always already present in every dimension of the universe. As redeemer God, he is always wooing, forever courting, constantly wowing. God is relentless in his pursuit, by his Spirit; he's always on the scene long before we get there with our tracts and our religious formulas. He has always been there, waiting for us to become aware enough to show up, forever pointing us toward his Son in a gesture of appeal: "Hey, check out my magnificent Son! Isn't he utterly amazing? Go to him!" The great Hans Urs von Balthasar goes as far as to talk about God actually "hunting" us down like prey: "When man seeks God, God is long before in search of man, and like the woman looking for her lost coin, God turns the house of man upside down. Man may hunt for God like one pursuing a deer with bloodhounds through fire and water, against lance and pike, but God's hunt for man is even wilder."[9]

FINDING GOD IN A THORNY SHRUB

In Exodus 3, after four decades of walking around the same few hundred acres of desert, tending sheep and raising a family, the life of Moses was forever changed on one particular day. While tending his sheep, he came upon a burning bush ("a thorny shrub" in Hebrew) that did not burn up. Dry plants make good tinder, and lightning strikes can quickly set them ablaze, so this may not have necessarily been an uncommon sight. What is unusual in this scene is the fact that the bush does not burn up. As God speaks to Moses out of this thorny bush and changes the course of the Hebrew narrative, we retrospectively realize this is a phenomenon generally called a "theophany," a tug of the infinite, a visible manifestation of God. This theophany in particular includes a direct call from God to an incredibly important task. In Moses' case, the call was to bring the Israelites out of Egypt.

To read this story well, a few questions must be wrestled with, especially in light of our quest to become aware of the prevenience of God: how long had the bush been burning before Moses was able to stop long enough to notice it? How long did he have to stare at it to realize it wasn't going to burn up? And when God told him to take off his shoes for he was on holy ground, how long had the ground been holy? A long time? Had Moses just missed God calling him because he hadn't been able to pay attention to what God had been doing all along? Rabbi Lawrence Kushner writes,

"The burning bush was not a miracle. It was a test. God wanted to find out whether or not Moses could pay attention to something for more than a few minutes. When Moses did, God spoke."[10]

If Kushner is correct, we have to consider for ourselves—are we simply too busy and preoccupied to pay attention to the fact that we are standing on holy ground? (Not that we *might* be, but that we *are*.) Do our desires and longings lead us to fill our schedules to the brim, so much so that we fail to notice God speaking to us because we are just too busy "doing ministry"? And how long exactly has he been calling and we haven't noticed?

Can we learn the practice of paying attention and apply that rhythm to our lives?

> Day by day, year by year, your own story unfolds, your life's story. Things happen. People come and go. The scene shifts. Time runs by, runs out. Maybe it is all utterly meaningless. Maybe it is all unutterably meaningful. If you want to know which, pay attention.
>
> The unexpected sound of your name on somebody's lips. The good dream. The odd coincidence. The moment that brings tears to your eyes. The person who brings life to your life. Maybe even the smallest events hold the greatest clues. If it is God we are looking for [...] maybe the reason we haven't found him is that we are not looking in the right places. Pay attention.[11]

THE ART OF LISTENING

In addition to the practice of paying attention, if we are going to move toward a deeper anthropological understanding of a culture, we will need to learn to *listen* well. We must learn the rhythm of stopping, noticing the bush is burning, absolutely. But we must move beyond awareness and learn the art of listening.

Listening is one of the least practiced skills among the church (like a bad first date, we love to be the ones talking). And yet, if Jesus' followers are serious about entering into a culture with a story of good news that will change the world, we should probably seek to understand exactly what good news is to those we are in relationship with. If only we will listen, they are telling us how to love them, how to bring the gospel to them. Or, as the inventor of the stethoscope, René Laennec, famously stated, "Listen, listen, listen to your patients, they are telling you the answer."

British church leader Mike Breen tells the story of certain English missionaries, well-supplied with money and resources, who travel to a slum in a small village in India, prepared to start a ministry, build a clinic, establish a new church, whatever this impoverished village needed. Fortunately, the missionaries were smart enough to adopt a posture of listening. The leaders of the village were very clear what good news was to their people: "What we really need is a PIN [zip] code, a post box, and a post office." The missionaries responded with, "Yes, of course. We can do that, sure. But what about a 'big ticket item'? What can we build for you? What can we throw our money toward? Please tell us."

The response of the people was a simple: "No, really … what we'd like, what we need is a PIN code. In the poorest parts of our country, if you are considered a slum by the governmental system, and you don't have a PIN code then you don't exist on a map. There could be 20,000 people living in the village, but if you don't have a PIN code, you don't exist. Without a PIN code we're not entitled to social services, any forms of structure, or health care. Without a PIN code you are invisible. If you are really here to help, and if you're really listening to what we are saying, the whole world would open up to us if we could get a post box."

The missionaries listened. It took two years, but the place finally became registered as a neighborhood and this small village finally had a PIN code. It happened, partially because the privileged missionaries were able to posture themselves to listen to their "patients," rather than dictating the particulars of the good news for these villagers.[12]

Of course, multiple examples of how *not* to listen are happening every day, throughout the world; on busy city streets, men (it seems like it's always men) stand upon their literal soapboxes and inform each and every person passing by about their impending journey to hell. These one-way proclamations have not one ounce of demonstration or dialogue about them. Most of you reading this book would never engage in, or endorse, these kinds of methods. Yet, if we were really honest, how different do Sunday morning worship gatherings appear to onlookers, as men (again, mostly men) stand on stages higher than a soapbox and speak/shout in similar ways? When will the art of listening (and dialogue) ever become a regular practice? What if we could make people feel like they're not invisible anymore?

LISTENING TO EVERYONE'S STORY

The recent book *Church Refugees* is a deep dive into some very important questions that highlight our inability to listen well. Authors Josh Packard and Ashleigh Hope wrote the book in an attempt to ask and answer two key questions: "Why is church so bad to some people? And more important sociologically, what happens to our society if this central institution continues to drive people away?"[13] They entered into a culture and practiced the art of listening with the *dechurched* and the *dones*. The responses were many and varied, and while Packard and Hope acknowledge that each and every person's story is unique, they also identify and list some common tensions that emerged from the stories they heard:

- They wanted community ... and got judgment.
- They wanted to affect the life of the church ... and got bureaucracy.
- They wanted conversation ... and got doctrine.
- They wanted meaningful engagement with the world ... and got moral prescription.

The authors go on to comment that,

> More than anything what the dechurched want is a home in the truest sense of the word. A place that's safe and supportive and refreshing and challenging. An identifiable place, embedded in a larger community where they both know and are known by those around them and where they feel they can have a meaningful impact on the world. They long for the same kind of church that we all long for. They desire a church that's active and engaged with the world, where people can bring their full and authentic selves and receive love and community in return.[14]

Our purpose in this space is not to address the themes highlighted in Packard and Hope's research but instead to draw attention to *Church Refugees* as a great example of people asking the right questions and learning the art of listening.

Ultimately, we need to learn to reverse the megaphone. Those on the Camino and at Burning Man view followers of Jesus as using funnel-shaped megaphones to yell their message louder and louder. Instead, we need to learn to hold the small end of a megaphone up to our ear so that it acts as an amplifier for what people are saying to us, instead of what we're saying to them. This would greatly assist us in this practice of listening.

THE ART OF INTERPATHY

"Last night, for the first time in my life, I hugged a white man." There is no denying this might appear to be somewhat of an odd phrase. Roy Taylor, my (Mark) now dear friend, spoke those words to me in a tiny church in Hollis, Queens, New York over twenty-five years ago. I was part of a group that had been working all week at Brother Roy's church, helping with a variety of things, including holding what he referred to as "Revival Services" every evening. On one particular evening, I gave the message and when I had finished speaking, Brother Roy, all five foot, four inches of him, awkwardly hugged me as I stepped to my seat.

In my ignorance, I was completely unaware that this hug was such a significant and earth-shattering event. But it was to Brother Roy, and it should have been to me. His church consisted of about thirty people, all of whom had immigrated to the U.S. in the past twenty years or so. If I'd had any awareness of the weight of racial baggage that he and the other people in his church had carried for so long, I would have understood at least some of their pain. Not only did they live as people of a different color amongst a white-dominated world, but they also experienced the travails of coming to live in this different land where they were rarely treated fairly or with dignity.

I really did not understand how they saw the world and how the world saw them. I did not understand the story they had lived. Not because I wasn't there to see and understand, but because I had never bothered to really look. In the current racial climate in the United States (Ferguson, MO; Charlottesville, VA; Black Lives Matter; and the ever-widening gap between law enforcement and the people), there is an even greater urgency to learn and understand a world so different to our own. But in this situation, twenty-five years ago, I had not done the necessary work. In my cluelessness, I failed to work diligently to understand this community's societal narrative of oppression, racism, and utter brokenness.

Ours is a world that is still resistant to understanding and learning about any culture other than our own. This resistance can either be caused by defiance or simply naïveté, or sometimes a balance of the two. We do not love "the other" well because we do not *know* "the other." Either by commission or omission we are guilty of not paying attention and not listening.

In Harper Lee's Pulitzer Prize winning *To Kill a Mockingbird*, the protagonist and narrator, "Scout Finch," is a young girl in southern Alabama who is forced to grow up quickly in the ever-changing world of the

1930s. Her father, Atticus, becomes the attorney for a black man accused of raping a white woman. Six-year-old Scout and her older brother, Jem, are thrust into the middle of the complexities of race and social class and "the other."

In an attempt to help her understand the social intricacies of the 1930s culture, Atticus tells his daughter "If you can learn a simple trick, Scout, you'll get along a lot better with all kinds of folks. You never really understand a person until you consider things from his point of view ... until you climb into his skin and walk around in it."[15] Atticus' words seem to be instructional wisdom for us as we attempt to make our way forward toward a telling of the story of God and the world that reframes our sense of both.

A term that missiologists use to describe this strong sense of affinity with a group of people, a cross-cultural form of empathy, is *interpathy*. Interpathy is a sense of *feeling* with the other, *climbing into another's skin and walking around in it*. It describes that depth of relationship when an outsider to a particular community develops a burden in her/his heart for that group. It refers to the capacity for an outsider to pick up a community's sense of values, what has hurt them, and where they're headed as a people group. It's a form of identification so deep that the guest/missionary almost becomes one of the tribe ... an insider.[16] The practice of interpathy is key when empathy crosses cultural boundaries.[17]

"In interpathic 'feeling with,' empathy is extended beyond known borders to offer a grace that draws no lines, refuses limits, claims universal humanness as sufficient foundation for joining another in a unique world of experience."[18] The practice of interpathy

> involves "bracketing" one's own beliefs and values and temporarily entering a very different world of beliefs and values. This is a radical and serious attempt to engage across cultural boundaries. It seeks not only to recognize and respect another in their "otherness" but also to attempt to share that otherness in as much as one is able to. Such ability is required of the historian, anthropologist and translator.[19]

As anthropologists (learning to be cultural exegetes) and translators (of the good news of Jesus), are we able to practice interpathy?

The story is told of an encounter the French poet Jacques Prévert had with a beggar on the street. The man held a sign that said, "Blind man without a home." Prévert approached the man to learn if he was getting any donations. "Oh, no," the man replied. "People pass by and drop nothing in my hat, the swines." Rather than putting money in the man's cup, Prévert took the sign from him and altered it. A few days later, he came upon the beggar again and asked if things had changed. "Oh, yes. It's wonderful. My hat fills up three times a day." Prévert had changed the phrase on the sign to say, "Spring is coming, but I won't see it." And now, when people came upon the blind man, they entered into a different story with him. They were invited into the practice of interpathy. They put themselves in *his* place, crossed a boundary into *his* circumstance of life. By remembering their own springtime memories, they could understand the great tragedy this man was living.[20] We believe it is possible that practicing interpathy changes not only how someone views the world but how they respond to it.

IT'S ALL ABOUT HOW YOU BEGIN

Learning missional rhythms should always begin by first immersing ourselves in a given context, rather than presuming we know the answers. In other words, we cannot frontload our mission with preformed ideas and models, assuming that what works in one context will readily apply in another. Different people groups experience the world differently. You need to *listen* in order to *see*. It is all about how you begin: if you begin with a theory, you begin with the answers, and the theory will always confirm what you (think you) already know. But begin with observation, and you begin with questions.

NewStory Church in the Edgewater neighborhood of Chicago, founded by Dory and Rich Gorman, suggest that in order to understand the people to whom you wish to bring good news, you have to go into a neighborhood and ask five questions related to the following issues:

- *Power*: Who are the powerful? Who are the powerless and why? What has the gospel got to say about that?
- *Pennies*: Who are the rich? Who are the poor? What does the gospel have to say about that?
- *Pain*: Where is the pain of the neighborhood? What does the gospel have to say about that?
- *Parties*: Where are the celebrations? How can we affirm and join in?
- *Persons of Peace*: Who are the gatekeepers of the community and how can I serve them?[21]

Jon Ritner, the leader of Ecclesia Hollywood (the Hirschs' base church when they lived in Los Angeles), says that mission is really a pretty simple affair: just find out what sucks in the neighborhood, find others that agree with you, and do something about it. How hard is that?

LIKE FALLING IN LOVE FOR THE FIRST TIME

Ultimately, all these examples and practices should lead us to a wi[l]der appreciation of God, his story, and his world. Adopting these rhythms will help us grasp what truly sounds like ravishingly good news for people in all spaces of life and faith ... something that will make their hearts sing. When we are able to discern what good news looks like in each context, we will find the key to an individual's heart and by extension to the heart of their community.

British evangelist and missiologist Steve Hollinghurst writes:

> Cross-cultural evangelism is not about changing the cultural clothing of an explanation of Jesus' death, but finding which parts of the whole story are "good news" within each culture and starting from these to explore the rest. To use the seed-planting analogy, the gospel is not a single seed that we plant in foreign soil; it is a whole packet of different seeds that together make a harmonious garden. Certain seeds in the packet will take root better in certain soils, others will need a lot of soil cultivation before planting, and others will be best planted much later when the rest of the garden is established. The art of the skillful missionary is to read the unknown soil and understand the seeds in the gospel packet well enough to know which ones to plant first, to discern when they have taken root in a healthy way, and know when it is time to plant the seeds that will be harder to nurture.[22]

Sigmund Freud asserted that religion is "wishful thinking" that merely consoles us. If we reduce the good news to such an extent that Jesus simply serves as an illusion to relieve our anxieties around death, loneliness, and other such issues, then maybe Freud was right.[23] Instead, may we give the gift of news that is greater than our wildest imaginations, news that means death doesn't carry the same weight anymore and that the gospel is not just about where you go when you die, but about the chance you get to truly live *right now.*

When the author of the Gospel of Mark wrote, "The beginning of the good news about Jesus the Messiah, the Son of God" (Mark 1:1), the readers would have known the phrase *good news* or *gospel* or *good tidings* (all the same phrase) was a thoroughly Roman term. It was a phrase connected to pagan festivals and the cult of the emperor.[24] The original hearers of Mark's Gospel would therefore have immediately understood that Mark "was referring to good news that was a cause for a celebration, a historical event that would introduce a radically new situation to the world."[25]

Likewise, any communication or incarnation of good news today should convey something that is a cause for celebration; an event that introduces a radically new situation to the world. The gospel we are to bring to a culture, a city, and a people that we have romanced and loved is a good news that is deeper and greater and wi[l]der than we could ever imagine.

The good news comes knocking on doors that we didn't even know we had; it flings open the curtains on windows we didn't know existed to reveal the rising sun flooding the room with glory when we had imagined that all light came from candles; it woos our cold hearts and awakens them, like someone falling in love for the first time, to a joy and fulfillment never before imagined.[26]

AFTERWORD

MICHAEL FROST

Albert Einstein has been credited with decreeing that everything should be made as simple as possible, but not more so. Sadly, we live in a time when the "more so" is too prevalent. Everything, it seems, has to be oversimplified beyond all sense and purpose.

The President mocks the idea of climate change on snowy days, because climate science has been abridged to some nonspecific belief about things getting warmer.

Black Lives Matter, whose guiding principles include advocating on behalf of black victims who died at the hands of white police officers, as well as being concerned with black-on-black crime, is met with the dismissive and oversimplified "All lives matter!"

Ethical questions regarding reproductive health, indigenous people's rights, racial reconciliation or social welfare, are reduced to slogans and catchcries. People demand that we answer complex questions with a simple yes or no. Radio announcers and news commentators mock those who want to describe the complexity of something and offer multifaceted solutions to tough issues. They decry such answers as convoluted and disingenuous.

As Rev. Byron Williams says, "Whether it's Black Lives Matter, trade agreements, illegal immigration, the economy or something else, we crave oversimplification for a recipe that requires nuance. We seek the simplistic answer when only the difficult response will suffice."[1]

That's because life is complex. It is richly, beautifully, magnificently baffling at times. All the most splendid things in this world—coral reefs, child-raising, social justice, the raging sea, reconciliation, staying married, Antarctica, South Australian cabernet, extended family meals, a sensational cup of coffee—these things are not simple to describe, nor to sustain.

The dumbing down of our society is crushing the life out of us, flattening everything into two dimensions, dicing it all into bite-sized pieces.

And the church is just as guilty of this reductionism. We want to shrink-wrap our truth claims too.

So, the big, wide, expansive understanding of the reign of God that Christ taught us has been reduced to merely information about how to go to heaven when you die. The mission of God's people is downgraded to an ecclesial recruitment strategy. All the recent talk about a *missional* church is condensed into discussions about style and venue, as if all there is to being missional is to meet in a bar and have a pastor with a hipster beard and tattoos.

As Walter Brueggemann says,

> The gospel is [...] a truth widely held, but a truth greatly reduced. It is a truth that has been flattened, trivialized, and rendered inane. Partly, the gospel is simply an old habit among us, neither valued nor questioned. But more than that, our technical way of thinking reduces mystery to problem, transforms assurance into certitude, quality into quantity, and so takes the categories of biblical faith and represents them in manageable shapes.[2]

We want to take a truth that's as big as an ox and turn it into a bouillon cube. We want to talk before we listen; argue before we converse; assume before we know; reject before we honor.

This is what Alan discovered at Burning Man, and Mark was confronted by while walking the Camino.

That's why a book like *Reframation* is so refreshing. It throws open all the doors and flings open every window on the gospel, to broaden our vision and deepen our responsibility as God's people. It is invigorating to have truth reframed this way. Perhaps as you read it, you felt a frisson of recognition. Like me, maybe Alan and Mark spoke to your yearning for something richer in your faith than mere Sunday attendance and plastic nativity scenes and the latest outreach program? I believe they have opened our eyes to the stunning, complicated, beautiful truth of Christ.

Incidentally, the great G. K. Chesterton once contrasted how Christian saints are depicted in art as opposed to Buddhist saints:

> perhaps the shortest statement of it is that the Buddhist saint always has his eyes shut, while the Christian saint always has them wide open. The Buddhist saint has a sleek and harmonious body, but his eyes are heavy and sealed with sleep. The medieval saint's body is wasted to its crazy bones, but his eyes are frightfully alive [...] The Buddhist is looking with a peculiar intentness inwards. The Christian is staring with frantic intentness outwards.[3]

Not so these days. As I've mentioned, we seem to prefer our eyes closed to complexity. That is until a book like this one shakes us from our slumber and demands we look again. And having seen it, we cannot look away. We cannot *unsee* what has been revealed to us.

And so, it falls to me in this afterword to state the obvious—that the burden of responsibility now falls on you. Alan and Mark have discharged theirs. Those of us who have heard and seen, whose doors have been blown from their hinges, whose windows have been shattered, who now see as they hadn't seen before, we are charged with the duty to act on what we now know.

Alan and Mark began this book by saying that they held a deep conviction "that there is a great need for a reframation that allows us to see God, people, and mission through re/enchanted frames." Now, as you close the pages of this book, you are left with the incredible commission to tell and live the full story of God in your town or village or suburb or on the Camino or at Burning Man or wherever God may send you in this world.

APPENDIX 1

THE GREAT OMISSION

Perhaps the most significant factor contributing to the dilution of our sense of life and humanity is what we can call the non-discipleship of the church ... or what Dallas Willard called *The Great Omission* (as an inversion of the Great Commission of Matthew 28:16–20).[1] In fact, non-discipleship might be the single biggest flaw in the Western form of Christianity. It is almost as if church as we know it is designed to exclude active discipleship and to encourage stunted forms of Christianity (we know the tree by its fruit).

So what is discipleship and what is at stake when discipleship is not pursued as a core task of the church?

At core, discipleship is a Jesus-saturated affair: based squarely as it is on Jesus, discipleship involves the active modeling of my life on his (imitation of Christ) and the willingness to let him live his life in and through me (union or abiding in Christ). Discipleship is how Jesus gets into his church. It has rightly been said that discipleship is who Jesus would be if he were you.[2] Or perhaps it can be viewed as doing the same kind of things Jesus did for the same kind of reasons he did them. Discipleship is the means by which Jesus establishes a people and a community that is based on the ideal of human holiness, embodied and exemplified in Jesus. In other words, Jesus is not simply my Savior (and he is that), but he is also my Hero (someone I want to be like) and my Lord, whose life and words contain eternal life that can and must be accessed now.

Making disciples was clearly front and center to Jesus' own approach to changing the world. Over time the church became the dominant religion and settled down to a more domesticated form. Correspondingly, the active focus on the following and imitation of Jesus has been incrementally substituted with believing certain tenets *about* Jesus. Objective, theological-confessional language has replaced the more immediate and subjective knowledge of Jesus that is gained by actively adhering to him. The net result is that the more human—and revolutionary—image of Jesus himself has been effectively decentered. The idea of Jesus has been reduced to that of eternal Savior, and is less and less example and Lord.

So much is this the case in some Protestant circles (particularly Lutheran and Calvinist) that many of its theologians assert that Jesus cannot be held as the ideal human image because it's an impossible standard to follow, and any attempt to do so simply creates guilt. As a result, they have effectively abandoned the imitation of Christ as an ideal of the Christian life. In this view, the purpose of the Incarnation (let alone all the other dimensions of Christ's person and work) has no meaning in its own right; it can only be seen as substantiating the work that Jesus accomplished on the cross. Jesus simply became one of us in order to save us on the cross, and the model of his humanity (and therefore his teachings) have limited authority for the Christian life.

This is exactly what Bonhoeffer condemns as "cheap grace"—a highly selective view of the work of Christ.[3] In the diagram overleaf, the reduction can be seen as elevating the cross (and perhaps resurrection) over all the other key dimensions of Christology. Using theological jargon, one might say that these interpreters have reduced Christology to soteriology. It's yet another reduction and its heretical implications are easy to discern.

What is lost in this reduction related to the central person in the biblical story is phenomenal. Its impact on our understanding of Jesus and the gospel, as well as of discipleship and spirituality, is immeasurable. Because if Jesus is not put front and center in the cosmos and not just in the church (the Alpha and Omega), and if Jesus is not considered the archetypal human being (the Second Adam), then the theological system is broken where it matters the most. Without an active vision and following of Jesus, the gospel becomes another ideology. As a result, we have ended up with an attenuated, ideologically co-opted gospel that limits the work of Jesus to the private salvation of the soul but has little to say about anything beyond the narrow confines of the privatized individual.

And, even more dangerously perhaps, a church without discipleship always ends up with what Bonhoeffer calls a Christ-less Christianity, as the church in pre-war Germany amply demonstrated—and as does the culturally captive evangelical church in our day.

> Discipleship means adherence to Christ, and, because Christ is the object of that adherence, it must take the form of discipleship. An abstract Christology, a doctrinal system, a general religious knowledge on the subject of grace or on the forgiveness of sins, render discipleship superfluous, and in fact they positively exclude any idea of discipleship whatever, and are essentially inimical to the whole conception of following

Christ. With an abstract idea, it is possible to enter into a relation of formal knowledge, to become enthusiastic about it, and perhaps even to put it into practice but it can never be followed in personal obedience. Christianity without the living Christ is inevitably Christianity without discipleship, and Christianity without discipleship is always Christianity without Christ. It remains an abstract idea, a myth which has a place for the Fatherhood of God, but omits Christ as the living Son. And a Christianity of that kind is nothing more or less than the end of discipleship. In such a religion there is [...] no following of Christ.[4]

This is a very dangerous reduction that inevitably leads to false and oppressive religion—as history sadly demonstrates.[5]

The point in this context is not to offer some definition of discipleship but rather to highlight what we lose when we fail to make discipleship central in the life of the church. The loss of the living and active presence of Christ among his people means the loss of the life that he came to bring to those who adhere to him (John 10:10).

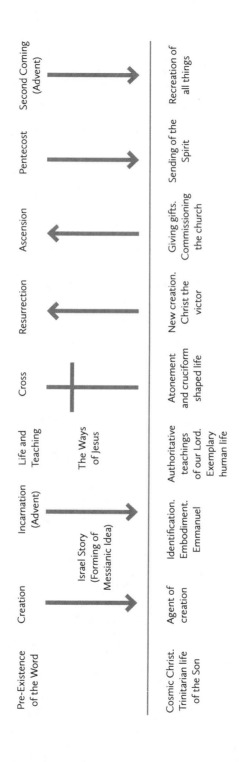

Pre-Existence of the Word	Creation	Incarnation (Advent)	Life and Teaching	Cross	Resurrection	Ascension	Pentecost	Second Coming (Advent)
	Israel Story (Forming of Messianic Idea)		The Ways of Jesus					
Cosmic Christ. Trinitarian life of the Son	Agent of creation	Identification. Embodiment. Emmanuel	Authoritative teachings of our Lord. Exemplary human life	Atonement and cruciform shaped life	New creation. Christ the victor	Giving gifts. Commissioning the church	Sending of the Spirit	Recreation of all things

APPENDIX 2

BLINDED BY DISOBEDIENCE

Visitors to the headquarters of the Central Intelligence Agency (CIA) at Langley, Virginia, are confronted with the following slogan: "And ye shall know the truth, and the truth shall make you free" (John 8:32 KJV). Besides this being a rather blasphemous appropriation of the words of our Lord, this application nonetheless reflects the generally held view that any old truth, no matter what it is about, where it came from, or how one arrived at it, can set the subjective knower free. But this is *not* what Jesus is saying here. This type of thinking always circumvents the essentially biblical idea that religious truth almost always requires repentance and change. Anything that involves theological truth—truths about God—requires something far more demanding and personal from the would-be knower.[1] The covenantal condition that Jesus attached to this promise in John 8 changes the frame entirely. Jesus actually says "*If* you hold to my teaching, you are really my disciples. *Then* you will know the truth, and the truth will set you free" (John 8:31–32, italics ours). The freedom Jesus promised here is conditional on discipleship.

Similarly, Jesus says in John 7:17 that one must be predisposed to obey God if one is to discern truth ("Anyone who chooses to do the will of God will find out whether my teaching comes from God or whether I speak on my own"). And in the parable of the wise and foolish builders, Jesus warns that "everyone who hears these words of mine and does not put them into practice is like a foolish man who built his house on sand" (Matthew 7:26). James explicitly admonishes, "Do not merely listen to the word, and so deceive yourselves. Do what it says. Anyone who listens to the word but does not do what it says is like someone who looks at his face in a mirror and, after looking at himself, goes away and immediately forgets what he looks like" (James 1:22–24).

In other words, true knowledge of God can only be gained though a relationship with God and obedience to him. Or, as Calvin says, "All knowledge is born in obedience [...] God cannot be truly served unless we obey his voice."[2] Without discipleship there can be no true (and liberating) knowledge of God. "Only he who believes is obedient, and only he who is obedient believes."[3] The Scriptures very clearly teach what we might call a bias toward obedient action. In other words, faith is not just about belief systems or dogmas and doctrines, as we have often made it. "The Word of God is telling us very clearly that if you do not do it, you, in fact, do not believe it and have not heard or understood it."[4]

For instance, "When believers confess who Jesus is, they also and inevitably confess what they must become. Jesus is not an objective datum that, like a rock under a microscope, can be observed and examined in supposed neutrality. The statement 'You are the Christ' (Mark 8:29) imposes a claim on the one who says it. *The Son of Man calls those who would know him to follow him*" (italics ours).[5] We cannot know Jesus without in principle first submitting to his claims over our lives and then following, and therefore learning to obey, him.

The intrinsic non-discipleship of our inherited forms of Christianity mean that we cannot truly interpret or understand the Scriptures— we have thus ended up with a severely reduced understanding of God's Word. This is precisely what Bonhoeffer was dealing with in the culturally captive Christianity of pre-war Germany. They just didn't understand the Scriptures and approached them as if they could distill abstract truth without orienting their lives to the living imperatives of God's Word expressed through the medium of Scripture. The result is that many German Christians missed the meaning of their own lives and ended up participating in a dangerously diluted form of Christianized (Nazi-fied) religion that legitimized some of the most brutal and murderous actions in history. We suspect a similar dynamic is at work in large sectors of American Christianity at the moment—grace is a doctrine, not an experience of Jesus that changes everything.

The Bible is consistent throughout: obedience is a critical element for the faithful interpretation of God's Word. In a whole chapter on the importance of obedience to the logic of the gospel and to discipleship, Bonhoeffer notes that, "By eliminating simple obedience on principle, we drift into an unevangelical interpretation of the Bible. We take it for granted as we open the Bible that we have a key to its interpretation."[6] This sounds all too familiar—when we too open the Bible, we assume we know what it means even if we don't act upon it. But this is a dangerous religious delusion.

Obedience unlocks the meaning of the Scripture and disobedience obscures and even distorts the intended meaning. This is what Scripture means when it calls us to *hear*—it means to listen with the view of obeying.[7] A would-be interpreter can only rightly understand theological truths by actually doing what the Scripture directs and commands. This means that mere intellectual engagement with the abstracted ideas and principles of Scripture can never produce an accurate understanding of God. "To deal with the word of Jesus otherwise than by doing it is to give him the lie [...] The word we thought we had was not Christ's, but a word we had wrested from him and made our own by reflecting on it instead of doing it."[8]

By leaving the obedience of discipleship out of the equation of interpretation, we will never faithfully understand the Scriptures, nor can we gain true knowledge of God. This greatly contributes to the reduced life many now live. A disobedient, non-discipling form of Christianity means we end up with that heretical, deistic, god-in-the-back-pocket-type religion that we have bemoaned throughout this book. In other words, discipleship is the right way for us to come to a knowledge of God. Conversely, non-discipleship cannot deliver a true knowledge of God.

APPENDIX 3

HAVING THE MIND OF CHRIST

One of the ways we have limited our seeing is by looking at the world through the distorting lens of what Paul calls the flesh and its associated rationality. The fleshly mind is contrasted with the spiritual mind. Each "mind" is what we might call a paradigm: a way of seeing and interpreting the world. The "fleshly" mind is one that interprets the world from a certain perspective, and, by its very nature, excludes information that can only be comprehended from the "spiritual" or the "mature" mind. The same issue is at stake in the interpretation of Scripture between the "Spirit and the letter" of the Word (2 Corinthians 3:4–6).

The fleshly person (or the one who focuses on the literal dimension of the Word) fails to recognize God and the things of God—they simply cannot get it. Or, to mix the metaphor a bit, they can't see the real meaning of things from within the darkened rationality of the cave.

It is because Christ lives in those who have received the Spirit that their stance and outlook can be those of Christ, and in this sense they are "spiritual." Life in the Spirit (as opposed to a life in the flesh) has to do with how we read the world and how the world in turn reads us.

The spiritual person sees the world as a space filled with the sacred and the possibility of sacredness. Everything has meaning, and the world is radically open to possibility because it is a world where God really does reign. Everything is connected to God and takes place under his auspices. Life in this view is dynamic and open. The spiritual person experiences God in all things. This does not mean that spiritual people are experts in every area of life. Rather, it means that they are able to appraise all things spiritually.

Conversely, the worldly (soulish – *psychichoi*) person has *a priori* refused this seeing and is thus enclosed in on self—the self and its survival has become the central concern. As what has sometimes been called "the false self," the worldly mind-set refuses the active reign of God, and in fact directly objects to his claims on our lives, actively seeking to obstruct God and the ways of God. Spiritual blindness is already built into the belief system. It cannot see God and the things of God. It is because of this that life in the flesh is closed and unmitigatedly tragic. Unable to see beyond the confines of his/her own thinking, the worldly must make their own way in the world which will always be ultimately meaningless. At the very least, there are depths and dimensions to life in the Spirit, which the person who lives on an entirely human level (1 Corinthians 2:14) simply cannot fathom. Aspects of Christian existence remain an enigma, unless others share the same insight of the Spirit of God.

Jesus, Paul, and John particularly write about the issue of perception; of seeing through the worldly or through the spiritual eye ... a way of seeing. This is what it means to have our perceptions cleansed, opened up to the realm of God through the power of the Spirit; to see things from the perspective of God ... of eternity. This is a big challenge to a church that has reduced faith to formula, and worship to mere ritual.

But we have the mind of Christ (1 Corinthians 2:16, Philippians 2:5–8)![1] Did you hear that? Whatever else this means, at the very least it means that the believer is able to understand Jesus' *nous* or paradigm, his way of thinking as it is revealed in and through God's Spirit who mediates Jesus to us. Jesus' *nous* is the realm of the real; it is a worldview in sync with God's will; it is a soul that is in accordance with the new life God has put within ("I only do/see/speak as I see the Father doing/seeing/speaking" John 5:19, 8:28, 12:49).[2] It's a way of perceiving the world that opens up a whole new way of seeing for the believer. It's a flinging open of the doors of perception to see the world as the Son sees it, to experience it in the same way he experienced it.

Living under the sovereign lordship of Jesus we can, and must, do everything in our power to see the world through the very distinct mind, rationality, and perspective of Christ. The Holy Spirit is God with us and will enable us to live into that dimension that the Bible calls the reign of God.

Perhaps the easiest, and soundest, way to start the journey of escape from the cloying confines of cave-rationality is to engage Jesus as if you were a participant of his original audiences. He uses metaphors all the time (seeds, birds, vineyards, trees, servants-master)—parables that invoke questioning and require a quest. His vision of the world can hardly be called small and cave-minded. In fact, he called all out of the cave in order to see things as they really are ... eternal.

Encountering the Lord Jesus always gives the seeker a wider and deeper perspective on God ... *always* ... then and now. In his earthly ministry, Jesus engages with the all-too-predetermined dungeon-rationality of his time. For instance, he says to traditionalist cave-dwellers, "You have heard that it was said ... *But* I tell you" (Matthew 5:17–48, our italics), and then proceeds to give them a radically different take on the interpretation that had locked people into thinking about God and reality in a certain predetermined way. No matter the situation, in word and deed, Jesus always surprises and does the unexpected. He speaks in puzzling parables and uses life metaphors (not rational code) that force people to see God in new and different ways. He appeals to a deeper perception than was bequeathed to them by their forbears: "Whoever has ears, let them hear" (Matthew 11:15). We need to hear and see beyond that which is merely heard and said. Jesus requires the radical openness of a heart engagement that is searching for deeper and truer perceptions of the truth.

NOTES

FOREWORD

[1] See Mt 11:3 MSG.

PREFACE

[1] *Ecclesia reformata, semper reformanda, est secundum verbum Dei*—"The church reformed ought always to be reforming, according to the Word of God". (We recognize the last phrase was a later addition added to insure the priority of Scripture in efforts to reform the church.) The idea here is that the historical church never attains to its perfect form—it never arrives at ecclesial perfection, but must always strive to appropriate more authentic ways of expressing itself.

[2] Quoted from J. D. Douglas, ed. *Proclaim Christ Until He Comes* (Minneapolis: Worldwide Publications, 1986), 198.

[3] "Christless Christianity" was Bonhoeffer's paradoxical term that he used to describe the Lutheranism of pre-war Germany.

[4] T. S. Eliot, "Little Gidding."

[5] Frederick Buechner, *Wishful Thinking: A Seeker's ABC* (New York: Harper & Row, 1973), 95.

[6] Frederick Buechner, *Telling the Truth: The Gospel as Tragedy, Comedy, and Fairy Tale* (New York: HarperCollins Publishers, 1977), 84.

[7] Franz Kafka, *Letters to Friends, Family, and Editors* (New York: Shocken, 1990), 16.

[8] We recognize that most, if not all, of the Protestant church's theology has been formulated by men. It is clear that men tend to think somewhat differently to women and therefore the theological code is somewhat imbalanced as a result.

INTRODUCTION: A TALE OF TWO PILGRIMS

[1] E.g., Greg Stier, "3 Things Millennials Aren't Finding in Church," *ChurchLeaders*, May 27, 2018, https://churchleaders.com/youth/youth-leaders-articles/254533-millennials-church.html .

[2] Walter Brueggemann, *Finally Comes the Poet: Daring Speech for Proclamation* (Minneapolis: Augsburg Fortress, 1989), ix.

[3] Pádraig Ó Tuama and Marilyn Nelson, "Choosing Words That Deepen The Argument of Being Alive," September 6, 2018, in *On Being*, by Krista Tippett, podcast, https://onbeing.org/programs/padraig-o-tuama-marilyn-nelson-choosing-words-that-deepen-the-argument-of-being-alive-sep2018/ .

[4] *Dead Poets Society*, film, directed by Peter Weir. USA: Touchstone Pictures and Silver Screen Partners IV, 1989.

[5] No specific reference found. This is quoted regularly without citation.

1 MOVING THE MOON

[1] Martin Buber, *Eclipse of God: Studies in the Relation Between Religion and Philosophy* (New York: Humanities Press International Inc., U.S., 1988).

[2] In the Bible, the concept of an eclipse of God is expressed in the idea of *hester panim*, the act of God whereby he conceals his face as a way of punishing his disobedient subjects; the "darkness of God" that results from his concealment is considered a direct consequence of accumulated human sin, and is therefore regarded as a clear sign of human culpability. But, true to the concept of the eclipse, the hiddenness of God's face was never about the absence of God (he is always present). Rather it was about concealment of his light.

[3] Charles Taylor, *A Secular Age* (Cambridge MS: Harvard University Press, 2007).

[4] C. S. Lewis, Karl Barth, Hans Urs von Balthasar, James K. A. Smith, Morris Berman, Charles Taylor, John Paul II, and Benedict XVI, among many others.

[5] Call it disenchantment, secularism, scientism, positivism, the immanent frame, idolatry, atheism, or whatever, but we can be sure that the processes have not taken place in God himself, but rather in our human perception and construal of him. We no longer have the epistemological tools by which to apprehend God in most arenas of life beyond the church. God has always been there; the problem is that *we* can no longer see or recognize him (namely to "glorify him" in the Scriptures. See Rom 1:18–22). In many ways, the obscuring of God is not new, and has been operative since the Fall, in which sin imposes a kind of theological amnesia on the rebellious human. This is such an important idea, but we have little time to unpack it here. See Charles

Taylor's monumental *A Secular Age*; James K. A. Smith's brilliant and more accessible analysis of it in *How (Not) to Be Secular: Reading Charles Taylor* (Grand Rapids: Eerdmans, 2014); Morris Berman's *The Reenchantment of the World* (New York: Cornel University Press, 1981). John Paul II's writings on this are contained in his *Evangelium Vitae*, https://goo.gl/zx7qfP .

[6] Benjamin Mann, "Understanding the 'Eclipse of God'," *Catholic Exchange*, February 7, 2014, https://catholicexchange.com/eclipse-of-god .

[7] John Paul II, *Evangelium Vitae*.

[8] John V. Taylor, *The Go-Between God* (London: SCM, 1973), 224.

[9] The beauty and glory of the divine life becomes invisible to us. The pressing reality of God slowly dissolves from our perception. In the language of Scripture, we have become *blind* and *insensitive* … seeing we no longer see, hearing we no longer hear, and this is a sign of God's judgment on us—we are handed over to our own blindness (Mt 13:13; Jn 12:36–45; Acts 28:26; Rom 1:18ff). We are no longer equipped to see things in the mode in which they are communicated and therefore how they are to be correctly comprehended and appropriated. Our capacity to see and to interpret— and therefore comprehend the meaning of—the world is thus diminished and distorted. This not only reshapes Christian perspectives of God, these ubiquitous cultural forces in broader Western society likewise shape how all people can know and experience God. We all carry the virus. The crisis really is universal in scope.

[10] It's not that God has moved out of his cosmos. God is still there. We just cannot seem to see or hear him. So if nothing has changed in God's relationship to his world, then what is the source of this age's "obscuring of God," indeed, "darkness of God"? Von Balthasar suggests that the reason for the eclipse of God "lies in the changed position of man vis-à-vis the things of the world, which are no longer the occasion for him to rise up in contemplation to the Absolute but for him to dominate them practically in technological instrumentality." In the premodern approach to the world, the human spirit looks through things upward; in the modern and postmodern attitude, it looks from its exalted height down on things. Hans Urs von Balthasar, *Explorations in Theology, III: Creator Spirit* (San Francisco: Ignatius Press, 1993), 300–2.

[11] Tom Wright, *Acts for Everyone, Part 2* (London: SPCK, 2008), 137–8. Von Balthasar, himself a brilliant theologian, noted that "Theologians have the bad habit of interrupting the Word before it has finished speaking; on the basis of some fragment they begin putting forward their own speculations, importing principles which may seem evident to man but which, from the perspective of God's Word, are by no means evident." Hans Urs von Balthasar, *Theo-Drama: Theological Dramatic Theory, Vol. II* (San Francisco, Ignatius Press, 1990), 124–5.

12 The term heresy is from the Greek αἵρεσις, originally meaning "choice" or "thing chosen," but it came to mean "the party or school of a man's choice and also referred to that process whereby a young person would examine various philosophies to determine how to live. It is easy here to see how the term indicates a self-selected reality that has lost its connection with total truth." See F. L. Cross and E. A. Livingstone, eds., "Heresy," *The Oxford Dictionary of the Christian Church* (2nd ed.) (Oxford: Oxford University Press, 1974), and F. F. Bruce, *The Spreading Flame* (Exeter: Paternoster 1964), 249. The founder or leader of a heretical movement is called a heresiarch, while individuals who espouse heresy or commit heresy are known as heretics.

13 Mawlana Jalal-al-Din Rumi.

14 Walter Brueggemann warns that "if our technical reason does not manage to pervert the truth of the gospel in relative naïveté, our unwitting embrace of social ideology [very effectively] distorts the news so that it can be accommodated to a variety of social ideologies, of the right and of the left. [...] Any ideology—by which I mean closed, managed, useful truth—destroys the power and claim of the gospel. When we embrace ideology uncritically, it is assumed that the Bible squares easily with capitalist ideology, or narcissistic psychology, or revolutionary politics, or conformist morality, or romantic liberalism. There is then no danger, no energy, no possibility, no opening for newness!" Brueggemann, *Finally Comes The Poet*, Kindle Edition, Kindle Location 44.

15 E. F. Schumacher, *A Guide for the Perplexed* (New York: Harper & Row, 1977), 5.

16 Walter Brueggemann, "Walter Brueggemann: Jesus Acted Out the Alternative to Empire," *Sojo*, June 22, 2018, https://sojo.net/articles/walter-brueggemann-jesus-acted-out-alternative-empire .

17 Von Balthasar, *Creator Spirit*, 363ff. Earlier on, von Balthasar says that even reform movements can become heretical when they make their emphases the main thing. "The indivisible unity is shown in the fact that every individual mystery, which becomes alienated when it is isolated, receives its light from the totality and takes on its theological 'necessity'(as Anselm calls it) within this totality; if one dislikes the term 'necessity', one can also call this the 'highest appropriateness'. To the extent that the individual mystery can be illuminated by the central light, it is shown to belong to the fundamental substance of the faith; but to the extent that it resists such an illumination, it will belong to what is ordained by the Church in a purely positive and disciplinary sense and must then be understood, and if necessary accepted, by the believer from this point of view. The fact that today much of what belongs to the fundamental substance of the Faith is given a place in the second category by believers, who consequently marginalize it and leave it on one side as something irrelevant, is the aftereffect of an atomism in

catechisms and sermons over a long period in which propositions of the Faith were drawn up in a list but produced no self-evident figure when taken together." *Creator Spirit*, 75–6.

[18] Whether we like it or not, Western Christianity (both Protestant and Catholic, and everything in between) has some pretty serious reductions in its core theology. Whether it be in our narrow understandings of God's ways and purposes in the world; a selective Christology where Jesus is understood as effectively limited to being my personal Savior but not my effective Lord nor the ideal human exemplar; a seriously diminished understanding of the missional purposes of the church; or a reduction of its ministry down from the fivefold of the New Testament to Christendom's option of the shepherd and the teacher, among many others, *Christian tradition has seriously narrowed the doors of our missional perception.* In this book, we are simply going to highlight *again* something of the mysterious ways of God and how he is always surprisingly involved in the redemption of the world. We don't have God in our back pocket ... we never will. He is always infinitely more than we think he is. We will also try to highlight some of the dangerous reductions in our understanding of God's gospel, which limit the way in which we understand God can save the world. We will show that the gospel is always bigger and way more potent than we have made it to be. And we will also look into ways in which we—perhaps especially evangelicals—have reduced our understanding of the human person into narrow legal and forensic categories, thereby limiting our understanding of how God can, and clearly does, touch people's everyday lives in a myriad of ways.

[19] Darrell Guder, *The Continuing Conversion of the Church* (Grand Rapids: Eerdmans, 2000), 77.

[20] Moses is told in reply to his question: *"Ehyeh asher ehyeh."* Buber interprets this to mean: "I will be there as I will be there"; that is, in whatever appearance I choose to be there, I will be there. Israel's God is, above all, the God who is present: "I am and remain present." And God is present as God chooses to be present, not as Israel desires this presence. "Thus YHWH does not say that He exists absolutely or eternally, but—without pledging Himself to any particular way of revelation ('as I will be there')— that He wants to remain with His people, to go with them, to lead them [...] The Biblical verb does not include this shade of meaning of pure being. It means happening, coming into being, being there, being present [...] but not being in an abstract sense. God promises that He will always be present, but not in any known or expected form. He identifies Himself only as the Presence which comes and departs, as the imageless God who hides and reveals Himself [...] Thus Moses at the burning bush clearly experiences the identity of the God whom he meets in the full and timeless present with the God of tradition revealed in time. He recognizes the God of the fathers as

the eternal Thou, and he understands the present revelation of God as the assurance of His future presence." Maurice Friedman, *Martin Buber: The Life of Dialogue* (London: Forgotten Books, 2018), 179–80.

[21] Guder (quoting Blauw), *The Continuing Conversion of the Church*, Kindle Edition, Kindle Location 937.

[22] Ibid., Kindle Location 1067.

[23] Ibid., Kindle Location 894. Guder advises us that "The missional purpose of all faith communities, Christ's definition of the church as his witnesses, must guide the formation of every Christian church in every culture. When other criteria and interests replace this priority of God's mission, then gospel reductionism is at work." Kindle Location 1060.

[24] L. Callid Keefe-Perry, *Way to Water: A Theopoetics Primer* (Eugene, OR: Cascade Books, 2014), 7.

[25] Brad Brisco, Facebook post, 8.55 a.m., February 14, 2019.

[26] Matthew Skinner, *Intrusive God, Disruptive Gospel: Encountering the Divine in the Book of Acts* (Grand Rapids: Brazos, 2015). 48–9.

[27] Ibid., 48–9. And we do well to remember that the book of Acts, given its connection to the Gospel of Luke, always keeps our attention on Jesus and the example he set for us. Here we see not a high-octane, butt-kicking Messiah, but rather one who is not only almost always surprising, but one who is willing to risk vulnerability, a Savior who knows the dynamics of aggression and coercion up close, having suffered from them himself. And it is because of this, or perhaps despite it, that he nevertheless remains committed to delivering us from our worst proclivities—even from our very violent selves.

[28] Ibid., 50.

[29] *A Grief Observed*, 76–7. Quoted in Wayne Martindale and Jerry Root, eds., *The Quotable Lewis* (Anna Maria, FL: Tyndale House Publishers, 2012), Kindle Edition, Kindle Locations 6349–56.

[30] Richard Bucher, "Luther's Anfechtungen: Setting for the Reformation," *Ev. Trinity Lutheran Church*, http://www.trinitylutheranms.org/MartinLuther/Anfechtungen.html .

[31] This so often happens with far-reaching ideas that have transformative impact on people and culture. For evangelicals particularly, "the gospel" has come to be almost solely understood as the way in which God forensically justifies and saves guilty sinners by forgiving our sins through what Jesus did on the cross.

[32] Lesslie Newbigin, *The Gospel in a Pluralist Society* (Grand Rapids: Eerdmans, 1989), 227.

33 Let's apply this to a tough urban context like New York City, for instance. Using Luther's experience as the missional lens to view the city, ask yourself how many people do you think are having *anfechtungen* today in New York City when they think about this holy God—i.e., how many experience overwhelming times of spiritual fear, despair and religious crisis? Obviously we cannot know for sure, but it would be hard to imagine many. Would they consider themselves guilty before a holy God? Generally, no. Westerners just don't live in that religious universe anymore. Do they consider and reflect on the idea of God? As has been stated earlier in the book, we believe all have a depth of divine longing (whether conscious or subconscious), so the answer is yes. Do they struggle with various aspects of the world's brokenness, including their own? Again, yes, but they are framing it in different language—for instance, the struggle with life-controlling forces that seem to dominate their lives. In other words, while they would not likely call their struggle with the capricious lures of money, power, success, and lust as a struggle with false gods, that is precisely what they are dealing with. They are enslaved to ideas and forces that promise the world but, in the end, deliver nothing but disappointment, hopelessness and meaninglessness.

34 Debra Hirsch, *Redeeming Sex* (Downers Grove, IL: InterVarsity Press, 2015), 170.

35 Richard Rohr, "Beginning with Blessing," *Center for Action and Contemplation*, October 6, 2015, https://cac.org/beginning-with-blessing-2015-10-06/ .

36 Abraham Kaplan, *The Conduct of Inquiry: Methodology for Behavioral Science* (New Brunswick: Transaction Publishers, 1964), 28. Similarly, people have a tendency to construct stories around facts to the point where the story obscures the facts and distorts them. Of course, stories may well serve the purpose of illustrating the facts. This is all good and well, but problems occur when people begin to believe the stories themselves rather than the facts that the stories are meant to illustrate. This is called "the narrative fallacy" or "the illusory correlation": it happens when people accommodate facts to the stories and not the other way around. We construct a narrative without any inherent explanation and then subsequently believe in it. Sound familiar? Marketers, politicians, and televangelists use this technique all the time to obscure facts, to gain adherence, or to sell you something. In other words, beware of the too compelling narrative.

37 Abraham H. Maslow, *The Psychology of Science* (Anna Maria, FL: Maurice Bassett Publishing, 2002), 15. Ironically, the English slang for a hammer is a "Birmingham Screwdriver." Apparently Birmingham industry gave the impression that everything should be pounded.

38 *My Big Fat Greek Wedding*, film, directed by Joel Zwick, USA: Gold Circle Films, HBO Films, MPH Entertainment, and Playtone, 2002.

[39] Von Balthasar, *Theo-Drama, Vol. II*, 124–5.

[40] The Crusades and the Inquisition were particularly violent manifestations of the reductionist disease. The church authorities settled on a very specific and authoritarian form of the church, which came along with a set of highly prescriptive beliefs (magisterium and canon law) that were used as a measure (imprimatur) of what was to be considered to be acceptable belief and behavior. For methods of torture used, see for instance Shanna Freeman, "How the Spanish Inquisition Worked," *How Stuff Works*, https://history.howstuffworks.com/historical-figures/spanish-inquisition3.htm .

[41] See article "The Facts and Stats on '33,000 Denominations' The 20,000 30,000 numbers and David Barrett's statistics Part II," http://www.philvaz.com/apologetics/a106.htm . For a list of the larger and more discernible denominations, see "List of Christian denominations," *Wikipedia*, https://en.wikipedia.org/wiki/List_of_Christian_denominations .

2 A CURD MADE FROM MASHED SOYBEANS

[1] Brueggemann, *Finally Comes the Poet*, 1.

[2] Don Everts, in a sermon given at Ivy Jungle Conference, approximately 2001.

[3] Timothy Keller, (@timkellernyc), Twitter post, 4:11 a.m., December 10, 2018, https://twitter.com/timkellernyc/status/1072101373410451456 .

[4] Jonathan Gottschall, in his book *The Storytelling Animal: How Stories Make Us Human* (New York: Mariner Books, 2013), describes this as a "story instinct." It is this story instinct in children that produces a natural ability to "make up stories, to tell stories, to live inside stories, to make believe." TEDx Talks, 2014. *The Storytelling Animal: Jonathan Gottschall at TEDxFurmanU*, online video, https://www.youtube.com/watch?v=Vhd0XdedLpY .

[5] Mike Melia, "Conversation: Jonathan Gottschall, Author of 'The Storytelling Animal'," *PBS News Hour*, June 13, 2012, https://www.pbs.org/newshour/arts/the-storytelling-animal .

[6] Richard Kearney, *On Stories* (London: Routledge, 2002), 3.

[7] Alasdair MacIntyre, *After Virtue: A Study in Moral Theory* (Notre Dame: University of Notre Dame Press, 2007 [if 3rd ed]), 216.

[8] Buechner, *Telling the Truth*, 79–80.

[9] From a dialogue with Jeff Wischkaemper, used with permission.

[10] Hans Urs von Balthasar, *Theo-Drama, Vol. I* (San Francisco: Ignatius Press, 1988), 15. Von Balthasar wrote five solid volumes on what he called "the theo-

dramatic" in which he explored in detail the dramatic events of salvation and the unfolding of the goodness of God. While he is by no means the only theologian to explore this (and the narrative/story-based aspects of biblical revelation), he is credited as having taken the conversation to a whole new level.

11 Abraham Joshua Heschel, *God in Search of Man: A Philosophy of Judaism* (New York: Farrar, Straus and Giroux, 1976) Kindle Edition, Kindle Locations 20–1.

12 See Thomas Cahill's fascinating book on how a relatively insignificant tribe in an insignificant part of the world changed the way we experience our world: *The Gifts of the Jews: How a Tribe of Desert Nomads Changed the Way Everyone Thinks and Feels* (New York: Anchor, 2010).

13 We are indebted to various thinkers who have explored the nature and reasons for this "disenchantment" of the Western mind. C. S. Lewis, J. R. R. Tolkien, Charles Taylor, Hans Urs von Balthasar, and Morris Berman come to mind.

14 Throughout the last few decades, there have been many who have written and spoken on the place of myth in our world, including theologians Reinhold Niebuhr, Paul Tillich, and Paul Ricœur as well as psychologists Sigmund Freud, Carl Jung and Rollo May. In addition, writers such as J. R. R. Tolkien and C. S. Lewis are especially known for their work on myth. All these scholars submit that a myth is so much more than how the word is used in common parlance: as a false belief, "an intentional misrepresentation of the truth," or "a fabrication," or "an exaggeration containing no truth."

15 But there is another reason in our day for the mistaken definition of myths as falsehood. Most of us have been taught to think only in rationalistic terms. We seem to be victims of the prejudice that the more rationalistic our statements, the more true they are … This monopoly on the part of left brain activity expresses not real science but pseudo-science. Gregory Bateson rightly reminds us that "mere purposive rationality unaided by such phenomena as art, religion, dream, and the like, is necessarily pathogenic and destructive of life." As we have said earlier, our first reaction when the myths have not sufficed is mythoclasm; we attack the very concept of myth. The denial of myths is itself part of our refusal to confront our own reality and that of our society.

16 Myth is that form of story that "gives an interpretation of the human in his relationship to the divine and thus gives him his being and his self-understanding." C. S. Lewis, "Myth Became Fact" in *C. S. Lewis Essay Collection: Faith, Christianity and the Church*, ed. Lesley Walmsley (London: HarperCollins, 2002), 138–42 and "Reflections on the Psalms" in *C. S. Lewis Selected Books* (London: HarperCollins, 2002), 363–8.

[17] James W. Menzies, *True Myth: C. S. Lewis and Joseph Campbell on the Veracity of Christianity* (Eugene, OR: Wipf & Stock Publishers, 2014), iBooks, location 9–25. The seminal Christian psychologist Rollo May says that "A myth is a way of making sense in a senseless world. Myths are narrative patterns that give significance to our existence. Myths are like the beams in a house: not exposed to outside view, they are the structure which holds the house together so people can live in it. They are narrations by which our society is unified. Myths are essential to the process of keeping our souls alive and bringing us new meaning in a difficult and often meaningless world." Rollo May, *The Cry for Myth* (New York: W. W. Norton & Company, 1991), 20.

[18] Dusty Gates, "Reality & Imagination: When Myth is Truer than Matter," *Eighth Day Institute*, June 21, 2015.

[19] "Balthasar does not conceive of humanity as ever bereft of knowledge of God. Man was created to know God—in the words of Acts which he is fond of quoting (the Areopagrede), man was created to seek God 'if maybe he might find Him': [...] Religion is the longing for a fulfilment in a way that the world cannot give. In this sense, there really is a general concept of religion, no matter how varied the types of religion may be. On one point, all religions are interchangeable. This presupposes that there is a level in the human which penetrates its entire essence. The locus classicus of this is found in St Paul's speech on the Areopagus. Beginning with the altar to the Unknown God, he speaks to the pagans of the God of Heaven and Earth who 'has caused the entire human race to proceed from one person [...] They should seek God, to see if they could touch and perhaps find Him, the One who is indeed not far from each one of us (Acts 17:23ff).'

"What the religions have in common is not at first blush any answer, but rather a question, a searching implanted in the human heart. Thus, humanity does, in fact, come trailing clouds of 'glory,' as it were. In his typically nuanced manner, Balthasar writes that the religious creations of the human imagination are certainly understandable, for man has a hunger for God which must be satisfied, and should God not speak to man, man must yet strive on his own to ascend—yet he hastens to add that in fact God has been revealing Himself to man from the beginning. 'Student of the Alexandrines that he was, Balthasar certainly does not deny the notion of a "logos spermatikos," seeing traces of knowledge of God throughout humanity. It is in the Christian dispensation that these logoi come "openly to light": man is "graced" not only since the time of Christ, but "in a hidden, but effective, way 'before the foundation of the world' (Eph 1:4)."' That which came to light in Christ was hidden 'in myths and conjectures concerning the beginning, end, and meaning of life.'" See Raymond Gawronski, *Word and Silence: Hans Urs von Balthasar and the Spiritual Encounter Between East and West* (Kettering: Angelico Press, 2015), 15–6.

[20] Hans Urs von Balthasar, *The Glory of the Lord: The Realm of Metaphysics in Antiquity. Vol. IV* (San Francisco: Ignatius Press, 1989), 21.

[21] Krystal Alexandria Pothier, *The True Myth: C. S. Lewis and Remythologization* (Honors thesis Baylor University, 2014), 1. See also Jacob J. Prahlow, "C. S. Lewis, Myth, and Fact," *Pursuing Veritas*, May 7, 2014, https://pursuingveritas.com/2014/05/07/c-s-lewis-myth-and-fact/ .

[22] Lewis is here referring to Tolkien's *Lord of the Rings*. See C. S. Lewis, "Tolkien's Lord of the Rings," in *Essay Collection and Other Short Pieces* (London: HarperCollins, 2000), 525–6. Tolkien, himself one of the greatest mythic writers of all time, used myth throughout his writings to steep his story with a mysterious "otherness," a sense of mystery and magic that hints at a reality beyond that which human reason can fathom.

[23] In many ways, even the various "searches for the historical Jesus" were manifestations of an attempt to move beyond the crude faith in Christ and describe the Jesus of history. This anti-supernatural bias, while it is not limited to theological liberalism, remains a cornerstone of the liberal Protestant theology of the past century. And it's still very much with us today, both in the academy and the sciences but also in the church. In fact, the irony is that evangelicals—who claim to be theists and have a high view of Scripture—pretty much build their house on the selfsame modernist principles of interpretation (historical, grammatical, literary, critical) and are themselves profoundly anti-supernatural in bias. Witness the severe reaction of fundamentalism to the charismatic movement.

[24] Browsing the standard Bible commentaries quickly proves the point—in our experience, the majority of the commentaries produced are products of modernist (reductionist) scholarship. They inevitably lack artfulness and poetry, and are largely dry and technical, dealing mainly with textural, grammatical, and historical factors. Few are they that have mythic *resonance* in that they seldom speak to the heart because they have effectively extracted the story. And from our experience, they rarely seek to truly grapple existentially with the purposes of God in the text or to submit to the Word of God pulsating throughout.

[25] Demythologizing has a long and successful history in Western culture. The roots are generally traced from the seminal modern philosophers Spinoza, Descartes, Kant, who provided the basic outlines for what is called the modern or enlightenment worldview. In terms of Christianity, which has been deeply influenced by this philosophical process in Western culture, demythologization finds its most thoroughgoing expression in the influential New Testament scholar Rudolf Bultmann and the various interpretive movements that emerged from him. "Bultmann suggested that, in order to make the gospel acceptable and relevant to the modern thinker, the New Testament must be demythologized. In other words, the mythical (i.e. miraculous) components must be removed, and the

universal truth underlying the stories can then be seen. For Bultmann, the universal truth was that, in Christ, God had acted for the good of humanity. However, the New Testament accounts of the virgin birth, walking on water, multiplying bread and fish, giving sight to the blind, and even Jesus' resurrection must be removed as mythical additions to the essential message. Today, there are many expressions of Christianity that follow this line of thinking, whether they attribute it to Bultmann or not. What may be called 'mainline liberalism' relies on a demythologized Bible. Classical theological liberalism teaches a vague goodness of God and brotherhood of man with an emphasis on following the example of Christ while downplaying or denying the miraculous." "What is Liberal Christian theology?", *Got Questions,* https://www.gotquestions.org/demythologization.html .

[26] Thankful for some of Preston Pouteaux's insights here: "Plesionology is theology's long lost twin, and why it's renewing my faith," January 23, 2019. https://medium.com/@pouteaux/plesionology-is-theologys-long-lost-twin-and-why-it-s-renewing-my-faith-a3c14bc6ad85 .

[27] Rollo May quotes Max Muller: "Depend upon it, there is mythology now as there was in the time of Homer, only we do not perceive it, because we ourselves live in the very shadow of it, and because we all shrink from the full meridian light of truth." *The Cry for Myth* (New York: W. W. Norton & Company, 1991), Kindle Edition, Kindle Locations 269–71.

[28] "They saw the overwhelming order of the world, the shining mathematical harmony that blazed out most purely [...] in the world of the constellations; and so the small human understanding was not the measure of all things but had to look upward to a higher, divine reason that rules all things in providence and shows itself in an epiphany in the order of the world." Von Balthasar, *Explorations*, III, 300ff.

[29] Or as the philosopher Paul Ricœur put it: "Modern persons no longer have a sacred space, a center, a *templum*, a holy mountain, or an *axis mundi.* Our existence therefore is decentered, eccentric, a-centered. We lack holy festivals, and therefore our time is as homogenous as our sense of space." Johan Cilliers, *Mysterium Tremendum et Fascinans. Liturgical Perspectives on the Approach to God*, 3, http://academic.sun.ac.za/tsv/profiles/profile_documents/johan_cilliers_mysterium_tremendum_et_fascinans.pdf .

[30] Gerard Manley Hopkins, "God's Grandeur."

[31] John V. Taylor, *The Christlike God* (London: SCM, 2004), 117.

[32] C. S. Lewis described the Numinous experience as follows: "Suppose you were told there was a tiger in the next room: you would know that you were in danger and would probably feel fear. But if you were told 'There is a ghost in the next room,' and believed it, you would feel, indeed, what is often called fear, but of a different kind. It would not be based on the knowledge of danger, for no one is primarily afraid of what a ghost may

do to him, but of the mere fact that it is a ghost. It is 'uncanny' rather than dangerous, and the special kind of fear it excites may be called Dread. With the Uncanny one has reached the fringes of the Numinous. Now suppose that you were told simply 'There is a mighty spirit in the room,' and believed it. Your feelings would then be even less like the mere fear of danger: but the disturbance would be profound. You would feel wonder and a certain shrinking—a sense of inadequacy to cope with such a visitant and of prostration before it […] This feeling may be described as awe, and the object which excites it as the *Numinous*." *The Problem of Pain* (New York: Harper Collins, 1996), 6–7.

[33] In many ways, the experience of the "trembling" is the quintessential religious experience, one that touches the believers directly and makes them perceive their identity as creatures without any introduction of rational reasoning. "Otto felt that in the religious experience, the three elements of mystery, awe, and fascination (or attraction) are so intimately related as to form an irreducible synthetic whole. The paradoxical tension between the fear inspired by the otherworldly Sacred and the irresistible attraction it exerts at the same time on the believer was the very essence of religious consciousness. Since human reason is unable to break its code, the Numinous also appears as the mystery." "Rudolf Otto," *New World Encyclopedia*, http://www.newworldencyclopedia.org/entry/Rudolf_Otto .

[34] All authentic encounters with God must maintain some admixture of these elements or else it is not the biblical God that one is encountering. So for instance, in every encounter with the Holy, with God, one experiences something of the divine comfort/succor of being loved and accepted at the most profound level, but at the same time there must also be some element of being humbled, or what the Scriptures call "the fear of God," a sense of feeling overawed simply by being in the presence of a Being who is wholly other than myself.

[35] "Rudolf Otto," *New World Encyclopedia*. With regards to mystery, with Norman Geisler we can say that "a mystery is not something that can be attained by unaided human reason (see Faith and Reason). A mystery is known only by special divine revelation (see Revelation, Special). Hence, mysteries are not the subject of natural theology but only of revealed theology […] Another characteristic of a mystery is that while we know that both elements making up the mystery are true and ultimately fit together, nevertheless, we do not know how they are compatible. For example, we know that Christ is both God and human, but it is a mystery just how these two natures unite in one person […] Finally, a mystery is distinguished from a problem. A problem has a solution; a mystery is the object of meditation. A problem calls for extensive knowledge; a mystery for intensive concentration. Like a missing word in a crossword puzzle, a problem can be solved by more knowledge; a mystery cannot. If it could, it

would not be a mystery. Mysteries do not call for answers, but for insights."
N. L. Geisler, "Mystery" in *Baker Encyclopedia of Christian Apologetics*
(Grand Rapids: Baker Books, 1999), 515.

[36] "The ineffable is not a synonym for the unknown or the nondescript;
its essence is not in its being an enigma, in its being hidden behind the
curtain. What we encounter in our perception of the sublime, in our
radical amazement, is a spiritual suggestiveness of reality, an allusiveness
to transcendent meaning." Abraham Joshua Heschel, *Man Is Not Alone:
A Philosophy of Religion* (New York: Farrar, Straus and Giroux, 1976),
Kindle Edition, Kindle Locations 385–9.

[37] Richard T. Hughes and Thomas H. Olbricht, *Scholarship, Pepperdine
University, and the Legacy of the Churches of Christ* (Pepperdine University
Center for Faith and Learning, 2004), no page numbers supplied, https://
community.pepperdine.edu/cfl/content/scholarship-booklet.pdf .

[38] Ibid., no page numbers supplied.

[39] Donald Davie, "The Translatability of Poetry," *The Poet in the Imaginary
Museum: Essays of Two Decades*, ed. Barry Alpert (Manchester: Carcanet
Press, 1977), 153.

[40] John Piper, "Obey God with Your Creativity," *Desiring God*, October 8,
2018, https://www.desiringgod.org/articles/obey-god-with-your-creativity .

[41] Eugene Peterson, "The Bible, Poetry and Active Imagination," August 30,
2018, in *On Being*, by Krista Tippett, podcast, https://onbeing.org/programs/
eugene-peterson-the-bible-poetry-and-active-imagination-aug2018/ .

[42] Think for a moment about the songs (Psalms) found in the Hebrew
Scriptures. In what belongs among the greatest of any poetry, in any culture,
in any time period, anywhere in the world, the Psalms are not systematized
theologies or ordered doctrines but instances of language that are full of
the very stuff of life—of misery and joy, love and hate, power and passion,
which speak to the personal experiences of this mystery. These songs do not
seek to contain or simply comprehend God; rather they convey beautiful
and heart-wrenching expressions of the human experience. They are songs
and poems, and their function is not to explain but to offer images, stories,
and emotions that expand our vision of reality.

[43] As told in the Christians in Theatre Arts Conference, Chicago, date and
speaker unknown.

3 STRANDED IN GREY TOWN

1   *Stranger Than Fiction*, film, directed by Marc Forster. USA: Columbia Pictures, Mandate Pictures, Three Strange Angels, 2006.

2   Jn 10:10.

3   Jerry Walls in Robert MacSwain and Michael Ward (eds.), *The Cambridge Companion to C. S. Lewis* (Cambridge: Cambridge University Press, 2010), 254.

4   Louis A. Markos, *A to Z with C. S. Lewis* (Silverton, OR: Lampion Press, 2012), Kindle Edition, Kindle Locations 302–5.

5   C. S. Lewis, *The Great Divorce* (New York: HarperCollins, 2001), 70. Lewis continues "But Heaven is not a state of mind. Heaven is reality itself. All that is fully real is Heavenly. For all that can be shaken will be shaken and only the unshakeable remains."

6   C. S. Lewis, *Mere Christianity* (New York: HarperOne, 1980), 92.

7   "There is always something [those in hell] insist on keeping even at the price of misery. There is always something they prefer to joy—that is, to reality." *The Great Divorce*, 64; "there are only two kinds of people in the end: those who say to God, 'Thy will be done,' and those to whom God says, in the end, 'Thy will be done.' All that are in Hell choose it. Without that self-choice, there could be no Hell. No soul that seriously and constantly desires joy will ever miss it," 66–7; and again, "Hell is a state of mind [...] And every state of mind, left to itself, every shutting up of the creature within the dungeon of its own mind— is, in the end, Hell," 68; "So if heaven is reality, and reality is joy, then hell is the loss of reality and consequently the loss of joy," 69. In Robert MacSwain and Michael Ward (eds.), *The Cambridge Companion to C. S. Lewis* (Cambridge: Cambridge University Press, 2010).

8   "'both good and evil, when they are full grown, become retrospective. Not only this valley but all this earthly past will have been Heaven to those who are saved. Not only the twilight in that town, but all their life on earth too, will then be seen by the damned to have been Hell. That is what mortals misunderstand. They say of some temporal suffering, "No future bliss can make up for it," not knowing that Heaven, once attained, will work backwards and turn even that agony into a glory. And of some sinful pleasure they say "Let me but have this and I'll take the consequences": little dreaming how damnation will spread back and back into their past and contaminate the pleasure of the sin ... And that is why, at the end of all things, when the sun rises here and the twilight turns to blackness down there, the Blessed will say, "We have never lived anywhere except in Heaven," and the Lost, "We were always in Hell." And both will speak truly.' 'Is not that very hard, Sir?' 'I mean, that is the real sense of what they will say. In the actual language of the Lost, the words will be different, no doubt. One

will say he has always served his country right or wrong; and another that he has sacrificed everything to his Art; and some that they've never been taken in, and some that, thank God, they've always looked after Number One, and nearly all, that, at least they've been true to themselves.'" Lewis, *The Great Divorce*, 69.

9   Timothy C. Tennent, *Invitation to World Missions: A Trinitarian Missiology for the Twenty-first Century* (Grand Rapids: Kregel, 2010), 22–3.

10 David Bosch, *Transforming Mission: Paradigm Shifts in the Theology of Mission* (Maryknoll: Orbis, 2011), 466.

11 *Rocky III*, film, directed by Sylvester Stallone. USA: United Artists, 1982.

12 From a conversation with Lonny Davis. Used with permission.

13 Melinda Lundquist Denton and Christian Smith, *Soul Searching: The Religious and Spiritual Lives of American Teenagers* (Oxford: Oxford University Press, 2005).

14 See Alan Hirsch, *The Forgotten Ways: Reactivating Apostolic Movements Second Edition* (Grand Rapids: Brazos, 2016), 35, 116–8, 161, 172 for further analysis on middle-class consumerism and how it attenuates biblical faithfulness. Also see Alan Hirsch and Deb Hirsch, *Untamed: Reactivating a Missional Form of Discipleship* (Grand Rapids: Baker, 2010) chapters 4–6.

15 C. S. Lewis, *The Four Loves* (New York: Harcourt Brace, 1988), 121.

16 Brené Brown, *Daring Greatly: How the Courage to Be Vulnerable Transforms the Way We Live, Love, Parent and Lead* (New York: Avery, 2012), 35.

17 Gregory Boyle, *Barking to the Choir: The Power of Radical Kinship* (New York: Simon & Schuster, 2017), 2.

18 C. S. Lewis, "First and Second Things," *God in the Dock* (Grand Rapids: William B. Eerdmans Publishing Co., 1970), 278–80.

19 "The thief comes only to steal and kill and destroy; I have come that they may have life, and have it to the full" (Jn 10:10).

20 Walker Percy, *The Moviegoer* (New York: Random House, 1961), 223.

21 Gregory A. Boyd, *Benefit of the Doubt: Breaking the Idol of Certainty* (Grand Rapids: Baker, 2013), 62–5.

22 The sin of idolatry appears on almost every page of the Old Testament and is coded into the monotheistic worldview that generated the entire Bible, including of course the New Testament: in the Bible itself it is variously associated with the sovereignty or the reign (kingdom) of God—clearly the central aspect of Jesus' teaching. Furthermore, Jesus affirms that the central, defining confession of the people of God is the *shema*: "Hear o'

Israel, Yahweh is our God, Yahweh is One! And you shall love Yahweh your God with all your heart, with all your soul, and with all your mind, and all your strength." And just in case we try to reduce religion to that of a private affair between God and our souls, Jesus adds, "'Love your neighbor as yourself.' There is no commandment greater than these" (Mk 12:29–31). See Alan Hirsch and Michael Frost, *ReJesus: A Wild Messiah for a Missional Church* (Grand Rapids: Baker, 2008), chapter 5 for a deeper analysis of monotheism and its implications.

[23] John P. Dourley, C. G. *Jung and Paul Tillich: The Psyche as Sacrament* (Ann Arbor, Michigan: Inner City Books, 1981), 14.

[24] Paul S. Minear, *Eyes of Faith* (Philadelphia: Westminster, 1946), 17. See the sections 17–22.

[25] Boyd, *Benefit of the Doubt*, 64. He adds "Augustine spoke a profound truth when he said our hearts are restless until we rest in God. So long as we try to meet our core needs with idols, we experience disappointment, frustration, and a host of other negative emotions. Yet we find ourselves unable to discontinue our searching, for our hunger never dissipates. We may try to numb it with the novocaine of alcohol, drugs, or pornography. Or we may try to forget about it by distracting ourselves with work, television, movies, sports, politics, and the like. But the novocaine eventually wears off and the distractions are only momentary."

[26] Biblical faith is exclusive. It disallows all that intrudes into, or dilutes, the exclusive claim that God makes over our lives … and thus it forbids all idolatry. "The sole sovereignty of God is realized only by stern struggle with other gods, with all the forces that oppose his will. This is to say that, to the biblical writers themselves, monotheism begins, not as a stage of metaphysical speculation, not as a final step in the development out of polytheism, not as a merging of all gods into one (as in Hinduism), but when the One God becomes the decisive reality for a particular man and thereby calls for the dethronement of all his other gods." Paul S. Minear, *Eyes of Faith* (St. Louis: Bethany Press, 1966), 25–6. Christian belief does not consist in merely believing that there is one God … even the devil knows that. No, Christians respond to God by faith in what he has done, trust in his power, hope in his promise, along with a passionate abandonment of self to do his will. "Only within the context of such a passionate vocation does the knowledge of the one Lord live" (Minear). And this knowledge necessitates rather than eliminates the struggle with the devil and all his works. Only in unconditional obedience, spurred on by passion and surrender, is the rule of God rightly manifested in human existence, as for example, in Jesus.

[27] David Foster Wallace, "This is Water by David Foster Wallace," *Farnam Street*, April, 2012, https://fs.blog/2012/04/david-foster-wallace-this-is-water/ .

[28] Buber, *Eclipse of God*, 158.

[29] Jacques Ellul, *False Presence of the Kingdom*, (Seabury Press, 1972).

[30] Truth is, when we look at the type of faith lived out in the various heroes throughout the Scriptures and history—the so called "cloud of witnesses" of Heb 11—we *can* talk about biblical faithfulness as a kind of receptivity which, consistent with the name YHWH ("I will appear as I will appear"), involves a radical openness to the present moment in which God calls us to respond. The kingdom of God does involve exposure to a kind of holy danger and risk, of new beginnings and of ever new becoming, and it requires an opened spirit and a willingness to live life "on the narrow ridge" (Martin Buber's favored image for the authentic life of responsive faith). Buber, *Eclipse of God*, 158

[31] Ibid., 158. "The kingdom of God is a kingdom of danger and risk, a kingdom of eternal beginnings and eternal becomings, of open spirit and deep realization, a kingdom of holy insecurity," 73.

[32] Hans Urs von Balthasar, *The Glory of the Lord, Vol. VI* (Edinburgh: T&T Clark, 1991), 163.

[33] "So, if we remain open and attentive and *responsible* to God, we will lose a [false] sense of security but we *will* gain a sense of direction and meaning. As all our saints and heroes have attested to this ... God will be near us at all times. And by being radically open and attentive to God we will actually attain to a much more authentic and true comprehension of the world. We will be able to discern the voice of God addressing us; and we will answer responsibly and strive for the hallowing of all things in the everyday. Here we will find our true task; we will be participating in God's work of creating and redeeming the world." Ibid., 157.

[34] Albert Einstein, *Ideas and Opinions* (New York: Crown, 1982), 11.

[35] Donald J. Moore, *The Human and the Holy: The Spirituality of Abraham Joshua Heschel* (New York: Fordham University Press, 1989), 37–41.

[36] Ibid.,

[37] Claire Danes, Ellen Burstyn, Tracy K. Smith, et al., "Stories About Mystery," December 28, 2017, in *On Being*, by Krista Tippett, podcast, https://onbeing.org/programs/claire-danes-ellen-burstyn-tracy-k-smith-et-al-stories-about-mystery-dec2017/ .

4 THE HUMMING OF UNSEEN HARPS

[1] The London Underground is the public rapid transit system serving London, England and some of its adjacent counties.

[2] David Brooks, "The Subtle Sensations of Faith," *The New York Times*, December 23, 2014, https://www.nytimes.com/2014/12/23/opinion/david-brooks-the-subtle-sensations-of-faith.html?smid=tw-share .

[3] Albert Einstein, *Physique, Philosophie, Politique* (English and French Edition), (Mass Market Paperback, 2002).

[4] Clotaire Rapaille, *The Culture Code: An Ingenious Way to Understand Why People Around the World Buy and Live As They Do* (New York: Broadway Books, 2007), 1.

[5] For a brilliant exploration of the implications of Bourdieu's ideas for spiritual and theological formation, see James K. A. Smith, *Desiring the Kingdom: Worship, Worldview, and Cultural Formation* (Grand Rapids: Baker Academic, 2009), and the subsequent *Imagining the Kingdom: How Worship Works* (Grand Rapids: Baker Academic, 2013).

[6] Rapaille, *The Culture Code*, 5.

[7] The concept of a cultural code supports the notion that the stories we have grown up in are *the* determining factor of our understanding and perception of a thing, an idea, a belief, etc. Our stories, all so obviously different, establish a foundation for us that, of course, leads us to processing the same information in so many different ways.

[8] Rapaille, *The Culture Code*, 2.

[9] Redeemer CFW, 2012, *James K. A. Smith, Culture as Liturgy*, online video, https://www.youtube.com/watch?v=vdVkXk3NADE .

Smith develops this approach in his more recent, *You Are What You Love: The Spiritual Power of Habit* (Grand Rapids: Brazos, 2016). See also Gregory E. Ganssle, *Our Deepest Desires: How the Christian Story Fulfills Human Aspirations* (Downers Grove: IVP, 2017).

[10] Rapaille, *The Culture Code*. If we allow people to define themselves by what they know, or what they think or what they believe, we are still a far distance from understanding *who* someone is. As much as we'd like to think that someone can know us by knowing what it is we believe about the latest issue, or by reading our latest Facebook post, or hearing our rational explanation of "my system of thought and approach to life," these do not tell others *who* we are.

11 Our future depends on our citizenship, on the direction of our will and the object of our loves ... We are called out of our loyalty to the earthly city and its account of where we belong and what gives us hope of eternal life, so that we can transfer our loyalty to the heavenly city "whose builder and maker is God" (Heb 11:10 KJV).

12 Saint Augustine, *The Confessions of Saint Augustine* (Mount Vernon: Peter Pauper Press), 1.

13 "The concept of yearning (desiderium) is central for Augustine; thus, while pointing to the innermost dynamism of finite freedom, he also makes it clear that such movement cannot in any way force the divine self-disclosure. Yearning is 'the soul's thirst ... for God', and it is by thirsting that the soul becomes able to seize him: 'The whole life of a proper Christian is holy yearning. You yearn for what you do not yet see, but the yearning itself makes you ready for being filled by it when it eventually presents itself to your sight.' Yearning is not a demand: it is a plea: 'Your yearning is your prayer; if it is constant, so is your prayer. You will fall dumb if you stop loving. If love remains awake, you will always be crying out; and as long as you thus cry out, your yearning remains.' And in order to show that genuine yearning is always directed toward a divinely planned and divinely willed encounter with God's free grace in the world, Augustine stresses that the saints of all ages, even before Christ, yearned for the advent of the Son in the flesh." Hans Urs von Balthasar, *Theo-Drama: Theological Dramatic Theory, Vol IV: The Action* (San Francisco: Ignatius, 1994), 372.

14 Alan Watts, *Behold the Spirit: A Study in the Necessity of Mystical Religion* (New York: Random House, 1971), 65.

15 Ibid.,

16 Smith, *How (Not) to Be Secular*, 131.

17 Alister E. McGrath, *Intellectuals Don't Need God and Other Modern Myths: Building Bridges to Faith Through Apologetics* (Grand Rapids: Zondervan) iBooks, 48.

18 Ibid., 48.

19 "It is the sad realization that one is yet separated from what is desired ... a ceaseless longing which always points beyond." Corbin S. Carnell, *Bright Shadow of Reality: C. S. Lewis and the Feeling Intellect* (Grand Rapids: William B. Eerdmans Publishing Co. 1974), 22–3. Simone Weil writes "When we possess a beautiful thing, we still desire something. We do not in the least know what it is. We want to get behind the beauty, but it [...] like a mirror sends back our own desire for goodness. It is a [...] mystery that is painfully tantalizing." Quoted in 28–9.

[20] Susan Scheibe and Alexandra Freund, "Approaching Sehnsucht (Life Longings) from a Life-Span Perspective: The Role of Personal Utopias in Development," *Research in Human Development*, Journal of Research in Personality 5(2), (2018): 121–33.

[21] C. S. Lewis, *Surprised by Joy* (London: Collins, 1959), 19.

[22] C. S. Lewis, *The Problem of Pain* (New York: Harper Collins, 1996), 153.

[23] C. S. Lewis, *Surprised by Joy: The Shape of My Early Life* (New York: Harper and Collins, 1955), 86. Elsewhere he notes, "We are born helpless. As soon as we are fully conscious we discover loneliness. Our whole being by its very nature is one vast need; incomplete, preparatory, empty yet cluttered, crying out for Him who can untie things that are knotted together and tie up things that are still dangling loose." C. S. Lewis, *The Four Loves* (New York: Harper Collins, 1960), 2.

[24] See Carnell's outstanding exploration of sehnsucht in Lewis, *Bright Shadow of Reality*, 163. "It is Sehnsucht which both expresses and helps satisfy longing and the desire for mystery. It has been present in every age, but it seems to be far more obvious in our time than in any previous period. It defies any final definition or analysis, and yet if we avoid considering it on these grounds, we fail to deal with an exciting and crucial concept." 157–8.

[25] C. S. Lewis, *The Weight of Glory and Other Addresses* (New York: HarperCollins, 2001), 42.

[26] It is worth quoting Lewis here more fully as it makes room for the poetic yearnings. "Our lifelong nostalgia, our longing to be reunited with something in the universe from which we now feel cut off, to be on the inside of some door which we have always seen from the outside, is no mere neurotic fancy, but the truest index of our real situation. [...] Ah, but we want something so much more—something the books on aesthetics take little notice of. But the poets and mythologies know all about it. We do not want merely to see beauty, though, God knows, even that is bounty enough. We want something else which can hardly be put into words—to be united with the beauty we see, to pass into it, to receive it into ourselves, to bathe in it, to become part of it." Ibid., 42.

[27] Jeffrey Hocking, *Liberating Language: Rubem Alves, Theopoetics, and the Democratization of God-Talk*, 17. https://www.academia.edu/1395368/Liberating_Language_Rubem_Alves_Theopoetics_and_the_Democratization_of_God-Talk .

[28] N.T. Wright, *Simply Christian: Why Christianity Makes Sense* (New York: HarperOne, 2010), see chapters 1–4.

[29] Frederick Buechner, *Whistling in the Dark* (New York: Harper & Row, 1988), 20.

[30] Robert Sibley, *A Rumour of God: Rekindling Belief in an Age of Disenchantment* (Toronto, Ontario, Canada: Novalis, 2010), 51.

5 THRO' NARROW CHINKS OF THE CAVERN

[1] William Blake, *The Marriage of Heaven and Hell* (Oxford: Oxford University Press, 1975), verse 115.

[2] "So with us. 'We know not what we shall be;' but we may be sure we shall be more, not less, than we were on earth. Our natural experiences (sensory, emotional, imaginative) are only like the drawing, like penciled lines on flat paper. If they vanish in the risen life, they will vanish only as pencil lines vanish from the real landscape; not as a candle flame that is put out but as a candle flame which becomes invisible because someone has pulled up the blind, thrown open the shutters, and let in the blaze of the risen sun." C. S. Lewis, *The Business of Heaven* (San Diego: Harcourt, 1984), 114–5.

[3] Interestingly, the Christian philosopher Søren Kierkegaard believed that one of the main causes of human angst (anxiety) arose from the failure to ground oneself in the ground of all existence [God] and that this refusal that lies at the very roots of consciousness caused huge problems of despair in soul and psyche. "In his The Sickness unto Death (1849), Kierkegaard has given a peerless description of this state of affairs [...] Man, he says, is a synthesis of the infinite and the finite, of the eternal and the temporal, of the possible and the necessary (that is, he is the locus of possible decisions, but he is also constrained by facts and earthly necessities). This objective relationship 'relates to itself', that is, it is subjective, reflex, and thus it provides a first definition of man as 'spirit' or 'self'. On the basis of this definition, this relation-to-itself is free: 'The self is freedom.' But the self, in its free self-consciousness, recognizes that the entire relationship is not something it has created: it has been established 'by another', in whom alone it can reach 'equilibrium and rest'. This 'other' is 'an infinite self', namely, God. And, in the presence of God, the self is given its second definition: it is a 'theological self'. The only ontological attitude appropriate to the self is this: 'In relating itself to itself and in willing to be itself, the self rests transparently in the power that established it. Kierkegaard calls every other attitude 'despair', whether man despairs and refuses to be himself or despairs and resolves to be himself [...] In the Christian perspective, all these forms of despair constitute a sickness of the spirit, the sickness unto death, in which man endeavors to destroy himself. As such, they are sin." Von Balthasar, *Theo-Drama*, Vol. IV, 371.

[4] Martin Buber, *The Way of Man* (Wallingford: Pendle Hill Publications, 1960), 10–11.

5   Moore, *The Human and the Holy*, 95–6. As children of Adam, humans are born fleeing from an encounter with God, fleeing into the abstractions of the spirit or into the dulled exile of the cave. But we cannot escape the pursuing God whose grace from the outset has tracked us down and ejected us from our respective hideouts. We cannot, it seems, hide ourselves from the face of God.

6   See Hans Urs von Balthasar, *Spirit and Institution: Explorations in Theology* (San Francisco: Ignatius, 1995), 445.

7   Huw Twiston Davis, "Sir Anthony Hopkins: I couldn't be an atheist," *Catholic Herald*, February 11, 2011, https://catholicherald.co.uk/news/2011/02/11/sir-anthony-hopkins-i-couldnt-be-an-atheist/ .

8   "Perhaps even the actual eating of the forbidden fruit by Adam might actually be less serious than his hiding from God after he had eaten it. Adam represents each one of us; his hiding from God is thus our hiding from God. The will of God is to be present in our midst and to be manifest to the world, but by betraying His trust and defying His will we have turned our back on Him and walked away." Moore, *The Human and the Holy*, 95–6.

9   A. C. Thiselton, *The First Epistle to the Corinthians: A Commentary on the Greek Text* (Grand Rapids: Eerdmans, 2000), 19. See also *Dianoia* in D. Mangum, *Lexham Theological Wordbook* (Bellingham: Lexham Press, 2014).

10   Consider that image of the old and young woman. You can only view one at a time. Seeing the one means deselecting the other.

11   Theologians have long pondered the so-called "noetic effects of the fall"— the darkening of the human mind. But we will also want to note that the Holy Spirit, who makes God real to the believer, brings about a renewal of the *nous* in ways that enable the disciple to come to genuine illumination and knowledge of God.

12   *The Great Divorce*, 70. In this book, Lewis describes his unique vision of heaven and hell in terms strikingly similar to Blake's. He shows us a heaven in which things are so real that in fact they are too real for the cave-adjusted senses of Grey Town, at least at first. The light is so bright it hurts the eyes. The grass so real that upon viewing it, one is forced to realize that we have never really seen grass before, but rather something of a dull, obscure vision of it, as if through grimy glass. To walk on this grass would at first hurt the feet because it's so much more real than the grass we are used to on earth. Through this imagery, Lewis is forcing us to realize that our perceptions of everything have been severely impaired. And now, for the first time, we are seeing things as they were meant to be. But the effect is so overwhelming that it takes us considerable time to acclimate ourselves to it.

13 Mk 10:13–16; Mt 18:2–5, 10.

14 George Bernanos, quoted in Hans Urs von Balthasar, *Bernanos: An Ecclesial Experience* (San Francisco: Communio, 1996), ebook.

15 According to Morris Berman, this disenchantment of the *nous* is a recent phenomenon. "For more than 99 percent of human history, the world was enchanted and man saw himself as an integral part of it. The complete reversal of this perception in a mere four hundred years or so has destroyed the continuity of the human experience and the integrity of the human psyche. It has very nearly wrecked the planet as well. We have, as Dante wrote in the Divine Comedy, awoken to find ourselves in a dark woods." *The Reenchantment of the World*, 23.

16 See Appendix three, "Having the Mind of Christ" at the end of this book.

17 George Orwell, *Why I Write* (New York: Penguin, 1946), 52.

18 This phenomenon (variously called *sustained inattention* or *inattentional blindness*) is not as unusual as it might sound. In fact it happens all the time: consider the experience of Laotian refugees brought to the United States in the 1970s from a remote mountainous region in which there were virtually none of the ordinary things that make up the modern American world. They described how, when they were first brought to Seattle and saw its tall buildings from the airplane windows, they perceived them as mountains. Their only experience with anything so high were the mountains that their village nestled among. It took sometimes painful effort for them to learn to interpret the objects in their new world as they actually were, not as they perceived them. Eugene Webb, *Worldview and Mind: Religious Thought and Psychological Development* (Columbia: Missouri University Press, 2009), 18.

19 Another example involves the classic experiment on visual processing, which asks people to watch a film clip of six people passing a basketball back and forth, and to press a button every time they notice a particular team has possession. While the players are passing the ball back and forth, a woman dressed in a gorilla suit walks directly through the players, looks into the camera, beats her chest and walks off the screen. Invariably only about half the people tested ever notice the gorilla, the others saying they saw nothing unusual or surprising during the video. Carina Kreitz, Robert Schnuerch, Henning Gibbons, Daniel Memmert, "Some See It, Some Don't: Exploring the Relation between Inattentional Blindness and Personality Factors," *Plos One* (May 26, 2015). https://doi.org/10.1371/journal.pone.0128158 .

It is worth noting that highly open people are less susceptible to inattentional blindness: they tend to see the things that others screen out. Inattentional blindness is a phenomenon in just about every arena in life, from the university to the kitchen—it involves the screening-out of visual information that is beyond our immediate attentional focus. This is similar to the term "not seeing the forest amid the trees" or "not seeing the trees amid the forest", depending on discussion, and it's related to the glass walls phenomenon. See "Ships Not Seen," Hmolpedia, http://www.eoht.info/page/Ships+not+seen , and Carina Kreitz, et al., "Some See It, Some Don't: Exploring the Relation between Inattentional Blindness and Personality Factors."

20 Webb, *Worldview and Mind*, 18.

21 The mind thinks in categories … by being able to separate what is different from other categorization. It's one of the bases of brain function and rationality. Therefore, if a person does not have the intellectual categories for something, they cannot recognize the categories and distinctions as they present themselves to the perceiver in the phenomenal world. One needs a subjective mental model (along with an approbate language) to be able to name what is real in the objective world.

22 "For people who are stumbling toward ruin, the message of the cross is nothing but a tall tale for fools by a fool. But for those of us who are already experiencing the reality of being rescued *and made right*, it is nothing short of God's power" (1 Cor 1:18 The Voice).

23 N. T. Wright, *Simply Good News: Why the Gospel is News and What Makes it Good* (New York: HarperCollins, 2015), 61.

24 Ibid., 85.

25 Maurice Friedman, *A Heart of Wisdom: Religion and Human Wholeness* (New York: State University of New York Press, 1992), 19.

26 See Jean Daniélou, *God and the Ways of Knowing* (San Francisco: Ignatius, 1957), 91–98, and Matthew A. Moser, *Love Itself is Understanding: Balthasar, Truth, and the Saints* (PhD thesis, Baylor University, 2013), 70ff.

27 *The Truman Show*, film, directed by Peter Weir. USA: Paramount Pictures and Scott Rudin Productions, 1998.

28 John Bowen, "The Gospel according to The Truman Show," *Institute of Evangelism*, February 10, 2001, https://institute.wycliffecollege.ca/2001/02/the-gospel-according-to-the-truman-show/ .

29 William James, *The Varieties of Religious Experience* (New York: Cosimo Classics, 2007), see especially lectures VI–VII.

30 Mt 13:14–15; Mk 4:12; 8:18; Jn 12:40; Acts 28:26–27; Rom 11:8.

31 Abraham Joshua Heschel, *Moral Grandeur and Spiritual Audacity: Essays* (Farrar, Straus and Giroux), Kindle Edition, Kindle Location 20.

32 According to some experts, this mentality is only getting worse. "The gap between what we know and what we think we know is widening every day," says Nate Silver, founder and editor-in-chief of website *FiveThirtyEight*, which uses statistical analysis to tell compelling stories about our world, especially in forecasting what is to come. Most people, especially the

so-called experts, tend to focus on "signals that reinforce their view of reality" while ignoring the presence of anything beyond their known experience. The problem intensifies when those who are "in the know" fail to disclose how uncertain they actually are. Sanjay Bhatt, "Nate Silver lives by data, whether on politicians or burritos," *The Seattle Times*, May 11, 2014, http://www.seattletimes.com/business/nate-silver-lives-by-data-whether-on-politicians-or-burritos/ .

[33] From a dialogue with Dr. Mark Weedman, September 11, 2015. Used with permission.

[34] Frederick Buechner, *Secrets in the Dark: A Life in Sermons* (New York: HarperCollins, 2006), 67.

[35] Murray Rae, *Kierkegaard's Vision of the Incarnation: By Faith Transformed* (Oxford: Clarendon Press, 1998), xi.

[36] Ibid., xi.

[37] The Inklings was an informal literary discussion group that included C. S. Lewis, J. R. R. Tolkien, and Charles Williams.

[38] Owen Barfield, *History, Guilt and Habit* (London: Barfield Press, 2012), 74.

[39] Don Everts and Doug Shaupp, *Pathways to Jesus: Crossing the Thresholds of Faith* (Nottingham: IVP, 2009), 71.

[40] From a dialogue with Anna Robinson. Used with permission.

[41] "limabean03," "Dante, Sin, Repentance, and Desire," *A Glorious Revolution*, December 17, 2008, https://trinitypastor.wordpress.com/2008/12/17/dante-sin-repentance-and-desire/ .

[42] Ibid.

[43] Hans Urs von Balthasar in Aidan Nichols, *Divine Fruitfulness: A Guide Through Balthasar's Theology Beyond the Trilogy* (London: T & T Clark, 1997), 97.

[44] Martin Buber, *Israel and the World* (New York: Schocken Books, 1963), 163.

6 THE ART OF SEEING

[1] Aldous Huxley, *The Art of Seeing* (London: Chatto & Windus, 1942), vii–x. This illustration about Huxley is drawn from Phillip Vannini, Dennis Waskul, and Simon Gottschalk, *The Senses in Self, Society, and Culture: A Sociology of the Senses* (New York: Routledge, 2012), 17–8.

[2] Huxley, *The Art of Seeing*, ix

[3] Ibid., x.

[4] Ibid., 42. For the balance of his book, Huxley offers scathing criticism

of standard medical approaches to eye treatment. By rejecting the facile assumption that vision is merely a passive product of properly functioning organs, he goes on to detail various techniques and practices for visual re-education.

5   F. Scott Fitzgerald pointed out, "The test of a first-rate intelligence is the ability to hold two opposed ideas in the mind at the same time, and still retain the ability to function." Quoted in Jim Collins, "Genius of the And." https://www.jimcollins.com/concepts/genius-of-the-and.html . Also in Collins' book with Jerry Porras, *Built to Last: Successful Habits of Visionary Companies* (New York: HarperCollins, 2004).

6   I (Alan) am convinced that almost all the problems we face as the church are the result of fragmentations of a once-greater truth, that the church by and large is a victim of its own rationalistic, formulaic, and reductionist thinking. In my book *5Q*, I spend a whole chapter on the difference between analytic and synthetic thinking on the understanding that we have reduced ministry down to unbiblical proportions—that of the Shepherd/Pastor and Teacher alone. The only way to heal a broken ministry is to reset it into its biblical whole as APEST, which includes the ministry of the Apostle, Prophet, and Evangelist. See Alan Hirsch, *5Q* (Atlanta: 100Movements Publishing, 2017), preface and introduction.

7   Michael S. Heiser, *The Unseen Realm: Recovering the Supernatural Worldview of the Bible* (Bellingham: Lexham Press, 2015), iBooks, 19.

8   Frederick Buechner, *The Longing for Home* (New York: HarperCollins, 1996), 109–10.

9   In the Scriptures, this capacity to see things from the view of the whole and not just the parts is called *pleroma* or fullness. It is found and attained in Jesus, and it is what all of creation is aiming toward (Eph 1:10; 1:23; 3:19; 4:13; Col 1:19; 2:9).

   The believer's innate instinct for truth is called "the illative sense" by various theologians and philosophers ... especially John Henry Newman in his *An Essay in Aid of a Grammar of Ascent* (Assumption Press, 2013).

10 This idea that God is always greater than we can conceive has always been an intrinsic part of how the church has understood faith. For instance, we can see it in the works of St. Anselm of Canterbury: nothing greater than God can be conceived of, and human beings can only understand God in a way that recognizes they can never fully comprehend him. St. Anselm, *Works of St. Anselm: Proslogium, Monologium, An Appendix in Behalf of the Fool, and Cur Deus Homo* (London: Forgotten Books, 2007).

11 Krish Kandiah, *Paradoxology: Why Christianity Was Never Meant to Be Simple* (London: Hodder & Stoughton, 2014), 4–5. The back cover says: "As we search the Scriptures we find that even the most heroic figures, the

models of courageous faith in the Bible, those to whom we habitually look for strength, struggled with the conundrums of God's character. Their struggles illuminate and validate our struggles, and their faith and worship in the midst of despair can help us in our faith and worship too."

12   From an audio recording at Peggy Guggenheim Collection, Venice, Italy.

13   *Finding Neverland*, film, directed by Marc Forster. USA|UK: Miramax Pictures, FilmColony, Key Light Productions, 2004.

14   Von Balthasar maintains that theology, like aesthetics, is a matter of "learning to see," requiring an attitude of service to the object of perception, identical to the way in which a work of art reveals itself and inspires transformation in the perceiver: we are, for von Balthasar, "'enraptured' by our contemplation of these depths and are 'transported' to them," *The Glory of the Lord: A Theological Aesthetics, Vol. I: Seeing the Form* (Edinburgh: T. & T. Clark, 1982), 119. This in turn reintroduces wonder into theology, where we approach the world with a sense of reverence, and in appreciation that it is a free gift of God. The proper attitude for the Christian, then, is not fulfillment but awe, and von Balthasar therefore describes his theology as a "kneeling theology," in which "God's truth has ascendancy over our own truth," and one must attempt to live one's life from that perspective. A theological aesthetics, therefore, is a means of expressing the primacy of God's revelation over abstract theological systems and forms of natural theology that strive to "deduce" God's revelation; for von Balthasar, a theological aesthetics does not look to get a secure place to stand, but rather attempts to get sight of what cannot be securely grasped. See David Liptay, *Beauty And/As Theology: The Theological Aesthetics of Hans Urs von Balthasar* (PhD thesis, Syracuse University, 2010), 12–3.

15   Max Planck, *Scientific Autobiography* (New York: Citadel, 1949), 91–3.

16   Kallistos Ware, *The Orthodox Way* (Crestwood: St. Vladimir's Press, 1979), 157–8.

17   From Elizabeth Barrett Browning, "Aurora Leigh."

18   From William Blake, "Auguries of Innocence."

19   Cited in Basil De Selincourt, *William Blake* (London: Duckworth, 1909), 70.

20   "In natural knowledge, the quicker and more penetrating the mind is, the more effectively a slight clue suffices to lead it to a certain conclusion. The same happens in the case of supernatural knowledge. The more responsive the mind is to the promptings of the Holy Spirit, the more easily it will come to assent to the Christian faith by means of signs that are ordinary, everyday signs, in no way 'extraordinary' or 'miraculous.' That is why an incontrovertible tradition, going back to the Gospel itself, praises those who have no need of wonders. They are not praised for having believed

without reasons; that would only be reprehensible. But we see in them truly illuminated souls, capable of grasping a vast truth through a tiny clue. Does not experience show that, when the Holy Spirit visits the soul with His consolation, the soul is no longer capable of doubting, as it were, and glimpses manifest signs of the truth in everything. 'Think of anything you wish,' says the author of *L'Aiguillon d'amour*, 'and you will find in it many reasons for loving your Creator.' Some saints went into ecstasy on viewing a blade of grass. So, too, when it comes to faith. When responding to the divine light, the believer sees all of world history as proving the Church's mission; the most commonplace word or fact floods the soul with certitude and peace [...] But the lover recognizes the Spouse 'by a single hair of her neck.'" Pierre Rosoulett, *The Eyes of Faith* (New York: Fordham University Press, 1990), 35.

21 Barbara Brown Taylor, *The Preaching Life: A Memoir of Faith* (New York: HarperOne, 2009), 16.

22 J. B. Phillips, *Your God Is Too Small: A Guide for Believers and Skeptics Alike* (New York: Touchstone, 1952).

23 "The more a great work of art is known and grasped, the more concretely are we dazzled by its 'ungraspable' genius. We never outgrow something which we acknowledge to stand above us by its very nature. And this will in no way be different for us even when we contemplate God in the beatific vision, since then we will see that God is forever the greater. Even the figure of a person whom we love and know well permanently remains for us too wonderful to exhaust by description, and, if we truly are lovers, we would be incensed if someone offered an account of the loved person which resolved all mysteries about him." Von Balthasar, *The Glory of the Lord, Vol. I*, 181.

One of the "rules" for enlarging one's experience of God, one used by all the early church Fathers and Mothers, was that *the more you think you know about God, the more you realize you don't know* (the antithesis of *all I know is all there is*); if you think you comprehend it, then it is not God that you comprehend. We will always be seeking God, even when we have found him—and particularly then. This is not only because of the limitations of our all too finite intellects and vision, but because of the superabundant vitality of infinite life itself.

Actually, Christianity has well developed resources within it that can help us in our effort to encounter God in a larger frame. As prayerful seekers after God, the early church Fathers and Mothers modelled a way of seeing the world as a living metaphor that was only truly understood with the eyes of wonder. They saw the world as a sacred cosmic ecology where all things are related to the triune God who not only created the world, but who continually redeems, restores, and orders it according to his own purposes. Driven by an innate motivation towards transcendence, their passion to know and love God led them to the very frontiers of human thought and experience.

One of the reasons why they achieved so much is because they believed in (and lived) what was later called the "analogy of being" by Thomas Aquinas. Without getting too technical and metaphysical, to believe in the analogy of being claims that all created things have some analogue or proportion to that which created them, that in some way there is an ongoing corresponding relation between God and cosmos. The only way that anybody can say that "God is like this or that" is through the analogy of being. This opened the world up in ways that were indeed spiritual and revelatory, but it also opened people up to all sorts of errors of idolatrous thinking, as Karl Barth so passionately pointed out. But the Fourth Lateran Council settled the parameters in the way that we think, opening up the power of analogy for us today, which states, "And since, being as an essence is inconceivable, whatever similarity the creature has with the Creator, the dissimilarity is always greater." Which, simply stated, means that the more you think that you have got God all worked out, you will find a greater incomprehensibility occurs at the same time. The closer you zoom in on an aspect of God, you will find that God zooms out in infinite proportion. You can never get a bead on him.

[24] "This direct and wholly realized union with God itself continues to bear the implication of the 'ever-moreness' of the Divine Other's infinite unbounded—ever gracious and unanticipatable—personal love." David Schindler, "On Trivializing the Lives of 'Ordinary People' in Liberal Societies," *Communio* (Spring, 2017): Vol. 44, 1, 109.

"In these and all other Biblical experiences of God, the element that impels the subject forward lies, precisely, in the superabundance of their content, as compared with man's limited capacity to grasp it; and the longing which they awaken and leave behind is not the yearning for something more which would be something different, but the longing for the Always-More that resides in what has already been bestowed." Von Balthasar, *The Glory of the Lord*, Vol. I, 312.

[25] Augustine, Sermon 170.9. And also "If he who is sought can be found, why was it said Seek his face evermore (Ps 105:4)? Perhaps because he should still be sought even when found? For this is how we ought to seek incomprehensible things." See also Sermon 125.11; *De Trinitate* 15.2.2: quoted in Schindler, "On Trivializing," 109.

[26] Raymond Gawronski, *Word and Silence: Hans Urs von Balthasar and the Spiritual Encounter Between East and West* (Kettering: Angelico Press, 2015), 16. Or consider this from von Balthasar, "Even in eternity itself God will not cease, in the freest self-giving, to be our fulfillment; so that even when we enjoy the vision of God we shall always be hanging on his every

word, we shall always be listening to him. Here on earth, conversely, the word need not be apprehended as something alien, something 'other': it can be understood to be what is most our own, what is most intimate and close to us; it is my truth, the truth of me and about me; the word which reveals me and gives me to myself. For we have been created in this word, and so it contains our entire truth, the whole concept of each of us, a concept so unimaginably great and beatific that we would never have thought it possible. But this concept is something we only encounter in the word of God. And we cannot lift it out of the word of God and take it home with us. We are only true so long as we are in him, so long as we are branches of his vine, allowing ourselves to be shaped and governed by his sovereignly free life. He alone can tell us what, in truth, we are; one word sufficed for Mary Magdalen, blinded with tears at the tomb: 'Mary!' This personal name, uttered by the lips of him who is Eternal Life, is a person's true concept. In it the believer is given his true I in God on the basis of pure grace and the forgiveness of sins; but it comes with all the compelling force of a love which, of its very nature, demands and appropriates everything. Nothing in man can be understood apart from this love." Hans Urs von Balthasar, *Prayer*, (San Francisco: Ignatius, 1986), 25–6.

27   Hans Urs von Balthasar, *The Moment of Christian Witness* (San Francisco: Ignatius, 1969), 101.

28   E.g., "In fact, though by this time you ought to be teachers, you need someone to teach you the elementary truths of God's word all over again. You need milk, not solid food!" (Heb 5:12). See also 1 Cor 3:2.

29   David Bentley Hart, *The Experience of God: Being, Consciousness, Bliss* (New Haven: Yale University Press, 2013), 9–10.

30   We are indebted to the brilliant and pioneering work done by missiologists Jackson Wu, Jason Georges, Werner Mischke, and others who form part of the HonorShame.com and the associated movement and conference. These theologians ought to be read widely.

31   Dallas Willard, *The Divine Conspiracy: Rediscovering Our Hidden Life in God* (New York: HarperCollins, 2001). See short article by Ransomed Heart, "A Gospel of Sin Management," January 14, 2018 https://www.ransomedheart.com/daily-reading/gospel-sin-management .

32   Jayson Georges, "Honor/Shame Sub-Cultures in the U.S.," *Mission Frontiers*, January–February, 2015 http://www.missionfrontiers.org/issue/article/honor-shame-sub-cultures-in-the-u.s .

33   Jackson Wu, "Why has the Church Lost 'Face'?," *Mission Frontiers*, January–February, 2015 http://www.missionfrontiers.org/issue/article/why-has-the-church-lost-face .

34 Georges, "Honor/Shame Sub-Cultures in the U.S." Further, Georges writes, "Western theology leads us to read Paul's epistle to the Romans as a legal letter explaining heavenly acquittal of our individual transgressions. But Romans rarely uses courtroom terms like guilt (0x), forgiveness (1x), or innocence (1x). Rather it places much greater emphasis on shame (6x), honor (15x), and glory (20x). In Romans, Paul addresses the corrosive ethnic divisions between Roman Christians (Jew-Gentile and Roman-barbarian) by replacing their false claims to honor with their new basis for true honor in God, equally available to all who trust in God's honored Messiah. In other words, Romans confronts "group righteousness" (claims to superiority over other groups), not just "works righteousness" (pride in one's moral goodness). In this context, Paul reveals sin as the shameful manipulation of cultural systems that dishonors God (1:23–24, 2:23–24, 3:23). The trajectory of "The Romans Road" leads to a salvation of divine honor, eternal glory, and membership into God's family (Rom 2:7; 8:18, 10:10–11)."

35 http://honorshame.com/about/ .

36 Brené Brown, "Listening to Shame," March 16, 2012, TED Talk. https://www.youtube.com/watch?v=psN1DORYYV0 ; and Werner Mischke, *The Global Gospel: Achieving Missional Impact in our Global World* (Scottsdale: Mission One, 2015), section 1.5.

37 Dan DeWitt, "The Difference between Guilt and Shame," *The Gospel Coalition*, February 19, 2018, https://www.thegospelcoalition.org/article/difference-between-guilt-shame/ .

38 Two other key differences between this Eastern frame (shame culture) and the Western approach (guilt culture) are that: - In a guilt culture, God is Lawgiver and Judge; in a shame culture, God is Father. - In a guilt culture, Jesus' death on a cross satisfies divine justice and makes forgiveness possible; in a shame culture, his shameful death covers our shame and his faithfulness to God restores our honor with the Father.

39 Wu, "Why has the Church Lost 'Face'?"

40 This is one of the assumptions of the various conferences and forums that are highlighting the shame and honor dimensions of the gospel, e.g., http://honorshame.com/ .

41 By the way, many world religions have their own versions of the Prodigal Son story, but Christianity is the only one where the person of God "runs" to the son. The others have him waiting on the porch and impose hoops for the son to jump through before the love of the father is given.

42 See Scott McKnight, *A Community Called Atonement* (Nashville: Abingdon Press, 2007) and Douglas John Hall, *Professing the Faith: Christian Theology in North American Context* (Minneapolis: Augsburg

Fortress, 1993), 413ff, for excellent theological analysis of the ways in which God addresses discreet issues of human sin. In a nutshell, Hall categorizes the various theories of atonement into three groups, and correlates them with three types of anxiety. The correlation is as follows:

1) Rescue/deliverance atonement—Anxiety of fate and death;

2) Sacrifice atonement—Anxiety of guilt and condemnation;

3) Demonstration/revelation atonement—Anxiety of meaninglessness and despair.

[43] Georges, "Why has nobody told me this before?," *Mission Frontiers*, January–February 2015, http://www.missionfrontiers.org/issue/article/honor-shame-sub-cultures-in-the-u.s .

[44] Hirsch, *5Q*, xxiii.

[45] Richard Rohr, "Life as Participation," *Center for Action and Contemplation*, April 1, 2015, https://cac.org/life-as-participation-2015-04-01/ .

[46] Ibid.

[47] Hirsh, *5Q*, xxiii–xxiv.

[48] Adrienne von Speyr, *The Letter to the Ephesians* (San Francisco: Ignatius Press, 1996), ebook [no page numbers supplied].

7 THE GREAT RE[FRAMATION]

[1] C. S. Lewis, *The Lion, the Witch and the Wardrobe* (New York: HarperCollins, 1950), 163.

[2] Walter Hooper, *The Narnian Chronicles of C.S. Lewis: Past Watchful Dragons* (New York: Collier Books, 1971), ix.

[3] Ibid., ix.

[4] G. K. Chesterton suggested that fairy tales "make rivers run with wine only to make us remember, for one wild moment, that they run with water." They increase our wonder and enhance our reality. G. K. Chesterton, *Orthodoxy* (New York: John Lane, 1908), 96.

[5] Dave Radford, "Stealing Past the Watchful Dragons: The Power of Story and Song," CCM *Magazine*, February 15, 2015, https://www.ccmmagazine.com/news/stealing-past-the-watchful-dragons-the-power-of-story-and-song/ .

[6] Emily Dickinson, "Tell all the truth but tell it slant."

[7] Eugene H. Peterson, *The Word Made Flesh* (New York: Hodder & Stoughton, 2010), 13.

8   See Dan DeWitt, "Why C. S. Lewis Didn't Write for Christianity Today: Carl Henry wanted more 'Mere Christianity' and direct theology. Lewis didn't," *Christianity Today*, December 27, 2012 https://www.christianitytoday.com/ct/2012/december-web-only/why-cs-lewis-didnt-write-for-christianity-today .

9   Buechner, *Telling the Truth*, 62–3.

10 Strangely enough, the words unravel and ravel mean the same thing. Unravel (ən'ravəl); to become undone: part of the crew neck had unraveled. Ravel ('ravəl); to untangle or unravel something: he finished raveling out his fishing net.

11 See Mt 5:17–20.

12 N. T. Wright, *The New Testament and the People of God*, (Minneapolis: Fortress Press, 1992), 132.

13 In Scott Nelson, *Mission: Living for the Purposes of God* (Downers Grove: IVP, 2013), 39.

14 Richard Velkley, *Freedom and the Human Person* (Washington, DC: The Catholic University of America Press, 2007), 13.

15 Moore, *The Human and the Holy*, 39.

16 Donald Miller, *Searching for God Knows What* (Nashville, Tennessee: Thomas Nelson, 2004), 155.

17 Dr. Mary Catherine Bateson, "Composing a Life," October 1, 2015, in *On Being*, by Krista Tippett, podcast, https://onbeing.org/programs/mary-catherine-bateson-composing-a-life/ .

18 Ronald V. Evans, *Making Sense of the Old Testament* (Victoria, BC: Friesen Press, 2018), 119.

19 Bateson, "Composing a Life."

20 Von Balthasar, *Prayer*, 157–8.

21 Ibid., 159.

22 Don Everts, *Jesus with Dirty Feet* (Downers Grove, IL: InterVarsity Press, 1999), cover.

23 See Don Everts and Doug Schaupp, *I Once was Lost* (Downers Grove, IL: Intervarsity Press, 2008), 63–4.

24 Moore, *The Human and the Holy*, 37–41.

25 Amos N. Wilder, *Theopoetic: Theology and the Religious Imagination* (Philadelphia: Fortress Press, 1976), 1.

26 Ibid., 1.

[27] Walter Brueggemann, "The Prophetic Imagination," December 19, 2013, in *On Being*, by Krista Tippett, podcast, https://onbeing.org/programs/walter-brueggemann-the-prophetic-imagination/ . Coleridge wrote that poetry exists to "awaken the mind's attention from the lethargy of custom, and directing it to the loveliness and the wonders of the world before us"; to remove "the film of familiarity and selfish solicitude; we have eyes, yet see not, ears that hear not, and hearts that neither feel nor understand". We need to be awakened. Coleridge, *Biographica Literaria*, chapter fourteen.

[28] Eugene Peterson, *Answering God* (San Francisco: Harper & Row, 1989), 11–2.

[29] Eugene Peterson, *Subversive Spirituality* (Grand Rapids: Eerdmans, 1997), 126.

[30] Brueggemann, *Finally Comes the Poet*, 3.

[31] See Brueggemann, "The Prophetic Imagination," podcast.

[32] Percy Bysshe Shelley, "A Defence of Poetry," *Poetry Foundation*, https://www.poetryfoundation.org/articles/69388/a-defence-of-poetry .

[33] David Jeffrey, *Houses of the Interpreter: Reading Scripture, Reading Culture* (Waco: Baylor University Press, 2003), 186.

[34] Pothier, *The True Myth*, 1.

[35] Tolkien, himself one of the greatest mythic writers of all time, used myth throughout his writings to steep his stories with a mysterious "otherness", a sense of mystery and magic that hints at a reality beyond that which human reason can fathom.

[36] Alister McGrath, *C. S. Lewis—A Life: Eccentric Genius, Reluctant Prophet* (Carol Stream, IL: Tyndale House Publishers), 149.

[37] Lewis, *Surprised by Joy*, 279.

[38] McGrath, *C. S. Lewis*, 149.

[39] Ibid., 149.

[40] Louis A. Markos, "Myth Matters: Why C.S. Lewis's books remain models for Christian apologists in the 21st century," *Christianity Today*, April 23, 2001.

[41] McGrath, *C. S. Lewis*, 150.

[42] Ibid., 148.

[43] Ed. Lesley Walmsley, "Myth Became Fact," *C. S. Lewis Essay Collection: Faith, Christianity and the Church* (London: HarperCollins, 2002), 138–42.

[44] Adrienne von Speyr, *The Letter to the Ephesians* (San Francisco: Ignatius, 1996), no page numbers provided.

45 We must make every effort to try to read Paul beyond his captivity by the scholastic-rationalists—the forensic accountants of religion—of various denominational hues, who have effectively imprisoned him in the scholastic formula.

46 Gen 26:15.

47 Lin-Manuel Miranda, "Lin-Manuel Miranda," January 3, 2014, in *The Dramatists Guild's In the Room Series*, podcast, https://www. dramatistsguild.com/education-category/in-the-room/ .

48 McGrath, *C. S. Lewis*, 277.

49 Dickinson, "Tell all the truth but tell it slant."

50 Walter Hooper, "Walter Hooper Part 5," 2016, in *The Eric Metaxas Show*, podcast, https://soundcloud.com/the-eric-metaxas-show/walter-hooper-part-6 .

8 I'LL HAVE WHAT SHE'S HAVING

1 Ann M. Trousdale, *Cotton Patch Rebel: The Story of Clarence Jordan* (Eugene, OR: Resource Publications, 2015), Kindle Edition, Kindle Location 98.

2 Jordan was a student of biblical language (a PhD in New Testament Greek from Southern Baptist Seminary) and published the *Cotton Patch Gospel* in 1969. Jordan's take on the Gospels and a few of Paul's letters was his attempt to not only translate individual words and phrases but to contextualize the Scripture to the southern United States during the time of the Civil Rights Movement. It was a radical reframing. He believed the Bible related directly to his own life and time, and he wanted other people to see it that way too, not simply as a history of some remote time and place. So he began translating the stories of Scripture as if they had taken place in rural Georgia in the twentieth century.

Jesus wasn't born in Bethlehem, but in Gainesville, Georgia.

Jerusalem became Atlanta; Rome was translated as Washington, DC.

When Herod killed the newborns at the time of Jesus' birth, the tragedy was a result of a bomb being thrown into the nursery of the big church downtown.

"Jew and Gentile" became "white man and Negro."

Jesus wasn't "crucified"—he was "lynched," as Jordan believed that no other term could adequately communicate the horrific nature into a current context.

It was said that Jordan was "a witty storyteller, who could literally keep an audience of two or two thousand captivated for hours. His humor could have you rolling one minute and gasping for breath the next." Trousdale, *Cotton Patch Rebel*, xi.

3   Greg Carey, "Recalling Clarence Jordan, Radical Disciple," *Huffington Post*, June 3, 2012, https://www.huffingtonpost.com/greg-carey/clarence-jordan-radical-disciple_b_1548373.html .

4   *Briars in the Cotton Patch: The Story of Koinonia Farms*, film, directed by Faith Fuller. USA: Vision Video/Gateway Films, 2005.

5   Trousdale, *Cotton Patch Rebel*, 44; 86.

6   Gen 4:1.

7   Callid Keefe-Perry, *Way to Water*, 125.

8   Søren Kierkegaard, *Concluding Unscientific Postscript* (Princeton: Princeton University Press, 1992).

9   David Tracy, *The Analogical Imagination: Christian Theology and the Culture of Pluralism* (New York, 1991 edition), 77–8. See the whole of chapter two: "A theological portrait of the theologian." And consider this from von Balthasar: "Just as God does not show an abstract, theoretical, lifeless and 'dead' faithfulness toward man, concealing his divine truth in mere 'propositions' and 'laws', but causes his truth to become real, pulsating life and flesh in terms of living history, so he cannot be satisfied with a 'dead' faith as man's response. He is the living God, 'bodily' present with and for man, and so he calls for an 'embodied' response: man, in the entirety of his existence as a hearer and answerer of the word." Von Balthasar, *Prayer*, 36.

10   Hans Urs von Balthasar, *The Word Made Flesh: Explorations in Theology, Vol 1* (San Francisco, Ignatius Press, 1964), 182.

11   We are now more aware that theology is always founded upon and sustained by spiritual experience. Theology needs to be lived as well as studied. Theology as a whole, not merely spirituality, demands a practical dimension. A theologian is a theological person, not merely someone who uses theological tools. Personal faith is inextricably bound up with theological investigation. Being a theological person involves more than intellectual capacities. "A 'theological person' is someone whose self-consciousness is fully impregnated, without any residual space, by a sense of a proper belonging to Christ and to his history. This belonging is not to a Christ reduced to a personality, or to an ideal, or an enunciator of values, or pretext for social causes but, to the risen Christ, a person living and precious, loved with all the force of one's being." Antonio Sicari, "Mission, Ascesis, Crisis," *Communio* 17 (1990): 339.

12   "The 'perfect' Christian is also the perfect proof of the truth of Christianity: in the Christian's existential transparency, Christianity becomes comprehensible both in itself and to the world and itself exhibits a spiritual

transparency. The saint [that is, the holy human being] is the apology for the Christian religion." Von Balthasar, *The Glory of the Lord*, Vol. 1 229.

[13] Martin Buber, *Hasidism* (New York: Philosophical Library, 1948), 74. To the truly devout believer in Judaism, "the man who lives solely by his mind is further from the divine than the simple man, so long as he had not brought to unity the manifoldness of his life. Therefore, the Baal Shem Tov taught that man should do what he does with his whole being. Only that which one does with all his might is the truth, and only when one acts with his whole being does he begin to love. Thus to the Hasid it is not the specific character of the action that is important but the inner dedication and intention that is brought to it. [...] Rabbi Leib, the son of Sarah, said of those rabbis who expound the Torah: 'What does it amount to—their expounding the Torah? A man should see to it that all his actions are a Torah and that he himself becomes so entirely a Torah that one can learn from his habits and his motions and his motionless clinging to God.' In Hasidism 'the holiest teaching is rejected, if it is found in someone only as a content of his thinking.' If the soul is dissociated it is at the mercy of its organic life, but to the degree that it has attained wholeness and unity, to that degree it is the master of its body and saves and guards its health." Maurice Friedman, *Martin Buber: Mystic, Existentialist, Social Prophet: A Study in the Redemption of Evil* (PhD thesis, University of Chicago, 1950), 360.

[14] "There is simply no real truth which does not have to be incarnated in an act or in some action." This is the logic behind von Balthasar's theology of the heroic form of discipleship—that of the exemplary saint. "They know the truth by participating in it; their theology, philosophy, and metaphysics arise from the action of their lives, their receptivity and obedience, and their prayer. It is through their prayers that the saints perform the truth of Being, knowing it and making it known." Of course, von Balthasar realizes that such a level of integration is an ideal which is perhaps seldom realized in practice. Nonetheless, that does not deter him from making the further claim that unless the possibility of such an integration is presupposed, the activity of Christian theologians is unintelligible. Moser, *Love Itself is Understanding*, 38.

[15] "Love, therefore, shows itself more in works than in words: because works are the gravity of its words. Without proof through the deed, not only would love's word be not fully credible, but the lover himself would not really have exhibited or uttered his love. He would not have had the chance to unveil his own hidden mystery and to make visible its power, depth, and fullness." Hans Urs von Balthasar, *Theo-Logic: The Truth of the World*, Vol. 1 (San Francisco: Ignatius Press, 2001), 177–8.

[16] Ibid., 494.

[17] It is by observing the lives of holy people that one becomes personally compelled by what they do and then begins to imitate them as models of

what human holiness ought to look like. Hence, the living out of a holy lifestyle is what performs the essential role in moving others towards Christian faith. And here, imitation is crucial—for it is by imitating what holy people can be seen to do—for example in acts of selfless love and service of the poor, in the prayer-filled following of Jesus, and so on—that one is able to come to live the holy life oneself; and this then enables one to see God's reality in its fullness. It is their capacity to hear the Word and respond in obedience that sheds new light on the faith and makes it credible. See Gawronski, *Word and Silence*, iBook, no page numbers supplied.

[18] Taylor, *The Go-Between God*, 71.

[19] Newbigin, *The Gospel in a Pluralist Society*, 227.

[20] Hugh Halter and Matt Smay, *The Tangible Kingdom: Creating Incarnational Community* (San Francisco: Jossey-Bass, 2008), 81.

[21] We were introduced to the idea of *hiddur mitzvah* through Lauren Winner's chapter in *For the Beauty of the Church*. W. David O. Taylor, *For the Beauty of the Church* (Grand Rapids: Baker Books, 2010), 74–6.

[22] *Masechet Shabbat*, 133[b]. The rabbis go on to theorize about the ways to a beautiful tabernacle, a beautiful scroll, how to celebrate festivals, how to celebrate Sabbath, etc. This thinking finds its origins in Exodus 15:2. After God miraculously rescues the Israelites from Egypt, the people sing: "This is my God and I will *navah* him with praises." The Hebrew word *navah*, in verb form, translates as *to make beautiful*, or *to adorn*. In defining *hiddur mitzvah*, the rabbis wrestle with the idea of *just what does it mean to beautify God*? Their answer: "Adorn yourself before him by a truly elegant fulfillment of your religious duties."

[23] Markus Barth, *Ephesians: Introduction, Translation, and Commentary on Chapters 1–3* (New York: Doubleday, 1974), 114–5.

[24] Fred Rogers, "Revisiting Fred Rogers' 2002 Commencement Address," *Dartmouth News*, March 27, 2017, https://news.dartmouth.edu/news/2018/03/revisiting-fred-rogers-2002-commencement-address .

[25] Ibid.

[26] Chris Horst, "Gardening While the World Burns," *Values & Capitalism*, 2015, http://www.valuesandcapitalism.com/gardening-world-burns/ .

[27] McGrath, *C. S. Lewis*, 134.

[28] "Julian was concerned that the Christians' acts of hospitality and philanthropy were winning too many of his subjects. He decided to launch an offensive against them by mobilizing his officials and the pagan priesthood to *out-love* the Christians. He decreed that a system of food distribution be started and that hostels be built for poor travellers. He wrote:

'Why do we not observe that it is their benevolence to strangers, their care for the graves of the dead and the pretended holiness of their lives that have done most to increase atheism? I believe that we ought really and truly to practice every one of those virtues [...] For it is disgraceful that when the impious Galileans support not only their own poor but ours as well, all men see that our people lack aid from us.'

Perhaps not surprisingly, Julian's new social program utterly failed. He couldn't motivate pagan priests or Roman officials to care that much for the poor. He failed to realize that the Christians were filled with the Holy Spirit of love and motivated by his grace. The message they shared—that God loved the world—was patently absurd to the average Roman. The pagan gods cared nothing for humankind. And yet in the miserable world of the Roman Empire, the Christians not only proclaimed the mercy of God, they demonstrated it." Michael Frost, *The Five Habits of Highly Missional People: Taking the BELLS challenge to Fulfill the Mission of God* (Exponential Resources), 12–13.

[29] *When Harry Met Sally* ... , film, directed by Rob Reiner. USA: Castle Rock Entertainment and Nelson Entertainment, 1989.

[30] Maria Popova, "Ursula K. Le Guin on Art, Storytelling, and the Power of Language to Transform and Redeem," *Brain Pickings* January 30, 2018, https://www.brainpickings.org/2018/01/30/ursula-k-le-guin-walking-on-the-water/ .

[31] James K. A. Smith, (@james_ka_smith), Twitter post, 2.49 p.m., June 6, 2016.

[32] James K. A. Smith, "An Announcement from Image," *Image*, https://imagejournal.org/editorial-announcement/ .

[33] G. K. Chesterton, *Manalive* (London: Forgotten Books, 1912), 142.

[34] Eugene Peterson, *Practice Resurrection: A Conversation on Growing Up in Christ* (Grand Rapids: Eerdmans, 2010), 139.

[35] W. David O. Taylor, Taylor Worley (eds.), *Contemporary Art and the Church: A Conversation Between Two Worlds* (Downer's Grove: IVP Academic, 2017), 211.

[36] Dickinson, "Tell all the truth but tell it slant."

[37] The poet and writer George Bernanos exemplifies this radical prophetic openness to God when he cries: "Shall we die a wretched little death having ventured nothing, when the wind that comes from another universe is already striking us in the face? [...] I lie down on the bed of the waves and of the wind—I get my direction. Once we bring order into our thought, it overflows even in the heart." Hans Urs von Balthasar, *Bernanos: An Ecclesial Existence* (San Francisco: Ignatius Press, 1996), no page numbers supplied.

38 The great southern writer Walker Percy described the calling of an artist this way: "My theory is that the purpose of art is to transmit universal truths of a sort, but of a particular sort, that in art, whether it's poetry, fiction or painting, you are telling the reader or listener or viewer something he already knows but which he doesn't quite know that he knows, so that in the action of communication he experiences a recognition, a feeling that he has been there before, a shock of recognition. And so, what the artist does, or tries to do, is simply to validate the human experience and to tell people the deep human truths which they already unconsciously know." In David Zahl, "What Else Is There? A Few From Walker Percy's *Signposts in a Strange Land*," *Mockingbird*, February 5, 2008, https://www.mbird.com/2008/02/walker-percy-quote/ .

39 Allen Verhey and Joseph S. Harvard, *Ephesians: A Theological Commentary on the Bible* (Louisville: Westminster John Knox Press, 2011), 86.

40 *The Brothers Bloom* film, directed by Rian Johnson, USA: Endgame Entertainment, 2008.

41 N. T. Wright, "How Can the Bible be Authoritative?" *NTWrightPage*, http://ntwrightpage.com/2016/07/12/how-can-the-bible-be-authoritative/ .

42 Walt Whitman, *Leaves of Grass* (1892) (public domain). Or as von Balthasar says, "the good which God does to us can only be experienced as the truth if we share in performing it [...] and this is possible because God has already taken the drama of existence which plays on the world stage and inserted it into his quite different 'play' which, nonetheless, he wishes to play on our stage. It is a case of the play within the play: our play 'plays' in his play." Von Balthasar, *TheoDrama*, 1, 20.

9 SHARDS OF HEAVEN'S KALEIDOSCOPE

1 Willa Cather, *Death Comes for the Archbishop* (Nebraska: University of Nebraska Press, 1999), 216.

2 Erich von Däniken, *Chariots of the Gods: Was God an Astronaut?* (London: Souvenir Press, 1990).

3 Von Balthasar, *Prayer*, 23.

4 Michael Frost and Alan Hirsch, *The Shaping of Things to Come: Innovation and Mission for the 21st-Century Church* (Grand Rapids: Baker Books, 2013), 134.

5 Bruxy Cavey, (@Bruxy), Twitter post, 6.12 a.m., June 5, 2018, https://twitter.com/Bruxy/status/1003987963976577025 .

6 *Criminal Minds*, "Compulsion," 2005. https://www.imdb.com/title/tt0550487/characters/nm0001597 .

7   Tim Keller, *Counterfeit Gods: The Empty Promises of Money, Sex, and Power, and the Only Hope that Matters* (New York: Penguin, 2001). See also James Edders, "20 Idol Crushing Questions by Tim Keller," March 5, 2018, http://jamedders.com/heart-idols/ for a list of questions that expose idolatry .

8   We note at this point that his methodology was entirely different when he engaged in Jerusalem. In Jerusalem he is among God's chosen people with a long heritage in the biblical story and instruction. His preaching there is in effect a reinterpretation of the nation's story in light of the coming of the Messiah. He is exegeting the Scriptures. It is as if he has his huge King James Version out and he is preachin' in the Bible belt, "line-by-line, precept-by-precept." In Athens, he reverses the process; he does not exegete the Scriptures; rather, he starts with art, poetry, religion, and philosophy, and ends with the gospel. Two different starting points, same goal. If the point is not obvious, we suggest that we are now more in Athens than we are in Jerusalem. We need to adopt a missionary stance in relation to our culture.

9   "In any given situation theology should relate itself not only to the philosophical ideas of the time but to its symbolic life and creative impulses [...] In our time when the theological tradition has lost so much of its cogency it is particularly important that it should redefine itself in relation to the dominant myths, dreams, images of the age, that is, with the contemporary quest-patterns of a changing world." Wilder, *Theopoetic*, 25.

10 TEDx Talks, 2010. *The Power of Vulnerability: Brené Brown at TEDxHouston*, online video, https://www.ted.com/talks/brene_brown_on_vulnerability?language=en .

11 YouTube, *Childish Gambino - This Is America*, https://www.youtube.com/watch?v=VYOjWnS4cMY .

12 Von Balthasar, *The Glory of the Lord*, 12–3. He takes his cue here from the great poet Goethe who said that, "men are productive in poetry and art only as long as they remain religious."

13 Rapaille, *The Culture Code*, 8–9.

14 See for example, Mt 9:14–15; 15:1–3; Mk 2:1–11, 4:10,13; Lk 6:1–3; 12:41–43; Jn 8:3–10; 18:22–23.

15 In looking for the subtext, we are trying to identify the motivation and rationale that is behind the presenting issue. Both Jesus (e.g., Mt 15: 17–20) and Paul (e.g., Col 1:20–21) characterized the basic mind or disposition of a person as evil, and the evidence was to be seen in their evil works. The cause of their sinfulness was not their evil deeds; rather, their evil deeds came from their sinfulness. Evil works are simply evidence of the heart of the matter, which is the mind or disposition. An axiom of Scripture is that "by

their fruit you will recognize them" (Mt 7:16); it is "the mind," therefore, that produces the fruit of actions.

16 This will form the basis of a book that Deb is working on. Used with permission.

17 Wanda Mallette, Bob Morrison and Patti Ryan, "Lookin' For Love," Full Moon, 1980.

18 *Looking for par'Mach in All the Wrong Places, Star Trek: Deep Space Nine,* television, directed by Andrew J. Robinson. USA: Paramount Studios, 1996.

19 Redeemer CFS, 2012. James K. A. Smith, *Culture as Liturgy,* online video, https://www.youtube.com/watch?v=vdVkXk3NADE .

20 According to Marion, some phenomena are "saturated" with intention and exceed any concepts or limiting horizons that a constituting subject could impose upon them. Marion describes phenomena which are saturated according to quality as dazzling (*éblouissant*). The intensity of the intuition given by them exceeds our capacity to see and prevents us from perceiving them as objects. He discusses these phenomena exclusively in terms of visual perception, and proposes the idol as the paradigm of a phenomenon saturated according to quality, describing the way in which paintings can function as idols. See Jean-Luc Marion, *In Excess: Studies of Saturated Phenomena* (New York: Fordham University Press, 2002). For some brilliant analyses of the inner dynamics of idolatry, Jean-Luc Marion, *God Without Being* (Chicago: University of Chicago Press, 2012). And his key interpreter Shane Mackinlay, *Interpreting Excess: Jean-Luc Marion, Saturated Phenomena, and Hermeneutics* (New York: Fordham University Press, 2010). Also see Owen Barfield, *Saving the Appearances: A Study in Idolatry* (New York: Harcourt and Brace, 1988).

21 C. S. Lewis, *The Weight of Glory,* 30–1. Created objects, as Lewis explains, turn into idols when we mistake them for ultimate realities. Or, as he memorably expresses it elsewhere: "You can't get second things by putting them first; you can get second things only by putting first things first." C. S. Lewis, "First and Second Things," *God in the Dock: Essays on Theology and Ethics* (Grand Rapids: William B. Eerdmans Publishing Co., 1970), 278–80.

22 Even the types of drugs indicate something of these categorizations. For instance, there are the so-called "downers" (opiates/opioids, sedative-hypnotics, and alcohol), which are largely ways to escape through invoking a careless sense of the world. And then there are the "uppers" (cocaine, amphetamines, ecstasy, etc.), which are the party drugs.

23 For Augustine, the difference between enjoying (*frui*) something and using (*uti*) it is that "to enjoy something is to hold fast to it in love for its own sake." Accordingly, while we may use this good created order, only the triune

God—Father, Son, and Holy Spirit—is to be enjoyed. Only he can be loved strictly for his own sake. The temporal, created order may only be used with an eye to the eternal purpose of the enjoyment of God. (Needless to say, for Augustine, the word "use" did not have the negative connotation of "abuse," which it often carries today.) This point is important because it is precisely by celebrating created realities for their own sake that we unhinge them from their grounding in the eternal Word or *Logos* of God. Unhinged from their transcendent source, created objects lose their source of meaning; they become the unsuspecting victims of the objectifying human gaze and turn into the manageable playthings of the totalizing human grasp. The irony of a misunderstood focus on the goodness of creation is that it results in its mirror image: a Gnostic-type of devaluation of created life. Hans Boersma, *Heavenly Participation* (Grand Rapids: Eerdmans, 2011), 30. C. S. Lewis elaborated on this in his essays on ethics called *God in the Dock*.

[24] Lewis, *The Weight of Glory*, 27.

10 ROMANCING THE CITY

[1] iLovePrincessDiana, 2010, *Princess Diana's engagement interview*, online video, https://www.youtube.com/watch?v=wg_fib2gQaU .

[2] Much of the "romancing" language and thinking comes from Michael Frost, Exponential Conference, main session, 2011. Also here: Michael Frost, "Romancing the City," August 27, 2012, in Exponential Podcast, https://itunes.apple.com/us/podcast/exponential/id194168324 .

[3] This story was also used in Alan's book with Michael Frost, *The Shaping of Things to Come*, 198–200. Used with permission of John Smith.

[4] Actually, mission is something that God is always (eternally) doing and precedes the work of the church, individual or corporate. This was precisely the key point of David Bosch's seminal book *Transforming Mission*, that missiology is an intrinsic dimension of the doctrine of God *proper*, and not the doctrine of the church. The missiology precedes and informs ecclesiology and not the other way around. See *Transforming Mission: Paradigm Shifts in the Theology of Mission* (Maryknoll: Orbis, 2011).

[5] In a conversation, used with permission.

[6] Lesslie Newbigin, *The Open Secret: An Introduction to the Theology of Mission* (Grand Rapids: Eerdmans, 1995), 56. "Prevenience" here is a now defunct English word that simple means "preparatory"—a grace that goes before and prepares the way for faith and discipleship. It is particularly significant in all Wesleyan theology.

[7] John Drane, *The McDonaldization of the Church: Consumer Culture and the Church's Future* (London: Darton, Longman & Todd, 2000), 63.

8   Guder, *The Continuing Conversion of the Church*, Kindle Locations 1094–8.

9   "St Paul says: 'I find within myself an eternal struggle. My inner nature contends with the eternal hunt of the spirit, and I do what I do not want, and I do not do what I do want.' So these two hunt one another, and in between them comes God from above and hunts them both, and likewise grace, and where this hunt is truly understood, it is a very good thing, for 'all those hunted by the Spirit of God are children of God.'" Von Balthasar, *The Glory of the Lord*, 56.

10 Lawrence Kushner, *God Was in This Place and I, I Did Not Know: Finding Self, Spirituality and Ultimate Meaning* (Vermont: Jewish Lights Publishing, 2016), 27.

11 Buechner, *Secrets in the Dark*, 183.

12 Mike Breen story, told by Michael Frost at Exponential Conference, main session, 2011.

13 Josh Packard and Ashleigh Hope, *Church Refugees* (Loveland, Colorado: Group, 2015), 6.

14 Ibid., 28–9.

15 Harper Lee, *To Kill a Mockingbird* (New York: Popular Library, 1960), 34.

16 Frost and Hirsch, *The Shaping of Things to Come*, 88.

17 Similar to empathy (which takes place between people) we can learn from psychology in this matter. Drawing on his half-century practice as a therapist, Erich Fromm offers six guidelines for mastering the art of empathetic listening:

The basic rule for practicing this art is the complete concentration of the listener.

Nothing of importance must be on their mind, they must be optimally free from anxiety as well as from greed.

They must possess a freely working imagination which is sufficiently concrete to be expressed in words.

They must be endowed with a capacity for empathy with another person and strong enough to feel the experience of the other as if it were his own (com-passion).

The condition for such empathy is a crucial facet of the capacity for love. To understand another means to love that person—not in the erotic sense but in the sense of reaching out to him and of overcoming the fear of losing oneself.

Understanding and loving are inseparable. If they are separate, it is a cerebral process and the door to essential understanding remains closed.

Erich Fromm, *The Art of Listening* (New York: Continuum International, 1994), 192–3.

[18] David W. Augsburger, *Pastoral Counseling Across Cultures* (Louisville, Kentucky: Westminster John Knox Press, 1986), 31.

[19] Emmanuel Y. Lartey, *In Living Color: An Intercultural Approach to Pastoral Care and Counseling* (London: Jessica Kingsley Publishers, 2003), 93–4.

[20] John Wood, "David Ogilvy's Copywriting Technique That Made a Homeless Man's Cup Runneth Over ... ," *American Writers & Artists Inc.*, February, 2013, https://www.awai.com/2013/02/david-ogilvys-copywriting-technique/ .

[21] Rich Gorman, *Just Step In* (Exponential Resources, 2014), 17, ebook.

[22] Steve Hollinghurst, *Mission Shaped Evangelism: The Gospel in Contemporary Culture* (Norwich: Canterbury Press, 2010), 168.

[23] Richard Beck has written brilliantly, contrasting Freud in a world of "new apologetics" in *The Authenticity of Faith* (Abilene, Texas: Abilene Christian University Press, 2012).

[24] For example, an inscription celebrating the birth of Octavian reads, "The birthday of the god was for the world the beginning of 'joyful tidings.'" Michael Card, *Mark: The Gospel of Passion* (Downers Grove, IVP, 2012), 27–8.

[25] Ibid., 27–8.

[26] Wright, *Simply Good News*, 154.

AFTERWORD

[1] Byron Williams, "The Dangers of Oversimplification," *Huffington Post*, August 22, 2016, updated August 23, 2017. https://www.huffingtonpost.com/byron-williams/the-danger-of-oversimplif_b_11650440.html .

[2] Brueggemann, *Finally Comes the Poet*, 1–2.

[3] G. K. Chesterton, *The Romance of Orthodoxy*, on *Page by Page Books*, 5, https://www.pagebypagebooks.com/Gilbert_K_Chesterton/Orthodoxy/The_Romance_of_Orthodoxy_p5.html .

APPENDIX 1

[1] Dallas Willard, *The Great Omission: Reclaiming Jesus's Essential Teachings on Discipleship* (New York: HarperOne, 2014)

[2] Dallas Willard, "How Does the Disciple Live?" http://www.dwillard.org/articles/individual/how-does-the-disciple-live .

[3] Dietrich Bonhoeffer, *The Cost of Discipleship* (New York: Touchstone, 1995), 43ff.

[4] He continues ... "Because the Son of God became Man, because he is the Mediator, for that reason alone the only true relation we can have with him is to follow him. Discipleship is bound to Christ as the Mediator, and where it is properly understood, it necessarily implies faith in the Son of God as the Mediator. Only the Mediator, the God-Man, can call men to follow him [...] Discipleship without Jesus Christ is a way of our own choosing. It may be the ideal way. It may even lead to martyrdom, but it is devoid of all promise. Jesus will certainly reject it." Ibid., 59.

[5] See also Jaques Ellul, *The Subversion of Christianity* (Eugene, OR: Wipf & Stock, 2011), for detailed analysis of Christ-less Christian religion.

APPENDIX 2

[1] Many reading this book would be aware of the distinctive meaning of the Hebrew word for knowledge, a word that is used for sexual intercourse, as well as for knowledge of God. "The original meaning of the Hebrew verb 'to recognize, to know,' in distinction from Western languages, belongs not to the sphere of reflection but to that of personal contact. In biblical Hebrew, in order to know something, one doesn't observe it, but one must come into contact with it. This basic difference is developed in the realm of a relation of the soul to other beings, where the fact of mutuality changes everything. At the center is not a perceiving of one another but a contact of being—intercourse. This theme of knowing rises to a remarkable and incomparable height in the relation of God to those he has chosen.

"Closely allied to this way of knowing is the role played by passion or affection in spirituality. Passion requires participation, involvement, faith. Søren Kierkegaard can say, 'If passion is eliminated, faith no longer exists.' The truth of God can be found only by such a passionate search and by applying one's whole personality existentially. The criterion of the genuine search for truth is what Kierkegaard called *inwardness*, which requires an intense personal concern with it to be able to understand and assimilate it." Hirsch and Frost, *ReJesus*, 151.

[2] John Calvin, *Institutes of the Christian Religion* (Grand Rapids: Baker Academic, 1987), I. 6.2.

[3]   Bonhoeffer, *The Cost of Discipleship*, 69.

[4]   "The only way that we become convinced of our own sense of power, dignity, and the power of God is by actually doing it—by crossing a line, a line that has a certain degree of nonsensicalness and unprovability to it—and that's why we call it faith. In the crossing of that line, and acting in a new way, then and only then, can we really believe what we say we believe in the first place. We do not think ourselves into a new way of living as much as we live ourselves into new ways of thinking. Lifestyle issues ask much more of us than mere belief systems." Richard Rohr, *Preparing for Christmas: Daily Meditations for Advent* (Ohio: Franciscan Media, 2012), 48.

[5]   James Edwards, *The Gospel According to Mark: The Pillar New Testament Commentary Series* (Grand Rapids: Eerdmans, 2002), 261.

[6]   Bonhoeffer, *The Cost of Discipleship*, 92.

[7]   It is the same in the Hebrew *shema* and the Greek *hupakouo*. So, for instance, von Balthasar equates "hearing" with possessing Christian faith: "Believing and hearing the word of God are one and the same. Faith is the power to transcend one's own personal 'truth', merely human and of this world, and to attain the absolute truth of the God who unveils and offers himself to us, to let it be decisive in our regard and prevail. The person who believes, who declares himself a believer, thereby proclaims that he is ready to hear the word of God." In Victoria Harrison, *The Apologetic Value of Human Holiness: Von Balthasar's Christocentric Philosophical Anthropology* (Berlin: Springer Science and Business Media, 2000), 27.

[8]   Bonhoeffer, *The Cost of Discipleship*, 3; 219.

APPENDIX 3

[1]   This becomes still more evident when we recall that the word *mind* (νοῦς) constitutes "not an instrument of thought" but "a mode of thought" or "mind-set." Similarly, νοῦς denotes "a constellation of thoughts and beliefs which provides the criteria for judgments and actions." It speaks of character or disposition. It is because Christ lives in those who have received the Spirit that their stance and outlook can be those of Christ, and in this sense they are "spiritual." The Hebrew represented by the LXX in any case has רוח (*ruach*) of God, and Paul uses πνεῦμα θεοῦ, *Spirit of God*, and πνεῦμα Χριστοῦ, *Spirit of Christ*, in ways that are at times virtually interchangeable. Rom 8:9 offers one example: "the Spirit of God lives in you. And if anyone does not have the Spirit of Christ, they do not belong to Christ." Hanson argues that Paul is aware of this background in 1 Cor 2:16. Thus, when he prays that Christians may reflect "the mind of Christ," Paul cites the self-humiliation of Christ in the existence of a "slave" and the cross (Phil 2:5–11). "The change of expression from 'Lord' in 16[a] to 'Christ'

in 16[b] binds the true divine wisdom to the crucified Christ, and thereby excludes the gnostic gospel of a transcendent wisdom." Paul will expound practical entailments of this in 3:1–4. A. Thiselton, *The New International Greek Testament Commentary: The First Epistle to the Corinthians*, 278 (in logos).

2   For explorations on the idea of *nous*/mind, see D. R. Brown and E. T. Twist, *1 Corinthians* (Bellingham, WA: Lexham Press, 2013), and also P. H. Towner, "Mind/Reason," *Evangelical Dictionary of Biblical Theology* (Grand Rapids: Baker Book House, 1996) electronic ed., 529, as well as O. Chambers, *My Utmost for His Highest: Selections for the Year* (Grand Rapids: Oswald Chambers Publications; Marshall Pickering, 1986).

MOVEMENTS

PUBLISHING

100 Movements Publishing is a hybrid publisher, offering the benefits of both traditional and self-publishing.

OUR AUTHORS ARE **RISK-TAKERS,**

PARADIGM-SHIFTERS, INCARNATIONAL

MISSIONARIES, AND **INFLUENTIAL LEADERS**

WHO LOVE THE BODY OF CHRIST AND

WANT TO SPUR HER ON FOR MORE.

Our books aim to inspire and equip disciples
to take hold of their God-given call to make disciples
and to see kingdom impact in every sphere of society.

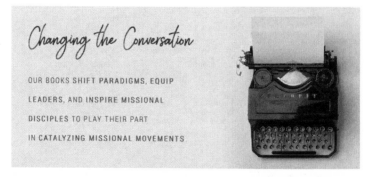

Changing the Conversation

OUR BOOKS SHIFT PARADIGMS, EQUIP
LEADERS, AND INSPIRE MISSIONAL
DISCIPLES TO PLAY THEIR PART
IN CATALYZING MISSIONAL MOVEMENTS.

For more information please visit us at 100Mpublishing.com

Made in the USA
Lexington, KY
09 September 2019